THE STATE OF BLACK AMERICA 2002

PUBLISHED BY NATIONAL URBAN LEAGUE ⊜

THE STATE OF BLACK AMERICA 2002

Editor
Lee A. Daniels

Associate Editors
David Brown
Serena K. Mayeri

Managing Editor
Rose Jefferson-Frazier

**IMAGE PARTNERS
CUSTOM PUBLISHING**

President and Creative Director
John Shearer

Vice President
Marianne Shearer

Design Director
Lisa Weber

Cover Image by
Cristy Briggs

Copyright© National Urban League, 2002
Library of Congress Catalog Number 77-647469
ISBN 0-914758-90-X
$24.95

NATIONAL URBAN LEAGUE

Our Children ⊜ Our Destiny

Kenneth D. Lewis
Chairman

Hugh B. Price
President and Chief Executive Officer

Milton J. Little, Jr.
Executive Vice President and Chief Operating Officer

Paul Wycisk
Senior Vice President and Chief Financial Officer

Mildred L. Love
Senior Vice President of Operations

Gena Davis Watkins
*Senior Vice President of
Development and Chief Development Officer*

Annelle Lewis
*Senior Vice President
Affiliate Development, Programs and Policy*

contents

DEDICATION Billy J. Tidwell, 1943 - 2001 7

OVERVIEW Still Worth Fighting For: America After 9/11
By Hugh B. Price 9

ESSAY 1 What Equality Would Look Like:
Reflections on the Past, Present and Future
By Franklin D. Raines 13

ESSAY 2 The National Urban League and Social
Welfare Policy: A Historical Perspective
By William E. Spriggs and Suzanne Bergeron 29

ESSAY 3 The Black Worker: Continuing Quest
for Economic Parity
By Bernard E. Anderson 51

ESSAY 4 The Geography of Discrimination:
Hypersegregation, Isolation and Fragmentation Within the
African-American Community
By Leland Ware and Antoine Allen 69

ESSAY 5 Military Organizations: Best Practices
and the Status of Black Americans
By John Sibley Butler 93

ESSAY 6 Holding the Accountants Accountable:
Why Are There So Few African-American CPAs?
By Theresa A. Hammond 109

THE STATE OF
BLACK AMERICA 2002

ESSAY 7 *African Americans Confront A Pandemic: Assessing Community Impact, Organization, and Advocacy in the Second Decade of AIDS*
By Maya Rockeymoore **123**

ESSAY 8 *African Americans and American Politics 2002: The Maturation Phase*
By Martin L. Kilson **147**

AFTERWORD
Praising the Mutilated World
By Lee A. Daniels **181**

FEATURE
Ten Important Contributions Black America Made to America in the Twentieth Century **189**

APPENDIX I
History of the National Urban League **195**

APPENDIX II
Statistical Overview **201**

APPENDIX III
Special Research Report: Negative Effects of TANF on College Enrollment **223**

APPENDIX IV
Index of Authors and Articles, 1987–2002 ....**253**

APPENDIX V
About the Authors **267**

dedication

Billy J. Tidwell
1943 - 2001

A longtime staff policy expert of the National Urban League; a co-founder and former editor of *The State of Black America;* an advocate of freedom; an activist who improved the quality of life for people in communities from east coast to west coast; a friend whose physical presence is deeply missed, but whose spiritual presence remains as vibrant as ever.

verview

Still Worth Fighting For: America After 9/11

By Hugh B. Price

A little more than a year ago, in my To Be Equal column of July 6, 2001, I wrote about the wonderful fireworks display over New York City's East River that was watched by tens of thousands of people who lined the river's Brooklyn and Manhattan banks. I noted that the display was an astonishing marriage of new-fangled high technology, old-fashioned sentiments, and time-honored principles.

On the one hand, there was the long, wondrous and color-coordinated explosion of fireworks from three substantial barges anchored near the United Nations complex, managed by computer and set to a varied score of well-known songs from European and American classical operas and symphonies, the repertoire of John Phillip Sousa, and even old popular standards. But what made the display emotionally thrilling was its essential old-fashioned element: the people who filled the usually car-choked Franklin Delano Roosevelt Drive that winds down the river's Manhattan bank were a mosaic of different races, colors, languages and economic classes, all drawn by the promised spectacle—and by the wish to celebrate en masse what the celebration of July 4th is supposed to represent: the American nation's commitment to guaranteeing for each individual life, liberty and the pursuit of happiness.

The moment inspired me to write that "One can't help but think of how much is 'right' about this nation, and of the advantages that exist for

overview

making things better. That is especially so when one looks around the world today—be it in parts of Latin America, or Europe, or Asia, or the Middle East, or Black Africa—and sees societies and peoples in alarming turmoil. The contrast between 'there' and here should not make us feel smug, however. Instead, it should intensify our commitment to use this nation's advantages to make things better, to extend the promise of the opportunity to pursue life, liberty and happiness to ever—widening circles of people."

I read those words now, when we are approaching the first-year anniversary of the tragedy of September 11, 2001, and in one sense, last year's balmy July 4, with its home-grown sense of feeling secure, seems so long ago. Our nation's future, and the future of humankind itself has become much more complicated—one could say, much more threatened—since last summer.

But then I understand all over again that that new reality has to become our inspiration. It's precisely because the world has become for us in America a more dangerous place that we must dedicate ourselves with greater urgency to the task we at the National Urban League have always held high: to make things better, to extend the promise of the opportunity to pursue life, liberty and happiness to ever-widening circles of people.

For more than a quarter-century, *The State of Black America* has helped to further that effort by providing the statistics and the scholarly perspectives that dissect and analyze what has occurred and what is occurring to Black America and America; and proposing what needs to occur if Black America and America are to prosper.

The need for both things to happen in tandem is more important than ever now.

In that regard, this volume continues the journal's tradition of responding to the urgency of the moment by helping America keep its eyes on the prize. Both of those things are reflected in the rich variety of our essays, ranging from a Franklin Raines' diagram, if you will, of what America would look like if we had reached the goal of equality of opportunity, to John Sibley Butler's assertion that the record of African Americans in the military offers valuable guidelines of how to do that. This volume includes Theresa A. Hammond's impressive discussion of the struggle of African Americans in one of the most rarefied of white-collar professions—certified public accountancy; as well as an essay and a special report (Appendix III) from William E. Spriggs and Suzanne Bergeron, of the Urban League's research arm, the Institute for Opportunity and Equality, that are vitally important to the discussion about reforming the welfare system so that it can help more of the poorest Americans.

Leland Ware and Antoine Allen continue *The State of Black America's* exploration of different facets of the class variegation among Black Americans; Martin L. Kilson provides a very necessary assessment of the political maturation blacks have charted since the 1960s and identifies some of the important dynamics which will affect the future of black politics; and Maya Rockeymoore, also of the Institute for Opportunity and Equality, offers a powerful examination of the response by the African-American community to the scourge of AIDS.

Together, these essays continue the exploration of the transformation of Black Civil Society and its interaction with the larger American society that has been the defining feature of *The State of Black America.* That is its legacy. That is its responsibility. September 11, 2001 set all Americans adrift in uncharted and dangerous waters. This particular situation is unprecedented. But, as Lee A. Daniels points out in his Afterword, the general predicament is hardly new to African Americans, a people who survived the moral and physical wilderness of Slavery and legal segregation. So, let us fortify our morale, praise the mutilated world, keep our eyes on the prize—and march on.

What Equality Would Look Like: Reflections on the Past, Present and Future

By Franklin D. Raines

Franklin D. Raines is chairman and CEO of Fannie Mae, and a trustee of the National Urban League. This essay is drawn from remarks he delivered at the closing dinner of the National Urban League Annual Conference in August of 2001.

What an extraordinary conference. So many great leaders. So many legends of our time. So many heroes of mine. It makes one proud to be a small part of the Urban League movement. From working with the Seattle Urban League in the early 1970s to the National Urban League Board today, I have always been impressed with the mission of the League.

I would like to reflect tonight on the mission of the National Urban League, which is "to enable African Americans to secure economic self-reliance, parity and power, and civil rights." The principle I want to underscore is at the root of all our efforts to expand equal rights in America. It is captured in six simple words from the inscription at Whitney Young's gravesite in Hartsdale, New York: "Where injustice reigns, all are unequal."

This is not a new concept. And we have made great progress on the march of civil and equal rights. But we all know the final miles are the hardest.

Will we ever get there? Will we ever achieve true equality in this country?

Roger Wilkins, in his new book, *Jefferson's Pillow*, asks the question this way: "My people and I have worked for America, and we have

Essay 1

changed it, made it richer and better," he says. "The question is whether we blacks can join other Americans—including more recent immigrants—and become the full emotional and civic owners of the place where we were once owned."[1]

What Professor Wilkins is proposing is very difficult, given how our history began. Some historians say it began this very day, August 1st, in 1619, the day the first 20 Africans arrived at Jamestown, Virginia. By 1776, there were over half a million slaves in this country, and by 1860, four million. Then one day, suddenly, they were set free. But they were not made whole.

As W.E.B. Du Bois has written, they were "left alone and unguided without capital, without land, without skill, without economic organization, without even the bald protection of law, order and decency."[2]

Frederick Douglass was even more pointed. "When the Russian serfs had their chains broken and given their liberty, the government of Russia gave to those poor emancipated serfs a few acres of land on which they could live and earn their bread. But when you turned us loose ... you turned us loose to the sky, to the storm, to the whirlwind, and worst of all, you turned us loose to our infuriated masters."[3]

At best they got work without a living wage. When slaves were freed in the District of Columbia, the slaveholders were paid $300 each. Their slaves were paid $100—if they left the country. They had fought to save the Union. But they were denied ballots to chart its course. As Frederick Douglass declared in demanding suffrage, "They now stand before Congress and the country, not complaining of the past, but simply asking for a better future."[4]

The nation has spent the next 136 years struggling to heed their call.

In that time we have gained voting rights. Outlawed discrimination. Embraced diversity. And taken affirmative action. Yet, it has not been enough. As President Johnson declared, "You do not take a person who, for years, has been hobbled by chains and liberate him, bring him up to the starting line of a race and then say, You are free to compete with all the others. And still justly believe that you have been completely fair."[5]

President Johnson was not the first to identify the need to provide help to the formerly enslaved. Two centuries earlier, in a column in a Philadelphia newspaper in 1774, a writer rhetorically asked, "Are we not bound in duty to him to repair these injuries?" That writer was the patriot Thomas Paine.

Imagine if these repairs had been made and that African Americans already shared in the full emotional and civic ownership of America. Imagine if the National Urban League had achieved its "Opportunity Agenda," the quest for economic and social equality in the new millennium.

What would this Promised Land look like? What if the average black American enjoyed the same status as the average white American? What would we have gained? What would be the state of Black America in the year 2001?

Let me try to offer a glimpse tonight.

Interestingly, the new survey just released jointly by *The Washington Post*, the Kaiser Family Foundation and Harvard University about Americans' attitudes about race says a majority of Americans think we have already achieved equality.[6] The results were eye opening: 40 to 60 percent of white Americans believe that the average black family is faring about as well as the average white family. Sometimes—even better.

To be generous, let us assume this opinion is not myopic, but optimistic. Fannie Mae's research team has looked at the state of Black America and roughly estimated what we would gain if the most optimistic Americans were right.[7]

Jobs

The Washington Post-Kaiser-Harvard survey said five out of ten white Americans believe the average black is about as well off as the average white in terms of the jobs they hold. The reality is that blacks are about twice as likely to hold lower-paying, less prestigious service jobs. Only 20 percent of blacks hold professional or managerial jobs, while more than 30 percent of whites do. African Americans are also twice as likely to be unemployed. Whitney Young once said, "The hardest work in the world is being out of work." What would happen if blacks and

Essay 1

whites had equal employment? It would mean 700,000 more African Americans would have jobs today. And nearly two million more African Americans would be promoted to higher paying and managerial jobs.

Income

It is interesting that when President Lincoln signed the Emancipation Proclamation, he didn't just free the slaves and command the military to protect their freedom. He included some advice for the newly freed: "I recommend to them that, in all cases when allowed, they labor faithfully for reasonable wages." Today, according to the racial attitudes survey, four out of ten white Americans believe that the typical African American earns as much or more than the typical white. The reality again is different. The poverty rate for African Americans is more than double the white rate. Nearly one out of every two blacks earns less than $25,000. Only one in three whites earn that little. The median income of a black household is $27,000 compared to $42,000 for a white household.

What would happen if we had income equality in America? The average black American household would get a 56-percent pay raise. Altogether, they would earn another $190 billion.

Wealth

Wealth is often conflated with income, but there is a critical distinction. When your grandfather's grandfather was "left alone and unguided without capital, without land, without skill, without economic organization," it is much harder for your family to amass and pass along a cushion of resources.[8]

It goes without saying that wealth gives you more choices in where and how you live, the quality of your schools, and whether your kids will go to college, medical school, law school—or even art school. Wealth lets you start a business and absorb losses. Investment income can help you weather stresses from job dislocation, illness or family break-up. You can improve the timing and quality of your retirement years. And you can buy a home more easily. The Urban League has summed it up best. Wealth improves the content and quality of your social, business and political influence.

Let's look at the wealth disparity. Right now, the average white household has a net worth of $84,000. The average black household has only about $7,500. If we had full equality, the wealth of black households would rise by $1 trillion. African Americans would have $200 million more in the stock market, $120 billion more in our pension plans, and $80 billion more in the bank. And we might have 31 African-American billionaires instead of one.

Education

In the mid-1880s when Frederick Douglass published the *North Star*, his goals went beyond abolishing slavery. He also wanted to "promote the intellectual improvement of the colored people" as a key to their full integration as American citizens.

According to the racial attitudes survey, half of all white Americans believe we have parity in education. In reality, there is a 10-percent gap in high school diplomas, an 11-percent gap in undergraduate degrees, and gaps in post-graduate degrees.

If we had achieved this quest for equality in education, two million more African Americans would have their high school diplomas. Nearly two million more would have undergraduate degrees. Nearly a half million more would have master's degrees. And 180,000 more African Americans would have their doctorates—250 percent more than today.

Other Measures

Beyond jobs, income and wealth, let us look at some other typical measures of status and influence in America.

In the survey about racial attitudes, 60 percent of white Americans say the average African American has equal or even better access to health care. In reality, African Americans are nearly twice as likely to be without health insurance. If we were insured at the same rate, 2.5 million more African Americans, including 620,000 children, would have health insurance. And 620,000 more African-American children would

Essay 1

have health coverage.

What if we closed the digital divide in this country? Three million more African-American households would own computers and have Internet access.

Equality would mean the automobile industry would sell 1.5 million more cars.

The prison system would lose 700,000 African-American adults, and 33,000 fewer juveniles now in detention. This would save the country over $15 billion in the cost of incarceration.

Equality would also transform the business world. For starters, African Americans would own over 600,000 more businesses, with $2.7 trillion more in revenues. We would have 62 African Americans running Fortune 500 companies, instead of just three. And we would have 590 more African Americans serving on boards of Fortune 1000 companies.

Equality would certainly change the face of democracy, as well. If we all voted at the same rate, over one million more African Americans would have cast ballots in the last presidential election. Over the years, voting equality would have put nearly 1,500 African Americans in Congress instead of 107. We would have had 14 African Americans on the U.S. Supreme Court instead of two. And yes, we would have had five Presidents of the United States.

Homeownership

What about the issue that is closest to my heart, homeownership?

Compared to white Americans and the rest of the nation, African Americans are still stuck in the pre-civil rights era when it comes to owning their homes. We all know the figures. The national homeownership rate is nearly 68 percent. For white families, it is 74 percent. For African Americans, it is 48 percent, which was the national rate in the early 1940s.

The gap is closing. But it is not disappearing soon. And, according to the Urban League's *The State of Black America 2001*, homeownership actually is declining among younger African Americans. Not necessarily because of discrimination. According to surveys by Fannie Mae and the Urban League, African Americans perceive less bias in lending than ever, although they are far more likely to be victims of predatory lending, or to use subprime loans where the rates are higher and extra costs are often added in.

So, if not increasing discrimination, why the decline? As the Urban League report notes, "African-American Generation X'ers have inherited an economic legacy which undermines their ability to enter the housing market." In simple terms, young African Americans are not in the best position to get help from their parents.

Indeed, according to Fannie Mae's national housing mortgage survey, African Americans are far more likely than the average family in America to be saving up to buy a home. While the number of Americans saving for a home dropped from 20 to 16 percent, 30 percent of African Americans are putting money away for the down payment and closing costs.

The lack of wealth to buy a home creates a vicious cycle, because owning a home is the single, most common and powerful way to build wealth in America. Many underestimate the importance of home equity in the overall balance sheet of consumers. We often talk about the values of the stock market and what impact that has on their consumption. But for the average family, their home equity is the largest source of wealth. Wealth that can be used to send their children to college, support retirement or invest in other ways.

You can ask William Harvey, president of Hampton University, who just joined the Fannie Mae board of directors. He's famous for telling graduates of the historically black college: "Today you get your degree. Tomorrow buy some property. Start small if you have to. Just start."

The many advantages of homeownership are well known. Homeownership creates more stable households in safer neighborhoods. Better schools. More cohesive communities. Citizens who are more active and involved. As William Harvey says, "Homeownership does a lot for a person other than putting a roof over their head. It helps with a person's psyche and discipline. They take ownership in their community and in their street."

Essay 1

Now even as Chairman of Fannie Mae, I know that homeownership is not a panacea. But it can improve the quality of life for African Americans in many ways.

As Dr. Du Bois noted in his epic work, *The Souls of Black Folk*, "the size and arrangements of a people's homes are no unfair index of their condition." Our index is still far below that of the nation as a whole.

But let us imagine the gap was closed. The difference it would make in wealth alone is staggering. On average, white homeowners have about $120,000 in home equity, while black homeowners have only $58,000 in home equity. If you were to close the home equity gap, the wealth of African Americans would jump by $760 billion. And if you were to close the homeownership gap, there would be 3 million more African-American homeowners.

Fannie Mae is fixated on narrowing that gap.

Most of you know that Fannie Mae is the nation's number one source of affordable home financing for African Americans. Through our American Dream Commitment, Fannie Mae has pledged to contribute at least $420 billion in mortgage investments to serve more than 3 million minority households over the decade. And we have pledged to lead the market in affordable lending to all racial and ethnic groups, and that effort is on track. We are proud to be working with the National Urban League to do that.

Our dream is that by closing the racial gap in homeownership, we can help to close some of the other gaps in the inclusion of African Americans into American society.

Tonight I have violated the cardinal rule of dinner speeches by throwing a lot of numbers at you. For that I apologize. But when many Americans believe this country has finally achieved racial equality, I wanted to make it clear that the numbers tell a different story. Black Americans are still 700,000 jobs behind, $190 billion in income behind, $1 trillion in wealth behind, 3 million health plans behind, 2.7 million college degrees behind, and 3 million homeowners behind.

The transition of black Americans from a formerly enslaved people to full and participating members of this society is far from complete. One hundred thirty-six years is too long. We have work to do. We have a lot of work to do.

But perhaps these numbers can provide the basis for the expression of a new national will to finish the work—work that begins with a more honest and realistic view of where we stand today.

We are Americans. To be an American is to be aspirational. And we have cause to have great aspirations. Slowly but steadily, generation after generation, step after difficult step, we have been making progress toward achieving the equality to which we and our nation aspire.

We must finish the job of including America's formerly enslaved into its economic and social mainstream. Let the inscription on Whitney Young's gravesite speak not only to black Americans but to all Americans, "Every man is our brother and every man's burden is our own."

I am proud that the Urban League continues to lead this fight.

Thank you.

Notes

[1] Wilkins, Roger, *Jefferson's Pillow: The Founding Fathers and the Dilemma of Black Patriotism.* (Boston, Massachusetts: Beacon Press, 2001), p. 7.

[2] Du Bois, W.E.B., *The Souls of Black Folk,* Chapter 9, "Of The Sons of Master and Man," Chicago, A.C. McClurg & Co., [Cambridge]: University Press John Wilson and Son, Cambridge, U.S.A., 1903; Bartleby.com, 1999. www.bartleby.com/114/

[3] Frederick Douglass speech, "Looking the Republican Party Squarely in the Face," delivered in Cincinnati, Ohio, June 14, 1876. Published in *The Frederick Douglass Papers, Series One: Speeches, Debates, and Interviews,* Volume 4: 1864-80, p. 442, Yale University Press, New Haven and London, 1991, John W. Blassingame and John R. McKivigan, eds.

[4] Douglass, Frederick, *"Appeal to Congress for Impartial Suffrage,"* (1867).

[5] President Lyndon Baines Johnson, *"To Fulfill These Rights,"* Commencement Address, Howard University, (June 4, 1965).

Essay 1

[6] "Race and Ethnicity in 2001: Attitudes, Perceptions and Experiences," *The Washington Post*, the Kaiser Family Foundation and Harvard University, (August 2001).

[7] 6/4/02 Fannie Mae's Editorial and Research Department undertook this research specifically for Mr. Raines' National Urban League speech. The following is a summary of the methodology used:

HOW WE ESTIMATE STATISTICS FOR BLACKS UNDER ASSUMPTION OF BLACK-WHITE PARITY

Employment:

* Total Employment: 700,000 more jobs

● Apply the employment rate for whites in 2000 to the black civilian labor force (16 years and over) in 2000 to arrive at total black employment in 2000 under the assumption of black-white parity. This is the "what-if" figure.

● The change in black employment brought about by black-white parity is the difference between this "what-if" figure and actual black employment in 2000.

* Managerial and Professional Occupations: Nearly 2 million more positions.

● Estimate the ratio of employed whites in managerial and professional occupations in 2000 to the white civilian labor force in 2000.

● Apply this ratio to the black civilian labor force in 2000 to arrive at the "what-if" figure of black employment in managerial and professional occupations.

● The change brought about by black-white parity is the difference between this "what-if" figure and actual black employment in managerial and professional occupations in 2000.

The sections that follow describe the ways to compute the "what-if" figures in various areas (income, wealth, billionaires, education, etc.).

Income: $190 billion more (or a 56 percent pay raise)

● Apply the three-year (1997-1999) average income for white households to the average number of black households for those three years.

Wealth: $1 trillion more

● Apply the median net worth of white households in 1999 to the number of black households in 2000 to get the total net worth of black households in 2000.

● Apply the percentages of bank accounts, stocks, IRA, respectively, in the net worth of white households in 1999 to the total net worth of black households (estimated in the previous step), to arrive at the estimates of the value of black households' bank accounts, stocks, and IRA in 2000.

Billionaires: 31 billionaires

● Estimate the ratio of white and black U.S. billionaires in 2000 to the number of White and Black Americans 30 years old and over in 2000. (Bill Gates became a billionaire at the age of 31.)

● Apply this ratio to the number of blacks 30 years old and over in 2000.

Education:

Holders of High-school Diploma: 2 million more

● Estimate the percentage of whites 25 years and over in 2000 who are high-school graduates and/or have a college education (including those having no college degree, an undergraduate degree, a master's degree, a professional degree, or a doctorate).

● Apply this percentage to the number of blacks 25 years and over in 2000.

Holders of Undergraduate College Degrees: 2 million more

● Apply the percentage of whites 25 years and over in 2000 who have an undergraduate degree (including associate degrees and bachelor's degrees) to the number of blacks 25 years and over in 2000.

Holders of Master's Degrees: Half a million more

● Apply the percentage of whites 25 years and over in 2000 who have a master's degree to the number of blacks 25 years and over in 2000.

Doctorates: 180,000 more

● Apply the percentage of whites 25 years and over in 2000 who have a doctorate to the number of blacks 25 years and over in 2000.

Essay 1

Health Insurance

* *All blacks: 2.5 million more insured*

● Apply the insurance coverage rate for all whites in 1999 to the number of blacks in 1999.

* *Children (under 18 years): 620,000 more insured*

● Apply the insurance coverage rate for white children in 1999 to the number of black children in 1999.

Computer Ownership: 3 million more households

● Apply the percentage of white households having a computer in 2000 to the number of black households in 2000.

Internet Access: 3 million more households

● Apply the percentage of white households having Internet access in 2000 to the number of black households in 2000.

Automobiles: 1.5 million more automobiles

● Estimate the ratio of the total number of white non-Hispanic households with a car in 1997 to the number of white non-Hispanic households in 1997.

● Apply this ratio to the number of black households in 1997.

Prisoners: 700,000 fewer

● Estimate the ratio of the number of white non-Hispanic adult (18 years and over) prisoners in 1999 to the white non-Hispanic adult population in 1999.

● Apply this ratio to the black non-Hispanic adult population in 1999.

Juveniles in Detention: 33,000 fewer

● Estimate the ratio of the number of white non-Hispanic juveniles (under 18 years) in detention in 1997 to the white non-Hispanic juvenile population in 1997.

● Apply this ratio to the black non-Hispanic juvenile population in 1997.

Business Establishments: 600,000 more businesses, $2.7 trillion more in revenue

● Estimate the ratio of white business establishments in 1997 to the number of white adults in 1997.
● Apply this ratio to the number of black adults in 1997 to get the "what-if" number of black businesses.
● Apply the average sales and receipts of white businesses in 1997 to this "what if" number of black businesses.

Fortune 500 CEOs: 62 Fortune 500 CEOs

● Estimate the ratio of white and black Fortune 500 CEOs in 2000 to the number of white and black adults in 2000.
● Apply this ratio to the number of black adults in 2000.

Membership on Fortune 1000 Companies' Boards of Directors: 590 more board members

● Apply the percentage of companies with blacks on their boards (from the *Board Book*) to the Fortune 1000.
● Subtract that figure from 1000 to get the number of boards without black members.
● Under the assumption of black-white parity, each of these boards would then have at least one black member.

Voting: Over 1 million more voters

● Estimate white and black voter turnouts in 2000 by multiplying total voter turnout in 2000 by white and black racial percentages from the exit polling survey.
● Estimate the white voter turnout rate by dividing the white voter turnout (estimated in the previous step) by the white adult population in 2000.
● Apply this rate to the black adult population in 2000.

Congressmen: Nearly 1,500 in Congress

● Estimate the ratio of the total number of elected congressmen and

Essay 1

senators since the legislature was established in 1789 (11,642) to the white and black adult population in 2000.
- Apply this ratio to the black adult population in 2000.

Supreme Court Justices: 14 justices
- Estimate the ratio of the total number of justices since the Supreme Court's inception in 1790 (108) to the white and black adult population in 2000.
- Apply this ratio to the black adult population in 2000.

Presidents: 5 presidents
- Estimate the ratio of the total number of white Presidents to-date to the U.S. native population 35 years old and over in 2000. (The minimum age for Presidents is 35.)
- Apply this ratio to the U.S. native black population 35 years old and over in 2000.

Homeownership: 3 million more homeowners
- Apply the homeownership rate for whites in 2000 to the number of black households in 2000.

Home Equity: $760 billion more
Two steps:
- Apply the homeownership rate for whites in 2000 to the number of black households in 2000 to get the number of black-owned homes under the assumption of black-white parity.
- Apply the average home equity of white homeowners in 2000 to the number of black homeowners in 2000 estimated in the previous step.

Prepared by: Lawrence Q. Newton and Maria E. Ugincius, Editorial and Research Services. Date prepared: 8/1/01

[8] Du Bois, W.E.B., *The Souls of Black Folk*, Chapter 9, "Of The Sons of Master and Man," Chicago, A.C. McClurg & Co., (Cambridge):

University Press John Wilson and Son, Cambridge, U.S.A., 1903;
Bartleby.com, 1999. www.bartleby.com/114/

The National Urban League and Social Welfare Policy: A Historical Perspective

By William E. Spriggs and Suzanne Bergeron

A Brief Overview

Open its history books, research its archives, peruse its annual reports and journals, attend its annual conferences, review its research, and it will be clear that the 90-plus-year-old National Urban League and its local affiliates have devoted themselves to improving the social and economic condition of African Americans through fair and equitable access to employment and economic justice. The motto of the League's first logo, "Not Alms, But Opportunity," best captures its guiding philosophy. From its inception, the Urban League concentrated on securing access to education, skills and the basic services that helped individuals get jobs. It has conducted its own research and pioneered in the training of black social workers. It operated a whole host of programs— vocational training, manpower training and development, youth employment, housing and community development, and social services. It has on numerous occasions recommended to congressional committees and presidential administrations alike how to improve the social and economic conditions of not only African Americans but all Americans who live in poverty. From the days of the Great Migration of African Americans from the rural South to America's urban centers early in the 20th century, to the digital age of information technology the National Urban League has fought for economic justice. (National Urban League, 1980, 1985;[1] Hamilton and Hamilton, 1997).[2] This is the perspective that undergirds the Urban League's participation in the ongoing debate about America's welfare policy.

Essay **2**

The Family Support Act of 1988

The National Urban League played a major role during the welfare reform debates and legislation that led to enactment of the Family Support Act (FSA) in 1988 (National Urban League, December 1988).[3] During the first term of the Reagan Administration in the early 1980s, major cuts were implemented in social welfare programs, particularly in the Aid to Families with Dependent Children (AFDC) program. In response, the League conducted public hearings in 16 cities around the country that documented the tremendous hardship imposed upon AFDC recipients and other working poor as a result of the budget cuts implemented by the Omnibus Budget Reconciliation Act of 1981 (OBRA) (National Urban League, May 1982).[4] In 1984, the League formally adopted a policy calling for full employment and offered specific recommendations to achieve it (National Urban League, September 1984).[5] In 1986-1987, a League policy research and analysis initiative on welfare reform and collaboration with another important national community-based organization, Opportunities Industrialization Centers of America (O.I.C.), produced two specific bipartisan legislative proposals that were introduced in both houses of Congress in June 1986, and reintroduced in 1987 (Bergeron, Dixon, Glasgow, April 1988).[6]

While no congressional action occurred on these bills, they provided a policy prism, if you will, through which to evaluate the House and Senate welfare reform bills then under consideration (Bergeron, Dixon, Glasgow, April 1988).[7] The Urban League-O.I.C.-related bills focused on the role community-based organizations (CBOs) needed to be given in helping long-term AFDC recipients make the transition from welfare to permanent and unsubsidized employment. Four of the seven guiding principles, which underlay the League's policy recommendations for welfare reform (National Urban League, April 1987),[8] were incorporated in the 1987 House-passed bill, the Family Welfare Reform Act (H.R.1720) (Bergeron, Dixon, Glasgow, April 1988,[9] National Urban League, December 1988);[10] (Note 1).

Unfortunately, the 1988 welfare reform effort in Congress ended with a final bill that the Urban League could not support. The League believed that the Senate welfare bill (S.1511) failed to meet the League's basic principles (National Urban League, October 1987)[11] and when a conference committee reconciled the House and Senate versions, the League found the final product more reflective of the Senate bill that leaned toward the more punitive and inadequate White House perspective (National Urban League, December 1988).[12] It should be noted that in congressional testimony before both houses, the National Urban League reminded Congress of the broader issues of poverty and unemployment throughout the country and that the AFDC program only included one-third of America's poor. The testimony provided extensive analysis and perspective on these two national problems, including the growing phenomenon of the working poor, their disproportionate impact upon African Americans, and outlined strategies for their resolution (National Urban League, October 1987).[13] When testifying before the Senate Finance Committee, the League stated boldly that it " ... fully intends to keep these issues [poverty and unemployment] before the nation and the Congress, and is committed to fashioning creative, humane, and effective plans for their resolution" (National Urban League, October 1987).[14]

Not long after enactment of the Family Support Act of 1988, the League's national headquarters and Urban League affiliates in Akron, Ohio; Bridgeport, Connecticut; Detroit, Michigan; New Orleans, Louisiana; and Tacoma, Washington conducted focus group sessions with welfare recipients for more than two years in order to document their perceptions of welfare and to assess from the recipients' perspective what would be needed to get off and stay off welfare assistance. The results, compiled in a Final Report issued in 1992 (National Urban League, 1992)[15] documented, from first-hand accounts, the myriad issues and problems that produced poverty and welfare participation. They included: loss of full-time employment; unwed teenage pregnancy; lack of various support services (for example, child care, transportation, and health care) that forced some to give up or not accept employment; inadequate education and training; and business and industry moving out of the central city (National Urban League, 1992).[16]

Essay **2**

Tackling Poverty and Unemployment Through A Marshall Plan for America

The National Urban League kept its 1987 promise to keep the issues of poverty and unemployment before the nation and the Congress, as well as its commitment to "fashioning creative, humane, and effective plans for their resolution" (National Urban League, October 1987)[17] when it launched a far-reaching, national initiative, *Playing to Win: A Marshall Plan for America* at its 1991 Annual Conference (Tidwell, 1991).[18] The League seized the political moment when this nation saw a massive global transition to a post-Cold War world that was to produce a "peace dividend." The Marshall Plan was billed not as a "social program," but an economic investment program designed to serve overriding national interests. It emphasized the mutual dependency between the needs of the African-American community and the interests of the nation as a whole. Through its Marshall Plan for America, the League proposed that $50 billion per year, above monies normally allocated to human resource and physical infrastructure purposes, be set aside to fund the program over a ten-year period. The human resource investments focused on early childhood development, education and job training, while the physical infrastructure proposals sought to promote efforts in job creation and advancement of telecommunications technology. The League also proposed administrative provisions to ensure the structural integrity of the Marshall Plan for America over time that included the Presidential appointment of a Cabinet-level Marshall Plan Administrator, and the establishment of an Interagency Council that would oversee the Plan's execution (Tidwell, 1991).[19]

Following the Plan's release, the League undertook a massive national promotion and advocacy campaign, which included urging the 1992 presidential candidates to address its recommendations (McAlpine, Bergeron, 1992;[20] McAlpine, 1992).[21] At the opening of the 103rd Congress, the League also called upon the new Clinton Administration and the Congress to translate its Marshall Plan proposals into legislation (National Urban League, 1993)[22] and alerted its affiliates throughout the country to support the Administration's economic plan and stimulus package as "key vehicles for moving Marshall Plan for America legislation." (National Urban League, March 8, 1993).[23]

Dismantling the Safety Net—The Personal Responsibility and Work Opportunity Reconciliation Act of 1996

During the Clinton Administration's initial attempt in 1993 and 1994 to fashion welfare reform legislation that matched his campaign promise to "End Welfare as We Know It" (Clinton, Gore, 1992),[24] a simultaneous policy debate was occurring both within the Administration and in Congress over how to reform and consolidate federal job training programs. The Urban League was actively involved in trying to shape the policies on both workforce-development and welfare-reform fronts.

The League attempted to re-shape the welfare debate by advancing the idea that the issue of welfare reform needed to be discussed within the broader context of a national comprehensive workforce development strategy that would provide every individual with the opportunity and resources to prepare for and participate in high wage, high skill employment in order to compete in a global economy. Undergirding this strategy was a strong civil rights enforcement component. The League's concern was that the Administration's welfare reform efforts under the Department of Health and Human Services would become isolated from the Department of Labor's initiatives under its newly created Office of the American Workplace, and ultimately result in a two-track employment and training policy, one that was separate and unequal (National Urban League, February and July 1993).[25] The League pressed this point repeatedly in discussions with Administration and Congressional officials (Note 2). For example, in a letter to members of the Congressional Black Caucus, the League stated that it envisioned,

> " ... a universal system whereby the service delivery and funding mechanisms are driven by the respective needs of individuals, rather than by pre-conceived notions about why they are not economically independent and by artificial time limits. A comprehensive workforce development strategy would begin the process of changing our national mindset on education and job training from a fragmented approach ... to

Essay 2

a developmental approach. Such a strategy would place value and invest resources in preparing every child, youth, and adult for career choices that lead to economic self-sufficiency either as employees or as employers. It would bring true meaning to the notion of 'lifelong learning.' [The League then expressed its deep concern] that unless we merge welfare and workforce proposals into a well coordinated national policy, we will end up with a two-track employment and training policy, separate and unequal: a quality investment package for displaced and dislocated workers; and underfunded, ineffective programs for AFDC recipients and the disadvantaged" (National Urban League, May 11, 1994).[26]

However, the looming congressional elections of 1994 fed a political climate that favored the politics of welfare stereotyping. Congressional proposals for welfare reform ran the gamut of political perspectives: from extremely punitive approaches espoused by far right conservatives in Congress, to the Clinton Administration's centrist approach that introduced the notion of two-year "time-limited" welfare coupled with subsidized jobs and increased funds for education, training and job placement; to more liberal proposals that rejected time limits and instead called for increased federal aid for educating and training welfare recipients (Congressional Quarterly Almanac, 1994, pp. 364-365). [27] When Republicans won control of the House and Senate in the November 1994 elections, House Republicans vowed to implement their ten-point campaign manifesto known as their "Contract With America" (Congressional Quarterly, 1994, p. 22). [28] The "Contract" included a set of unprecedented extremely punitive proposals on social welfare policy, including dismantling the AFDC cash benefit entitlement and imposing a five-year lifetime limit on public assistance with a state option to end benefits after two years.

The outcome of the 1994 congressional elections required the

National Urban League and others concerned about welfare reform to adjust their advocacy approaches within a political environment unlike any faced before (Note 3). The League did not waiver in stating that any viable welfare-reform effort had to provide for job-training programs, and such support-services components as health care and child care. A series of "To Be Equal" columns from the League's leadership hammered away at getting this message across to the Administration, the Congress, and the general public (Note 4).

In 1995, the League proposed Ten Principles for Economic Self-Sufficiency that it (Note 5) later presented in testimony before the Senate Finance Committee, saying that " ... the debate and rush to reform the 'welfare' system continues to be isolated from another critical debate that is evolving with regards to fashioning a national workforce development system in other congressional committees, both on the House and Senate sides" (National Urban League, March 29, 1995). [29] The League urged that the principles serve as "key criteria for transforming our fragmented welfare and workforce programs into one, coherent, effective workforce development system leading to economic self-sufficiency" (National Urban League, March 29, 1995).[30] After the House passed its version of welfare reform that dismantled the nation's 60-year safety net, the League expressed its strong opposition to the bill, stating in a "To Be Equal" column that, "There's a brand of welfare reform that we should reject out of hand. It's one that would tear a gaping hole in the social safety net, allowing poor mothers and children to fall through to the streets to beg. Make no mistake. That could happen if, as the House of Representatives has legislated, teen mothers and children are cut off and if rigid time limits are imposed on the receipt of benefits" (National Urban League, May 19, 1995).[31] The League continued its effort to influence the running debate on welfare reform as deliberations shifted from the House to the Senate. It convened a special media forum on Capitol Hill with scholars and practitioners, and kept its local Urban League affiliates updated. After the Senate passed its welfare bill, the League joined the NAACP and other national organizations in a press conference to reject both the House and Senate welfare bills (National Urban

Essay 2

League, October 5, 1995).[32] In October 1995, the League called upon its local affiliates around the country to mobilize their communities to defeat the House and Senate passed bills, and again in November 1995 to urge a Presidential veto of the final welfare bill approved by both houses (National Urban League, October 12, 1995;[33] National Urban League, November 7, 1995).[34]

President Clinton vetoed the welfare reform bill approved by both houses of Congress twice, in December 1995 as part of the FY1996 Budget Reconciliation bill, and again in January 1996, when the welfare overhaul bill was passed as a stand-alone bill (HR 4). The veto victory was short-lived, however, as the machinery of presidential election year politics once again drove congressional deliberations on welfare reform. The National Urban League sent a letter to the President expressing serious concerns about the direction the Administration was taking on this issue, especially with regards to time limits, the lack of jobs, and the dismantling of the entitlement to federal assistance (National Urban League, March 7, 1996).[35] The League kept its local affiliates around the country updated, and as the debate once again shifted to the Senate, the Urban League sent a letter to the Senate Minority Leader urging defeat of the Senate proposals (National Urban League, July 19, 1996).[36] Undaunted, the Senate passed its bill with bipartisan support. In late July 1996, the Senate and the House reconciled their two different new versions of welfare reform legislation, both of which were objectionable to the League, and on July 29, as the joint legislation neared a final vote, Urban League President Hugh Price joined with other members of the Leadership Conference on Civil Rights (LCCR) to urge Congress and the President not to sign the legislation. Hugh Price opened his statement with the following indictment:

> "Congress is putting the finishing touches on sweeping welfare reform legislation that changes the basic rules of public assistance that have prevailed for generations. The bill is an abomination for America's most vulnerable mothers and children. It appears that Congress has wearied of the war on poverty and

decided to wage war against poor people instead. The legislation is fundamentally flawed and beyond fixing by tinkering with isolated provisions. We of the National Urban League implore President Clinton to stand for mothers and children by vetoing the legislation." (National Urban League, July 29, 1996)[37]

To no avail. The landmark Personal Responsibility and Work Opportunity Reconciliation Act of 1996 was subsequently passed by the House on July 31, 1996, and by the Senate on August 1, 1996. The President signed the bill into Public Law 104-193 on August 22, 1996.

An Overview of What Has Happened Since 1996

In 1997, the first year of the new law, the welfare caseload stood at 2,679,716 adults: 36 percent were white, 35.4 percent were African American, and 21.2 percent Hispanic. By 1999, the caseload had fallen more than 500,000, to 2,068,024 adults. But, now 32.4 percent were white, 36.4 percent were African Americans, and 23.1 percent were Hispanic.

What happened that the drop in white women on welfare had been dramatic enough to lower their share of the program, but leave it with a much higher share of African-American and Hispanic women?

Researchers Cheryl Miller and Kenya Cox (2001) found that differences in the share of jobs that are in the service sector was the most consistent economic variable in explaining the reduction in African-American and Hispanic caseloads: That is, African-American and Hispanic caseloads declined the most in states with a high share of service sector employment.

But, they also found that welfare recipients who lived in metropolitan, rather than rural areas, tended to have more difficulty securing work—and a disproportionate share of the African-American and Latino-American recipients lived in urban areas. More importantly, they noted that two-state welfare policies had a significant impact on African-American women: work activity sanctions and family-cap policies. These two punitive policies were significant in explaining case load reductions for African Americans but not for whites. States were far more likely to sanction—thus remove African Americans—from public support for failure to meet work activity requirements, than to sanction whites. And family cap policies, which fixed benefits so that children born after the mother began receiving welfare benefits would not receive additional support, had a disproportionate affect on African Americans.

That disparity is at the heart of one of the National Urban League's major concerns about the operation of the Temporary Assistance to Needy Families program. The new program potentially added many work support mechanisms to aid women in getting off the welfare rolls, from transportation to child care to job training assistance. But, a body of research has now documented that the gap in rate at which white and African-American women have been able to get off the rolls is related to racial disparities in access to work support and to disparities in sanctions against women of color.

During a briefing for senior congressional staff on research on racial disparities in race and welfare in May 2001, Maya Rockeymoore (2001), Senior Resident Scholar for Health and Income Security of the Urban League's Institute for Opportunity and Equality, referred to three studies that highlight sources of racial disparities in the program. First, research by the Chicago Urban League has found that whites in Chicago and throughout Illinois were almost three times more likely than African Americans to be referred to educational programs. Secondly, research by Professor Susan Gooden, of Virginia Tech, found that in rural Virginia counties she surveyed, African Americans were less likely than whites to receive transportation assistance or get support for formal education. Finally, studies by Gooden, and other work by Professors Harry Holzer, of Georgetown University and the Urban Institute and Michael Stoll, of the University of California at Los Angeles determined that employers look less favorably on hiring African-American welfare recipients than white welfare recipients.

In April 2002, the League sponsored a briefing for the staff of the Congressional Black Caucus on the civil rights issues in TANF reform. At that briefing, Ronald Walters (2002), of the University of Maryland, shared the summary of a set of researchers who make up the "Scholar

Practitioner Program of the Devolution Initiative," a program funded by the Kellogg Foundation. He reported on findings in five states: In Milwaukee, researchers found that African-American recipients were more likely than whites to report negative treatment by caseworkers, including being less likely to receive work support assistance, and negative experiences with employers. In Washington state, researchers found that African Americans, Native Americans and Asian Americans had the most negative experiences with Washington state's WorkFirst program. In Miami, researchers found Haitians to have the most negative experiences with the state TANF plan in Florida. In Harlem and the Lower East Side of Manhattan, researchers found that African Americans and Latinos experienced more difficulty than whites in getting employment and were more likely to get sanctioned. Finally, in Mississippi, researchers found a statewide pattern of disproportionately negative treatment for African Americans compared to whites—except in the 2nd Congressional District of the state, where African Americans have political control of the county governments. Maya Rockeymoore made the point that when the Aid to Dependent Children program was created during the 1930s New Deal, compromises with Southern Democrats led to the exclusion of African Americans from this vital part of the country's safety-net legislation. Those barriers were not removed until the Civil Rights Movement of the 1960s forced President Lyndon Johnson's War on Poverty to correct racial disparities. The major change of the new law from AFDC was to put states back in control, and reopen the doors to discrimination in a program that had been an entitlement.

In August 1996, employment in the private non-farm sector stood at just over 100 million. By December of that year, employment in that sector had risen to nearly 101.5 million, a rate of about 280,000 new jobs a month. Three years later, in 1999, private-sector, non-farm employment was growing at the still enviable rate of 211,000 a month. The TANF program was launched during this period of rapid job growth, and the drop in the welfare rolls reflected it. In 2000, the work participation rate for all families on TANF reached 34 percent.

But, after the Federal Reserve Board of Governors took a series of steps

Essay 2

in 1999 and 2000 to slow the economy, and so in February 2001 employment had peaked at just under 112 million workers, and as of May of the following year stood at a little below 110 million. So, in a little over one year, employers dropped 1.8 million paychecks from their payrolls. It is in this environment—with jobs being lost at an average rate of 153,000 a month that TANF is being reauthorized.

When the Aid to Dependent Children program began during the New Deal, it was part of a set of programs that comprised the safety net. Not only did it help individuals experiencing hard times, it kept up the demand for goods and services when the economy itself slowed down, thereby saving the economy itself from sliding into a deeper recession.

What the 1996 law did was to remove that entitlement, and to limit eligibility for welfare benefits to five years, regardless of the health of the economy. Now the five-year limit has hit, and the economy is in need of protecting consumer demand.

The National Campaign for Jobs and Income Support (2002), in a report released at a League press conference in February 2002, noted that during the first ten months of the 1990-1991 recession, when the old AFDC program was in operation, 41 of 42 states reported rising unemployment and welfare caseloads. But, during the first ten months of this recession, only 32 of 47 states had rising unemployment and welfare caseloads. And, there were 14 states with rising unemployment and falling welfare caseloads. So, under TANF, as job opportunities have diminished, support for families is shrinking.

Further, we should not believe that, because employment was up and caseloads were down in the late 1990s, when the economy was producing jobs, TANF really addressed the issue of how best to reduce poverty. The Urban Institute (Zedlewski, Giannarelli, et al 2002) has noted that while the official poverty rate declined from 13.7 percent in 1996 to 11.8 percent in 1999, the incidence of extreme poverty—defined as living below half the official poverty line (for a family of three, extreme poverty is income below roughly $7,100)—increased. A key component of that increase, according to the study, is the smaller number of families benefiting from government anti-poverty programs like AFDC and food stamps.

What the Urban League Wants Now

To correct these clear failings of the revised welfare program—to eliminate discrimination in the program's operation; to protect recipients against downturns in the economy; and to extend benefits to the most needy—the National Urban League offers these specific recommendations:

- **Expand opportunities for education, including post-secondary education, and training.**
 The correlation between education and increased earnings is straightforward. According to the U.S. Census Bureau, in 2000, a woman without a high school degree earned $9,996, a high school degree earned an average of $15,119; and an Associate's degree earned her $23,269. In contrast, a woman with a Bachelor's degree received $30,487; and a Master's degree earned her $40,249. In short, the more education one has, the easier is the path out of poverty. The National Urban League Institute for Opportunity and Equality recently released a report showing that under AFDC, welfare recipients, with high school diplomas, were more likely to attend college than non-recipients, but that under TANF, welfare recipients are less likely to attend college (Cox and Spriggs, 2002).[38] There was a 20-percentage point swing in that change, significantly reducing college attendance of welfare recipients relative to non-recipient poor women. State restrictions that limited college enrollment by not considering it a valid work activity were significant in reducing college attendance for African Americans, while for all recipients, increased hours spent at work because of the TANF work requirements reduced college attendance. Given our shortage of teachers, nurses and computer programmers, we all lose out from policies that discourage college attendance. Thus, states must be allowed to count education and training as qualified work activities in their state-designed programs—to include postsecondary education and expanded quality training—and for the length of time the recipients need.

Essay 2

- **Ensure a continuum of pre- and post-work support services for TANF participants.**
  Study after study confirms the need to ensure that families have access to the various support services in order to be able to work steadily. These include: access to quality infant and child care, particularly during non-standard hours; the ability to take time off from work to deal with family or medical needs; access to transportation, health care, food assistance when needed, and housing. Research has shown that some families who remain on assistance are faced with multiple or severe problems that impede their ability to move to the labor market and stay employed. States must be allowed the flexibility to fashion realistic and proven interventions that meet the need, not satisfy artificial time limits to address such problems as substance abuse, mental and physical health, and domestic violence.

- **Ensure fair treatment in state welfare programs by improving program performance and accountability, improving data collection, and restoring benefits for legal immigrants.**
  There is mounting evidence that the discretion to offer assistance in child care, transportation, training and other work support programs is offered to a significant degree on a racially discriminatory basis. Studies show that there is less employer demand for African-American welfare recipients than for whites, and that welfare caseworkers are less likely to refer them to important education and training programs. With African-American unemployment rates consistently double the rate of whites in May 2002 (blacks had a 10.2 percent unemployment rate compared to 5.2 percent for whites), the Congress must take notice of the fact that disparate outcomes in the labor market based on race limit the options of black and other minority TANF recipients and make the proposed 70-percent workforce requirement a highly untenable Catch-22. Thus, TANF's reauthorization must include requirements that all existing civil rights laws be enforced, and mechanisms to improve accountability in state and county TANF delivery systems regarding

their fair treatment of and effective service delivery to all program participants—including persons with language barriers and disabilities. We urge adoption of specific improvements in how state welfare data is collected and made publicly available to better document how minorities and the disabled fare in state TANF programs and *across* state programs. Better data collection would also help document which interventions—child care assistance, transportation and other programs—are the most helpful in turning recipients into self-sufficient workers. Further, to insure quality and fair service delivery to all TANF participants through a stable and professional workforce, the reauthorization should also include measures that enable caseworkers to improve their ability to deliver service of the highest quality. Fairness also dictates that the current ban on legal immigrants' access to TANF be lifted.

- **Rescinding the drug felony conviction lifetime ban on receiving TANF and food stamps by repealing Section 115.**
  Section 115 of the 1996 welfare law, included after just two minutes of debate, has had a devastating impact on low-income women and children in African-American and Latino-American communities. Section 115 stipulates that persons convicted of a state or federal felony offense involving the use or sale of drugs be banned for life from getting cash assistance and food stamps. According to a recent study released by The Sentencing Project, the Washington-based think tank on criminal justice issues, the ban affects more than 92,000 women and 135,000 children—nearly half of whom are African American or Latino American. There is no such thing as "child well-being," under this provision when children are placed at risk of delinquency, neglect, and ultimately family dissolution through the prospect of reduced family income support. The reauthorized law must repeal this provision; access to TANF and food stamps is essential to the rehabilitative efforts of women ex-offenders and to the well-being of their children.

Essay 2

- **Reject super-waivers.**

    Some in Congress are proposing rolling all current support and human development programs into one block grant to states to let them rearrange the distribution of services as they see fit. Included in the block grant would be anti-poverty entitlements like Food Stamps, and such human-development programs as job training under the Workforce Investment Act. While the creativity and flexibility of the 1996 law allowed many governors to lower their states' welfare caseload, the flexibility did not lead to a drop in extreme poverty, nor did it prevent the reappearance of discrimination in the welfare system. Many of the programs to be lumped in the super waiver are programs now overseen by officials at the local level—which would transfer more power to governors—none of whom are African American and away from locally-elected officials—many of whom are African American. Bundling together into "super" block grants programs that were originally meant to stabilize consumer demand during economic recessions could threaten the stability of neighborhood-level economies with high pockets of unemployment, because the block grants will not automatically increase the flow of funds to where they are needed when the economy slows. In fact, as we have seen with TANF, they could have the perverse effect of moving in the opposite direction during an economic slowdown. Also, some governors have, unfortunately, raided their TANF funds for many programs that appear to be only marginally connected to directly aiding the poor. Already, under TANF, a much smaller share of the money is going to poor individuals and a larger share to programs.

Conclusion

The National Urban League will be monitoring the development of this debate, and continuing to raise concerns on behalf of its constituents. The aim will continue to be moving African Americans into the economic mainstream, and keeping the playing field level.

References

1 National Urban League, Inc. *70th Anniversary Journal 1910-1980.* 1980, and National Urban League, Inc. *75th Anniversary Journal 1910-1985.* 1985. These two journals provide condensed but comprehensive information about the history of the National Urban League and its affiliates as the Urban League Movement evolved, decade by decade, since its founding in 1910.

2 Hamilton, Dona Cooper, and Charles V. Hamilton. 1997. *The Dual Agenda, The African-American Struggle for Civil and Economic Equality.* New York: Columbia University Press. In this landmark book, the authors trace the social welfare policy positions taken by civil rights organizations (including the National Urban League) from the New Deal to the 1990s. The authors demonstrate the many ways in which the Civil Rights Movement fought not only to end racial segregation and discrimination but also to support social and economic justice for all Americans. Through extensive research they reveal an aspect of the civil rights struggle which has been too long overlooked or obscured—one that has fought for policies to expand social and economic welfare for blacks and whites alike.

3 National Urban League. December 1988. Internal paper, "A Case Study on the National Urban League's Policy Initiative on Welfare Reform and the Legislative Process." Office of the Vice President, Washington Operations, Washington, D.C. This case study provides a comprehensive and detailed account of the National Urban League's actions on welfare reform from 1984 to 1988, including testifying at several hearings before Congress, working with congressional staff and their members on key provisions and language, collaborating with other national community based organizations, and mobilizing Urban League affiliates throughout the country.

4 National Urban League. May 1982. "Don't Just Stand There and Kill Us." *A People's Report on AFDC by the Social Welfare Cluster.* New York.

5 National Urban League. September 1984. "A Policy Paper on Full Employment." Office of the Vice President for Washington Operations. Washington, D.C.

Essay 2

6 Bergeron, Suzanne; Johanne Dixon, and Douglas G. Glasgow. April 1988. "Welfare Reform: An Antipoverty Strategy." *Black Americans and Public Policy, Washington, D.C.: National Urban League.* The bills were The Opportunities for Employment Preparation Act of 1986 (H.R.5064/S.2578) and the Aid to Families and Employment Transition Act of 1986 (H.R.5065/S.2579) introduced on June 18, 1986.

7 See Reference 6 above.

8 National Urban League. April 1987. Testimony of Douglas G. Glasgow, Vice President for Washington Operations, National Urban League, Inc., before the House Committee on Education and Labor on Welfare Reform. April 29, 1987.

9 See Reference 6 above.

10 See Reference 3 above.

11 National Urban League. October 1987. Testimony of Douglas G. Glasgow, Vice President for Washington Operations, National Urban League, Inc., before the Committee on Finance on Welfare Reform. October 28, 1987.

12 See Reference 3 above.

13 See Reference 11 above.

14 See Reference 11 above.

15 National Urban League. 1992. National Urban League, Inc. Focus Group Sessions Family Support Act Final Report 1992. New York: National Urban League, Inc. Programs Department. During the second round of the Focus Group Sessions, the Bridgeport Urban League was forced to close its doors in 1991, unfortunately falling victim to the same poverty that had become a way of life for participants. States were in the process of implementing the Family Support Act of 1988 during this period.

16 See Reference 15 above.

17 See Reference 11 above.

18 Tidwell, Billy J., Ph.D. 1991. *Playing to Win: A Marshall Plan for America*. Washington, D.C.: National Urban League, July 1991. The plan included very specific proposals calling upon the nation to commit to a program of long-term, strategic investment in the development of its human resources and the physical infrastructure that supports economic activity in order to move the economy forward and secure our economic future.

19 See Reference 18 above.

20 McAlpine, Robert, and Suzanne Bergeron. 1992. Special Supplement to *The Urban League News*, 1992 Conference Issue, *Playing to Win: A Marshall Plan for America*. Washington, D.C.: National Urban League, 1992. This four-page document provides a detailed accounting of the history behind the Marshall Plan concept and the extensive advocacy actions taken for its promotion. It includes the various outcomes in Congress and gives the political context in which the League promoted its plan.

21 McAlpine, Robert. 1992. Internal Document. *"Legislative Briefing on the National Urban League's Marshall Plan for America, Actions in the 102nd Congress."* Prepared for National Urban League Board of Trustees Meeting. New York: November 17, 1992.

22 National Urban League, February 18, 1993. *Statement by John E. Jacob, President and Chief Executive Officer, National Urban League, Inc. on President Clinton's State of the Union Address*. New York. The statement made the connection between the Clinton Administration's initial plan for national economic development and the League's Marshall Plan for America when it noted, " ... The Administration's program embodies many of the aspects of the National Urban League's Marshall Plan for America, which is a comprehensive, targeted program of investments in our infrastructure and in our people. We strongly urge the Administration and the Congress to look closely at our Marshall Plan and ensure that as the President's program moves through the legislative process, it will embody the critical aspects of our proposal, especially those that sharply target investments in job creation and in human resources

Essay **2**

development to those most in need." The statement also signaled that the League found room for improvement when it stated that, " ... while [the President's plan] may fall short of what many, including the National Urban League, would desire, it is a solid step forward that should be supported by all citizens concerned for their nation's future."

23 National Urban League. March 8, 1993. *Legislative Action Alert.* Washington, D.C.

24 Clinton, Governor Bill, and Senator Al Gore. 1992. *Putting People First, How We Can All Change America.* New York: Times Books.

25 National Urban League, February 11, 1993 and July 23, 1993. Letters to Bruce Reed, Deputy Assistant to the President. Washington, D.C. Through these letters, the League placed a formal request to the White House to be included among the non-governmental experts for consultation on welfare reform and provided the League's perspective on a national comprehensive workforce development strategy.

26 National Urban League, May 11, 1994. Letter to members of the Congressional Black Caucus.

27 *Congressional Quarterly*, 1994. The 50th Annual CQ Almanac 1994, 103rd Congress, 2nd Session. Washington, D.C.: *Congressional Quarterly Inc.*, Volume L, pp. 364-365.

28 *Congressional Quarterly*, 1994. The 50th Annual CQ Almanac 1994, 103rd Congress, 2nd Session. Washington, D.C.: *Congressional Quarterly Inc.*, Volume L, p. 22.

29 National Urban League. March 29, 1995. Statement by Audrey Rowe, Executive Vice President, National Urban League, before the Senate Finance Committee. Washington, D.C.

30 See Reference 29 above.

31 National Urban League. May 19, 1995. "Investing in Infrastructure and Children." *To Be Equal*, by Hugh B. Price, Column #20.

32 National Urban League. October 5, 1995. Statement by Audrey Rowe, Executive Vice President, National Urban League on House/Senate Proposals for Welfare Reform, Washington, D.C.

33 National Urban League. October 12, 1995. *Action Alert*. Washington, D.C.

34 National Urban League. November 7, 1995. *Action Alert*. Washington, D.C.

35 National Urban League. March 7, 1996. Letter to the President from Hugh B. Price, president, National Urban League.

36 National Urban League. July 19, 1996. Letter to Thomas A. Daschle, Senate Minority Leader, from Audrey Rowe, executive vice president, National Urban League.

37 National Urban League. July 29, 1996. *Welfare Reform vs. Welfare Reality*. Press statement by Hugh B. Price, president, National Urban League.

38 Cox, Kenya and William Spriggs. June 2002. *Negative Effects of TANF on College Attendance of Welfare Recipients*. National Urban League Institute for Opportunity and Equality, Special Research Report 2002-01.

Notes

Note 1 The four National Urban League principles incorporated in the House-passed welfare reform bill, H.R. 1720, in December 1987 were: (1) The primary objective in reforming our system of social welfare must be to strengthen the family. (2) Families and individuals having multiple barriers to employment such as a lack of education, skills training, work experience, and long term spells of poverty and unemployment must be targeted for intensive services that facilitate their transition to the labor market. (3) To insure permanent entry or reentry into the labor force, special emphasis must be placed on the critical transition stage from public assistance to employment. Support services such as child care, transportation, extended Medicaid coverage and

Essay 2

income disregards must be provided. (4) A comprehensive continuum of service delivery systems must be utilized in national and local plans for improving the lives of poor families and individuals. Along with federal, state, and local private agencies, community based organizations must be strategically involved in both planning and service delivery levels.

Note 2 Internal League papers document that the League shared its concept for a comprehensive workforce development strategy through contact with: White House Deputy Assistant to the President for Domestic Policy, Bruce Reed; Co-Chair of the White House Working Group on Welfare Reform, David Ellwood; then Secretary of Labor, Robert Reich; Director of the Women's Bureau, Karen Nussbaum; congressional staff; members of the Congressional Black Caucus; Administration staff when participating in meetings to review and comment on their preliminary proposals for welfare reform; and external advocacy organizations.

Note 3 Internally, the National Urban League had gone through a major transition with the transfer of its leadership in mid-1994, from John E. Jacob (who retired) to its new president, Hugh B. Price. Mr. Price articulated a three-pronged agenda for the National Urban League: 1) the education and development of our children growing up in the inner city so that they have the academic and social skills to be successful; 2) to enable their families to become economically self-sufficient; and 3) to encourage racial inclusion so that our folk can participate fully in the mainstream economy (*The State of Black America* 1995, National Urban League).

Note 4 "Jobs and Welfare Reform." *To Be Equal*, by John E. Jacob, Column #6, 2/9/94; "Balancing Jobs and Training." *To Be Equal*, by John E. Jacob, Column #8, 2/23/94; "A New War on the Poor?" by John E. Jacob, Column #9, 3/2/94; "Make Work Pay." *To Be Equal*, by John E. Jacob, Column #14, 4/6/94; "Jobs for the Inner City." *To Be Equal*, by Hugh B. Price, Column #24, 9/30/94.

Note 5 This was spearheaded by the National Urban League's new Executive Vice President, Audrey Rowe, who came to the League as a former Commissioner of Social Services in both Washington, D.C. and Connecticut. Under her leadership, the League convened a special internal ad hoc committee of executive, program, policy and Urban League affiliate staff to develop a position on economic self-sufficiency. The committee produced a set of ten principles for consideration in the welfare reform debate.

3

The Black Worker: Continuing Quest for Economic Parity

By Bernard E. Anderson

In more ways than one might realize at first glance, the concept and the actual fact of work has always been central to the existence of African Americans in America. As National Urban League President Hugh B. Price noted in a recent issue of *Opportunity Journal*, "black Americans' relationship to work was—for centuries—profoundly distorted by slavery and the legal segregation that followed." But Price also asserted that, nonetheless, "Work is an African-American tradition, just as much as it has been for other peoples and ethnic groups ... because work is essentially the activity through which human beings define themselves and their relationship to, not merely society, but to life itself."

Examining the status of black workers provides a keen prism through which to consider the status of Black America itself for several reasons. One is that, because African Americans, compared with other groups, own significantly less capital, land, and other income producing assets, employment opportunity—having a job—is by far the major source of their economic well being. Secondly, black labor is an important part of the nation's workforce, and is indispensable for economic growth. Labor shortages can truncate growth and prevent the economy from reaching its full productive potential. Balanced economic growth requires the use of all the nation's human resources, including black labor. Third, the level and quality of black participation in the labor market is central to the quality of black civic life. We know all too well that the failure to fully utilize the black workforce contributes to welfare dependency and poverty. More positively, employment helps define individuals' social status, and provides an alternative to crime, youth delinquency, and other social problems.

The Employment Situation

In the first quarter of 2002, the non-farm labor force (the standard measure of the nation's army of workers) totaled 143 million people, of whom 133 million were employed, and 8.6 million were unemployed.[1] The black workforce included 16.9 million people, of whom roughly 15 million were employed, and nearly 1.9 million were unemployed. Thus, in early 2002, black workers comprised 11.9 percent of the workforce, 11.2 percent of the employed, and 22.1 percent (or slightly more than one of every five persons) who were unemployed.

Occupation and Industry Profile

About 7 of every 10 black workers hold white collar or service jobs.[2] Nearly one-fifth, or 4.4 million hold management or professional jobs. Fewer than a third of all black workers are in blue collar jobs, in contrast to the pattern of employment that was typical of the black workforce forty years ago (Table 1).

About 2.3 million black workers, mainly black women, hold clerical, administrative assistant, and similar jobs. There are 300,000 employed in the financial services sector, and 133,000 in retail trade. Another 2.3 million are black sales workers employed mainly in retail trade.

Blue-collar jobs include skilled craftsmen, semi-skilled production workers, and less skilled laborers and helpers. Fewer than one-third, or 6.4 million black workers are employed in such jobs, of whom 1.6 million are skilled craftsmen, 2.3 million production workers, and 1.4 million laborers and helpers. Such workers are broadly distributed across the industries that typically employ a large number of blue-collar workers, including manufacturing, transportation, public utilities, and construction.

Except for the construction industry, black workers are employed throughout American industry roughly in proportion to the industry distribution of all workers (Table 2). For example, slightly more than half of all workers, 57.4 percent, are employed in the services and trade industries, and 56.5 percent of black workers are so employed. In comparison, the construction industry employs 6.3 percent of all workers, but only 3.9 percent of all black workers.

The 5.5 million black workers in the services sector are more heavily concentrated (3.4 million) than other workers in personal services, including the hospitality industries, laundry, cleaning, and personal care. But black workers also hold a substantial number of jobs, about 1.8 million, in hospitals and health services. In fact, the health care industry is one of the major sources of employment for black professional and nonprofessional workers in urban areas throughout the country.

The financial services industry is one that black workers have penetrated with some success in recent years. Today, 735,000 black workers are employed in financial services, where 184,000 (7.2 percent of all) hold management and professional jobs; and 345,000 (12.6 percent) hold administrative and sales jobs.

Finally, the black worker has established a foothold in the public sector. Nearly one million (957,000) black employees are public administrators, representing about 18 percent of all employees in the public sector. Black public administrators hold 10.6 percent of all executive and legislative offices, 16.5 percent of jobs in public finance, and 14.3 percent of the jobs administering economic development programs.

Since 1960, public administration has emerged as a major venue for black professional and managerial talent. Indeed, in scope and level of responsibility, the public sector often provides greater opportunities than the private sector for black professionals and managers. Historically speaking, this stems from the greater freedom—that is, the lesser degree of racism—black Northerners and black Southern migrants enjoyed in the urban North in the decades after the Supreme Court's approval of legal segregation in the *Plessy v. Ferguson* decision of 1896 and before the civil rights victories of the 1960s. Since then, that pattern of employment has been most significantly due to the influence of black voters. The election of black office holders to mayor, city council, appointments to school boards, commissions and public authorities, all led to wider oppor-

Essay 3

tunities for black professionals, managers, and other skilled jobs in recent years.

Black Workers and Unions

About 12 percent of the civilian workforce are members of unions, but a slightly higher proportion of black workers, nearly 15 percent, hold union cards. These numbers include union representation of workers in both the private and public sectors.

Union membership is beneficial to workers for many reasons, but one of the most important is that union wages are usually higher than that for non-union workers. The union membership wage premium—the difference in wages for union and non-union workers—is larger for black workers than others in the labor force.

For example, in 2001, median weekly earnings for black full-time wage and salary workers were $487, and for similar white workers, $612. But black union members earned $603 weekly, compared with $463 for black non-union workers.[3] The wage difference represents nearly $8,000 per year more income for black families of union workers. Stated differently, black union members enjoy a 30-percent wage premium over black non-union workers, compared with the 25-percent advantage white union members have over their white non-union counterparts.

The industry concentration of black workers helps explain their union wage premium. As described above, black workers have a major presence in basic manufacturing, transportation, health services, and the public sector. These industries have long been areas with major union representation. Public sector unions, for example, are now among the largest organizations affiliated with the AFL-CIO, and they have thousands of black members. Also, the National Education Association, not affiliated with the labor federation, but heavily engaged in collective bargaining and worker representation, also includes many thousand black members. The emergence of black workers as major participants in organized labor is one of the most important developments affecting the American workforce in the last four decades.

Historical Redux

Before the 1960s, the black worker held an unfavorable position in the American economy. The number of black workers in most non-farm industries was small in relation to the total workforce, and relatively few black workers held skilled, technical, supervisory, or white collar jobs.[4] Black men were employed mainly in unskilled and semi-skilled production jobs, or worked as unskilled laborers in construction. Black women were employed primarily in private household jobs and service occupations. Black professional and managerial talent was employed almost entirely in the racially segregated market, where black people provided services to others within their own group.[5]

Partly as a result of their limited opportunity in the labor market, black workers often dropped out of the labor force entirely. For example, in 1960 the labor force participation rate for black workers was 57 percent, compared with a 63-percent participation rate for all workers. Black workers in non-farm industries were employed in jobs that were highly vulnerable to cyclical variations in business activity. They were the last hired when employment was growing, and the first fired in an economic downturn. They were also employed in the lowest-paid jobs, even in less cyclical industries, such as the service sector.

Substantial numbers of black workers were underemployed. They worked at less than the minimum wage; worked part time though they wanted full-time jobs; or worked in jobs for which their education and experience made them over-qualified. In short, prior to the 1960s, the black worker was a marginal presence in the American workforce, while at the same time playing an essential role in some occupations in which it was difficult to attract other workers.

That was the "state of black labor" when the Civil Rights Movement moved into its "high gear" in the 1950s and early 1960s. One of its major goals was to break the chain of racial exclusion in the American workforce in order to improve job opportunities and increase the income of black families.

It is important to note that the famous civil rights March on Washington in August 1963 was for "Jobs and Freedom." The juxtaposition of those words was carefully considered. They represented the views of A. Philip Randolph, the venerable labor and civil rights leader, that victory in the struggle for civil rights would be empty if it did not include victory in the pursuit of economic rights and opportunities for black workers.

The Civil Rights Movement included several leaders whose primary focus was better jobs and income for black workers. For example, Whitney M. Young, Jr., president of the National Urban League from 1961 to his tragic death in 1971, focused heavily on the effort to open jobs in the private sector for black professionals and managers. In doing so, Young intensified the long-held priority of the League's headquarters and its affiliates throughout the country of breaking job barriers.

Reverend Leon H. Sullivan, the Philadelphia Baptist activist preacher, led a major selective patronage campaign to break down the walls of racial discrimination that blocked black workers from most non-menial, private sector jobs in that city. He later organized the Opportunities Industrialization Centers, a network of local job training organizations, to prepare minorities for the jobs that were beginning to open up as employment discrimination started to weaken.

Other local civil rights protests focused on employment discrimination in the construction industry. Between 1963 and 1969, there were major direct action demonstrations against building contractors and unions in New York, Philadelphia, Pittsburgh, Cleveland, and Chicago.[6] Building trades unions representing electricians, carpenters, operating engineers, and plumbers were special targets in these mass protest demonstrations. Often the conflict was sparked by the anomalous situation in which a major project, involving the construction of a school, library, housing, or other public facility, was located in a predominantly black neighborhood, but no black skilled labor would be employed on the project. The building trade unions had few, if any, black members or apprentices, and most often, were unwilling to admit black workers or women into the trade.

Determinants of Change

Over the past four decades, many developments occurred in the American economy and society to bring black workers into the positions they occupy today. While many factors played a role, three loom large as key determinants of the "state of black labor": the pace and pattern of economic growth, the implementation of public policy to protect equal employment opportunity, and the educational advancement of African-American youth.

Black Workers and the American Economy

The economic status of the black workforce is closely bound up with the direction and pattern of economic growth. It is as though black workers bear a relationship to the economy similar to that of the caboose and the train. When the train speeds up, the caboose speeds up. And when the train slows down, so does the caboose. But in the natural order of things, the caboose never catches up with the engine.

During the 1960s and '70s the American economy never reached its full productive potential because as the economy grew and approached full employment, it encountered the threat of inflation. Job growth was stunted as the Federal Reserve Board raised interest rates, choking off growth at a relatively high level of unemployment—usually above 6.0 percent.

Throughout that period, the unemployment rate among black workers remained above 7.0 percent—twice the rate of unemployment among white workers. Unemployment rates for black teenagers also hovered in the neighborhood of 30 percent. Many black youth dropped out of the workforce, did not seek employment, and were not counted among the unemployed.

It is important to note that the unemployment rate reflects workers seeking employment but unable to find it. But job search can be interpreted as a sign of hopefulness about job prospects, as well as a response to the requirement that persons who receive unemployment compensation must continue to search for work. This reality might help explain why the labor force participation rate (LFPR) for black workers in the early 1970s exceeded that for white workers (72.0 percent vs. 70.1 percent). The widest gap was for four year college graduates (87.4 percent vs. 81.9 percent), but black high school graduates (76.8 percent) also showed a higher LFPR than white high school graduates (69.7 percent).

Essay 3

This suggests that both black high school and college graduates faced a more congenial labor market in the late 1960s and early 1970s than in earlier years when opportunities for both groups were very restricted. The more favorable labor market suggests that employers were beginning to open some doors to black workers and hire them in jobs from which they had previously been excluded. In fact, modest gains in employment for black workers were observed during the long period of economic growth from 1964 to 1969 when employment steadily rose at a rate of more than 4.0 percent per year.

The 1970s and 1980s

Black workers made few gains toward a better position in the labor market during the two decades between 1970 and 1990. That was a period when the economy struggled to reach full employment as policymakers worked hard to keep inflation under control. Throughout that period, the black unemployment rate slipped back above 9.0 percent and remained there, while the white unemployment rate remained below 5.0 percent.

At the same time, black employment prospects were adversely affected by the steadily changing structure of the American economy. Jobs were shifting from manufacturing to services, from the cities to the suburbs, and from the snowbelt to the sunbelt. The structural changes were generated by increasing competition from foreign producers, and technological change in the production process, both of which affected the domestic cost of production and the skill requirements of labor demand. These developments had a major impact on manufacturing industries, such as automobiles, machine tools, steel, and other basic industries where black workers had gained increased employment opportunity during and after World War II.

For example, during the 1970 and 1980 decades, the big-three U.S. auto makers steadily lost market share to foreign, mainly Japanese, producers, as more and more American consumers bought smaller, more gas efficient cars. As a result, the U.S. automakers introduced automation into the production process; reduced new hiring and expanded overtime hours of work; closed aging production plants in the Northeast and Midwest; and built new, more technologically based plants in the South and West. These developments had a significant impact in reducing employment opportunities for auto workers in New York, Pennsylvania, Ohio, Michigan, and Illinois. African-American auto workers, who accounted for about ten percent of the nearly two million auto workers at that time, were disproportionately affected by the structural change in the industry.

The structural change in the economy led some observers to ascribe non-racial causation to the worsening economic fortunes of black industrial workers during the postwar years. For example, Professor William J. Wilson argued that the changing economy of the past several decades created a situation in which institutional forces supplanted race as the dominant factor responsible for perpetuating racial inequality in American economic life.[7] The plight of black workers in the basic industries since the 1960s offers substantial evidence to support Professor Wilson's thesis. Not only did the number of jobs decline in the geographic areas where black workers lived, but also the skill requirements of jobs shifted to levels beyond that of large numbers of black job seekers.

The 1990 Decade

The best evidence for the proposition that a rising tide lifts all boats is the experience during the 1990 decade. Between 1993 and 2000, the economy created 22 million new jobs. During that time, in contrast to previous expansions, inflation remained under control. As a result, job creation continued unabated, as productivity gains led to increases in earnings for all income groups.

In the midst of the vibrant, balanced economic growth during the 1990s, the black unemployment rate fell from above 11 percent to below 8 percent—the lowest level in 30 years. Median black family income rose to more than $29,000, and the rate of poverty among black families fell to 26 percent—again, the lowest level ever recorded. Clearly, black workers benefited from the long, uninterrupted period of economic growth during the 1990s, and greatly improved their position in the American labor market.

Essay 3

Anti-Discrimination Policy

But economic growth alone will not produce economic equality. It is always necessary to implement policies that protect workers against discrimination, and assure equal job opportunities. Such policies were adopted during the 1960s, and contributed to improving the labor market status of black workers since that time.

In 1964, Congress enacted Title 7 of the Civil Rights Act, which created the U.S. Equal Employment Opportunity Commission. The Commission's charge was to require all employers of 15 or more employees to avoid discrimination based on race, gender, national origin, and religion. Later amendments of the act extended the Commission's authority beyond the private sector to state and local government, and gave the Commission power to enforce its rulings through the courts.

In September 1964, President Lyndon B. Johnson issued Executive Order 11246, which requires not only nondiscrimination, but also affirmative action by employers who have contracts to provide goods and services to the federal government. Affirmative action is a more powerful instrument than nondiscrimination alone for ending employment discrimination, because it requires employers to adopt measures for recruitment, applicant assessment, training, promotion, and compensation that assure that qualified minorities and women will have a fair chance to compete for available jobs.

In addition to the federal government initiatives for equal job opportunity during the 1960s, many states and municipalities adopted policies to prevent discrimination. While the scope and enforcement of such policies varied widely across the country, the breadth and visibility of anti-discrimination policies expressed a new national consensus that racial discrimination was no longer an acceptable part of doing business as usual.

Anti-discrimination policy contributed to the improvement in the labor market experience of black workers over the past three decades. The statistical evidence is not as robust as one might like, but it suggests that EEO policies played an important role in opening the doors of opportunity for black workers wider than they would have been in the absence of such policies.

For example, early studies of the impact of EEOC enforcement concluded that both black men and women gained more jobs in firms covered by the EEO policy than in firms that were not covered. The estimates of increases in black employment that were attributable to anti-discrimination enforcement varied from 3 to 7 percent.

Perhaps more compelling evidence is that obtained from changes in corporate business practices. From the late 1960s through the 1980s, black men and women increasingly found jobs in places where no black people previously had been employed. Perhaps the change was the result of a "change in the hearts of men," but a more reasonable interpretation of events is that the widespread turmoil associated with the Civil Rights Movement, coupled with the settlement of disputes through the equal employment enforcement agencies, contributed to a new awakening among employers that the black workforce was a resource that should be brought into the production process. Attitudes and behavior on equal job opportunity changed when the law made employment discrimination no longer acceptable.

Education and the Labor Market

The economic status of the workforce is influenced strongly by educational attainment. That is truer today than at any time in the past. With the onslaught of computerization in the workforce, technological change in most production processes, and frequent change in business methods, the skill level and "trainability" of workers is a major factor in determining who will get a job, what they will be paid, and how long they will keep the job.

That is the reality that black workers face in the labor market today. At a time of economic expansion, and in an environment of less employment discrimination, black workers will have a better chance to find good jobs if they have the requisite skills and capacity for training to meet employer demand. Their success should be reflected in higher labor force participation, lower unemployment, and higher income associated with higher levels of education. The evidence on the labor market experience of black workers during the 1990s confirms these expectations.

Essay 3

For example, the labor force participation rate for all adult workers averaged 78 percent, and for adult black workers, 77 percent during the 1990 decade. But during that time, black college graduates had a participation rate above 90 percent, i.e., about 9 of every 10 had a job or were seeking one, while black high school dropouts showed a participation rate of only 55 percent.

A similar difference in labor market experience was reflected in the rate of unemployment. From 1992 through 2000, the average unemployment rate for black workers was 6.6 percent. But black college graduates had an unemployment rate half that level (3.3 percent), while high school dropouts hovered at more than twice the total group level (13.1 percent).

Earnings also show the impact of education on the income of black workers. In 2000, weekly earnings of full-time adult workers were $611, with white workers earning $628, and black workers earning $494, or 79 percent that of white workers. Black college graduates earned $739 weekly, or 1.7 times the earnings of black high school dropouts, and 1.4 times that of high school graduates.

Viewed from another perspective, the increase in worker earnings over time was also affected by education. Over the past two decades, a period that included two recessions and the largest expansion since World War II, the weekly earnings of all adult workers rose from $286 to $611, or 114 percent. Black adult workers gained weekly earnings of $268, or 119 percent.

But black college graduates had the most rapid gain in earnings over the past two decades, rising from $318 to $739 per week, an increase of 132 percent. In contrast, black high school dropouts had earnings gains at only half the rate of college graduates (74.7 percent), and even high school graduates did not keep pace in earnings gains with those who completed four years of college.

The black college graduate earnings gains reflect black worker penetration into jobs from which they were previously excluded, as well as the labor market reward for skilled labor. During the booming '90s, employers increasingly faced labor shortages, and in many cases raised entry-level wages in order to attract the workers they needed. In many cases, the tight labor market also opened doors that were previously closed to black workers. The notable growth of employment of black women in financial services, health care, and retail trade reflects both the impact of tight labor markets, and a decline in labor market discrimination in those industries.

The Challenge Ahead

Black workers have made significant gains in the labor market over the past four decades. But regrettably, their success has done little to close the economic gap that separates black from white America.

While rapid employment expansion, coupled with vigorous anti-discrimination efforts opened many job doors that were previously closed, black workers, at best, kept pace with other workers in the economy. For example, the rate of unemployment among adult black workers fell from 9.8 percent in 1993 to 5.4 percent in 2000, but it remained at twice the rate of unemployment among white workers. Similarly, annual earnings for black workers who were employed full-time, all year rose to $25,688 in year 2000, but that was only 79 percent of the annual earnings of adult white workers. That is the position black workers occupied when the most recent recession struck in 2001.

Black Workers and the Recent Recession

The recession hit black workers harder than others. The prominent black economist and columnist Julianne Malveaux has pointed to the threat that in addition to likely layoffs of many black workers because of the recession, business corporations might well reduce their support of programs in inner-city areas that are helping black youth better prepare for entry into the "new economy." [8]

The statistical evidence shows that the unemployment rate for all adult workers peaked at 3.0 percent in 2000, but rose to 3.7 percent in 2001. The black adult unemployment rate bottomed out at 5.4 percent in 2000, but rose to 6.3 percent in 2001. These rates are lower than the widely reported unemployment rates for the workforce at large, which include teenagers, especially black teens whose unemployment is persistently higher than that for adults.

One of the major concerns about the impact of the recession is how it affected those who moved from welfare to work during the booming '90s. The 1996 welfare reforms embodied in the Temporary Assistance for Needy Families (TANF) Act included strong work requirements. Analysts agree that the reforms, coupled with tight labor markets, allowed many black women to move into the job market.[9] While all the evidence is not in, at least one observer has estimated that as a result of the recession, caseloads have risen, on average, by about 5 percent for each percentage point increase in unemployment.[10]

The consensus among economists is that the recession, which officially started in the second quarter of 2001, probably ended in the first quarter of 2002. The economy is now growing moderately, but without strong job creation. Month-to-month employment growth since January 2002 has averaged less than 100 thousand, a rate less than the growth of the labor force. Because of continuing layoffs (although the rate of layoffs has dropped sharply since early 2002), the unemployment rate has continued to rise. Of course, the unemployment rate is a lagging indicator, i.e., it will start to decline only after the recovery is well underway.

There are several reasons to believe that black workers will not lose as much ground from the recent recession as they did in previous economic downturns. First, the recession was relatively mild, and short-lived. It was driven by a decline in corporate profits, a buildup in business inventories, and a decline in business investment in new equipment. Further, it was exacerbated by the terrorist strike on New York and Washington in September 2001, and the resulting decline in the travel and hospitality industries.

But the impact of the recession was probably moderated by the $1.6 billion tax cut in 2001, the steady decline in interest rates set by the Federal Reserve Board, and the $40 billion increase in federal spending for defense and home security. If the economy continues to respond to these stimulative measures and the pace of growth picks up, the unemployment rate might begin to decline during the fourth quarter of 2002. That will surely benefit black workers, and reduce their unemployment rate.

Second, the climate in support of equal employment opportunity clearly has improved. As a result of the persistent emphasis by the federal government on affirmative action enforcement during 1995 through 2000, many employers have strengthened their human resource management systems to better assure EEO. Also, the successful private litigation cases involving Texaco ($170 million) and Coca Cola ($192 million) have sent a clear and unmistakable message that employment discrimination can be costly. These, and other positive developments on the anti-discrimination front are likely to enhance the job prospects of black workers, even in a slow-growth economy.

Finally, the penetration of black workers into a broad range of industries might have added more cyclical stability to black employment. During the past two decades, black workers in significant numbers moved into health services, financial services, communications, and transportation. They already held prominent positions in public service. These industries are less cyclical than others in which black workers were disproportionately concentrated forty years ago. The current inter-industry employment mix might well reduce, although not eliminate, the adverse effect of the mild recession on black workers.

A major caution about the future employment prospects for black workers stems from their continuing concentration in depressed areas of major cities, and the challenges facing black youth in the public schools. Community economic development in low-income urban areas would contribute much to the improvement of job opportunities for many black workers. And successful efforts to improve the basic skills and academic achievement of black youth will enhance their job prospects in the new economy. That is the major challenge facing those who want to assure the continuing advancement of black workers toward greater parity in the American economy.

TABLE 1. Employed Persons by Non-Farm Industry and Race (In Thousands)

INDUSTRY	ALL EMPLOYEES	BLACK	PERCENT BLACK
Total, 16 years and over	143,784	15557	10.8
Mining	569	26	4.6
Construction	7943	524	6.6
Manufacturing	20518	2154	10.5
Durable Goods	12202	1037	8.5
Nondurable Goods	8316	1056	12.7
Transportation	5715	886	15.5
Communications	1614	232	14.4
Utilities	1489	168	11.3
Wholesale and Retail Trade	26497	2332	8.8
Finance, Insurance, Real Estate	8076	735	9.1
Services	45043	5450	12.1
Public Administration	5802	957	16.5

Source: U.S. Bureau of Labor Statistics, Employment and Earnings Statistics, 1998

TABLE 2. Employed Persons by Occupation and Race (In Thousands)

OCCUPATION GROUP	TOTAL EMPLOYED	BLACK	PERCENT BLACK
All Occupations	135024	14804	10.9
White Collar	97431	8858	9.1
Managers and Professional	52745	4107	7.8
Technicians	5827	582	10.0
Sales	15590	1238	7.9
Administrative Support	23269	2931	12.6
Blue Collar	32683	3833	11.7
Craftsmen	13964	1113	8.0
Semi-Skilled Operatives	13622	1879	13.8
Laborers	5097	841	16.5
Service Workers	30482	4086	13.4

Source: U.S. Bureau of Labor Statistics, Employment and Earnings Statistics, 1998

Notes

[1] U. S. Bureau of Labor Statistics, Employment Situation, April 2002.

[2] U. S. Census Bureau, Employment and Earnings Statistics.

[3] U. S. Bureau of Labor Statistics, "Medium Weekly Wages of Full-Time Wage and Salary Workers, by Union Affiliation," April 2002.

[4] Northrop, Herbert R. and Richard L. Rowan, *Negro Employment in Basic Industry* (Philadelphia: University of Pennsylvania Press, 1970).

[5] Spero, Sterling D. and Abram L.Harris, *The Black Worker* (New York: Atheneum, 1968).

[6] Marshall, F. Ray, *The Negro and Organized Labor* (New York: John Wiley, 1965), and *The Negro and Apprenticeship* (New York: Draeger, 1968).

[7] Nelson, William J., *The Declining Significance of Race* (Chicago: University of Chicago Press, 1978).

[8] Freeman, Richard, "Changes in the Labor Market for Black American, 1948-72", *Brookings Papers for Economic Activity*, 1973, 1, pp. 67-120, and Bernard E. Anderson, "The Ebb and Flow of Enforcing Executive Order 11246," *American Economic Review, Papers and Proceedings*, June 1996.

[9] Malveaux, Julianne, "Slowdown into People of Color Hardest," *The Progressive Media Project*, March 13, 2001.

[10] Holzer, Harry and Michael J. Stall, "Employer Demand for Welfare Recipients by Race," *Urban Institute Working Paper*, July 2001.

The Geography of Discrimination: Hypersegregation, Isolation and Fragmentation Within the African-American Community[1]

By Leland Ware and Antoine Allen

Introduction

The Fair Housing Act of 1968 outlawed racial discrimination in the sale and rental of housing. Since that time, African Americans, as a group, have forged substantial progress in gaining access to an extended menu of housing choices. But, despite these advances, the 2000 census has underscored what has long been evident: that as America has become more racially and ethnically diverse, the nation's inner cities are more segregated now than they were 50 years ago.[2] Most urban neighborhoods in the North and Midwest are more segregated than they were before the 1960s, when segregation was enforced by laws in the southern half of the country and perpetuated by custom in other regions. Indeed, today's African Americans who reside in the nation's inner cities live in such extreme racial isolation, that social scientists refer to it as "hypersegregation."[3] Studies conducted regularly by the federal Department of Housing and Urban Development, by academic researchers, and by private organizations, all demonstrate conclusively that today's residential segregation stems not from the private choices of individual families but from decades of official segregation and the persistence of unlawful discriminatory practices.[4]

For example, one of the most harmful ways in which the adverse effects of segregated housing show themselves is in the racial composition of public schools. In most inner-city areas, student populations are primarily racial minorities while white students predominate in suburban schools. As school districts closely follow the boundaries of political districts—student populations mirror the racial make up of a given area's residents. As a result, because schools are financed by local property taxes, and communities that are predominantly African American and Latino tend to be much poorer than predominantly white areas, schools in these areas suffer from inadequate resources, a disproportionate number of inexperienced teachers and chronic under funding.

A generation of African Americans have benefited from opportunities created by the Civil Rights legislation of the 1960s. Those who were in a position to do so took advantage of the educational, employment and other opportunities that were foreclosed to African Americans during the first half of the 20th century. The success of middle- and upper-income African Americans and the growth in their numbers over the last thirty years is a testament to their intelligence, ambition and hard work. For these groups, the Civil Rights Movement created unprecedented avenues for advancement. However, for the one-third of the African-American population left behind in the nation's inner cities, the Civil Rights Movement might as well have never happened.

The increasing isolation of inner-city African Americans and the profoundly negative, often irreparable, effect this trend has on them should be a considerable cause for concern. These individuals live in conditions that are, in many ways, more oppressive than those African Americans endured during the depths of the segregation era—their levels of unemployment are higher, their families are less intact, their educational opportunities have not improved, the infrastructure of their neighborhood has deteriorated and their communities are far less safe. Not only is there extreme isolation and segregation from whites, there is also a growing separation of inner-city African Americans from middle- and upper-income African Americans. In most important respects, the bonds of commonality among African Americans have endured. However, the growing spatial separation and deepening economic disparities separating middle-class African Americans from impoverished, inner-city residents threatens to fragment the African-American community. For the last thirty years, civil rights organizations have devoted a considerable amount of their resources to efforts to secure equal educational opportunities. That focus must be broadened. Community leaders, elected officials, and civil rights organizations should direct more of their attention to the geography of discrimination.

The Origin and Development of Segregated Housing Patterns

Today's racially segregated housing patterns are a vestige of a pervasive system of government-sponsored discrimination the Supreme Court fostered by approving the doctrine of separate but equal put forth in *Plessy v. Ferguson*,[5] the 1896 decision that permitted segregation in public transportation and, by extension, to all sectors of public and private life. Segregated housing was merely one aspect of this elaborate system. But, it was a crucial part, because it legitimated the efforts that whites in the North and West took to establish segregated neighborhoods in reaction to the floodtide of African-American southern migrants that soon began to swell the African-American populations of urban industrial centers outside the South.[6]

The African-American migrants trekked North and West to escape the brutal restrictions and violence of the South in search of the broader employment opportunities that cities offered.[7] One response to search for jobs and housing was local governments enacting laws that prohibited African Americans from occupying properties except in certain locations. Because these laws involved state action that discriminated on the basis of race, they were challenged and declared unconstitutional in a 1917 Supreme Court decision, *Buchanan v. Warley*,[8] which held that the laws violated the Equal Protection Clause of the Fourteenth Amendment.

Buchanan led white property owners to resort to private covenants to enforce segregated housing patterns.[9] The covenants were restrictions in deeds that prevented property owners and subsequent purchasers from selling, renting or otherwise conveying property to racial and religious minorities—African Americans, Jews and Catholics—who were the intended targets of these covenants. The Supreme Court implicitly endorsed the validity of covenants in a 1926 decision, *Corrigan v. Buckley*,[10] suggesting that unlike Buchanan, the private covenants did not involve state action so there was no violation of the Constitution.

After *Corrigan*, the use of racially restrictive covenants accelerated rapidly in community after community throughout the U.S. In localities across the nation, African Americans and other people of color were confined to discrete residential districts whose most prominent features were substandard housing and overcrowded conditions. Despite the proliferation of the covenants, however, the continued heavy African-American migration created intense pressure among African Americans, sympathetic whites and profiteering realtors to find ways around the covenants.

The most prevalent of these was the use of the white "straw man" who would purchase property and immediately transfer title to an African-American purchaser, usually at a substantial profit. One of the bitter ironies of the covenants was that because of the scarcity of housing available to African Americans, the price per square foot of such housing was far more expensive than it was for similar housing in white areas. These economic realties gave white property owners a considerable financial incentive to violate the covenants. As more African-American families relocated to cities, the demand for housing increased, causing the continued circumvention of the covenants. This, in turn, prompted white homeowners to file civil actions to enforce the covenants.[11]

As part of its campaign against segregation during the 1930s and 1940s, the NAACP launched a litigation campaign against restrictive covenants.[12] This effort culminated in May of 1948 when the Supreme Court decided in *Shelley v. Kraemer*[13] that restrictive covenants were unenforceable because the use of the courts to enforce racially discriminatory agreements constituted state action that violated the Fourteenth Amendment. The NAACP's housing litigation campaign was important in another sense. The organization's "brain trust" used it to refine their legal strategy that would ultimately destroy government-sanctioned school segregation: After *Shelley*, the NAACP bore down on cases that resulted in the 1954 decision in *Brown v. Board of Education*. That decision, of course, struck down state sponsored segregation and helped to provoke the mass action, nonviolent campaign of the 1950s and early 1960s, which produced a sheaf of civil rights legislation, including the 1968 Fair Housing Act.[14]

Hypersegregation in Urban Communities

Despite the progress made possible by the Fair Housing Act, racially identifiable neighborhoods are as common in 2002 as they were in 1942. A traveler to any major metropolitan area can arrive at the local airport, hail a taxicab, and ask to be taken to the "black neighborhood." The driver will immediately know the traveler's destination. Its epicenter will almost invariably be located at the intersection of a Martin Luther King Boulevard and some other street. As Professors Douglas S. Massey and Nancy Denton explained in *American Apartheid: Segregation and the Making of the Underclass:*

"[O]ne-third of all African Americans in the United States live under conditions of intense racial segregation. They are unambiguously among the nation's most spatially isolated and geographically secluded people, suffering extreme segregation across multiple dimensions simultaneously. Black Americans in these metropolitan areas live within large contiguous settlements of densely inhabited neighborhoods that are tightly packed around the urban core. In plain terms, they live in ghettos."[15]

To measure up in the level of segregation in given areas, social scientists have developed a "dissimilarity index" which gauges the unevenness in the distribution of groups in a given area, that is to say, it measures the percentage of members of a particular racial group that would have to move to another area to achieve an even distribution of each group in proportion to its representations in the general population. To reflect complete integration, the index should reflect an even distribution of whites and African Americans relative to their proportion in the entire area. A score of 0 on the index represents full integration. A score of 100, on the other hand, reflects complete segregation. Communities are considered integrated when the dissimilarity index is lower than 33; moderately segregated when the index is 33-66; and highly segregated when the index is above 66.

The following chart compares patterns of segregation in the top 50 metropolitan areas based on the 1990 and 2000 census:

Essay 4

Black-White Segregation in Top 50 Metro Areas

2000 RANK	METRO AREA	2000 SEGREGATION	1990 SEGREGATION	1980 SEGREGATION
1	Detroit, MI	85	88	88
2	Milwaukee / Waukesha, WI	82	83	84
3	New York, NY	82	82	82
4	Chicago, IL	81	84	88
5	Newark, NJ	80	83	83
6	Cleveland / Lorain / Elyria, OH	77	83	86
7	Cincinnati, OH / KY / IN	75	77	79
8	Nassau / Suffolk, NY	74	77	78
9	St. Louis, MO / IL	74	78	83
10	Miami, FL	74	73	81
11	Birmingham, AL	73	74	76
12	Philadelphia, PA / NJ	72	77	78
13	Indianapolis, IN	71	75	80
14	New Orleans, LA	69	69	72
15	Kansas City, MO / KS	69	73	78
16	Memphis, TN / AR / MS	69	69	70
17	Baltimore, MD	68	72	75
18	Los Angeles / Long Beach, CA	68	73	81
19	Houston, TX	68	67	76
20	Pittsburgh, PA	67	71	73
21	Baton Rouge, LA	67	67	71
22	West Palm Beach / Boca Raton, FL	67	76	84
23	Boston, MA / NH	66	70	77
24	Atlanta, GA	66	69	77
25	Tampa / St. Petersburg / Clearwater, FL	65	71	79
26	Louisville, KY / IN	65	71	74
27	Mobile, AL	64	68	70

Black-White Segregation in Top 50 Metro Areas (continued)

2000 RANK	METRO AREA	2000 SEGREGATION	1990 SEGREGATION	1980 SEGREGATION
28	Columbus, OH	63	68	73
29	Washington, DC / MD / VA / WV	63	66	70
30	Oakland, CA	63	68	74
31	Fort Lauderdale, FL	62	71	84
32	Jackson, MS	62	70	71
33	Fort Worth / Arlington, TX	60	63	78
34	Dallas, TX	59	63	78
35	Greensboro / Winston-Salem / High Point, NC	59	62	67
36	Minneapolis / St. Paul, MN / WI	58	62	68
37	Shreveport / Bossier City, LA	57	62	65
38	Orlando, FL	57	61	74
39	Nashville, TN	57	61	66
40	Richmond / Petersburg, VA	57	61	65
41	Charlotte / Gastonia / Rock Hill, NC / SC	55	56	62
42	San Diego, CA	54	58	64
43	Jacksonville, FL	54	59	69
44	Columbia, SC	52	56	59
45	Charleston / North Charleston, SC	47	51	57
46	Greenville / Spartanburg / Anderson, SC	46	50	54
47	Riverside / San Bernardino, CA	46	45	55
48	Norfolk / Virginia Beach / Newport News, VA / NC	46	49	60
49	Raleigh / Durham / Chapel Hill, NC	46	49	52
50	Augusta / Aiken, GA / SC	46	46	49

Source: Lewis Mumford Center

Essay 4

This data shows that almost half of the top 50 metropolitan areas in the United States are highly segregated. The other half is moderately segregated. None is within the range of what would be considered integrated. This proves that hypersegregation persists; indeed, many areas have become more segregated since 1990. This is because study after study over the decades has shown that African Americans don't have the residential choices similarly situated whites do. At least one in four African Americans seeking housing can expect to encounter some form of discrimination.[16] One such obstacle involves "steering,"—by which realtors show homes to African Americans in "black" areas while white purchasers are directed to white neighborhoods.[17]

In addition, the rates at which African-American homebuyers are turned down for financing, or charged higher mortgage rates, is substantially higher than white purchasers with identical credit histories.[18] Also, African Americans who remain in identifiably African-American neighborhoods are frequently redlined out of the mainstream mortgage market and forced to rely on the predatory lending practices of the "sub-prime market," that is, financial institutions that specialize in loans to persons who are considered to be higher risk borrowers. These lenders typically charge interest rates and other fees that are substantially higher than those available to borrowers in the prime market.[19] A recent HUD report determined that the sub-prime market accounts for 50 percent of refinancing by minority borrowers.[20]

After paying usurious interest rates to predatory lenders, many African-American homebuyers will not be able to purchase homeowner's insurance from mainstream companies. The *American Family* case in Milwaukee[21] and the more recent *Nationwide Insurance* case in Richmond[22] revealed that major insurance companies are engaging in overt discrimination. The *American Family* case was a class action that resulted in a multi-million dollar settlement, based on evidence showing the agents were instructed in sales meetings to avoid selling policies in African-American neighborhoods and were disciplined when they did so. In the *Nationwide* case, a multi-million dollar verdict was entered in a class action in Richmond, Virginia, based on evidence that proved the company's systematic refusal to issue homeowner's policies in African-American neighborhoods. These few examples of the variety of discriminatory behavior African Americans seeking housing regularly encounter indicate that, at every level of the transaction—from the initial effort to identify housing, to the loan closing—African Americans and other minorities are likely to receive treatment that is different and less favorable than whites. These practices severely restrict the residential choices available to African Americans and they perpetuate segregated housing patterns.

There is another trend that contributes to the conditions in urban ghettoes. In the years since the enactment of the Fair Housing Act large numbers of middle- and upper-income African-American families have relocated from inner-city neighborhoods to suburban areas. In 1970, two years after the adoption of the Fair Housing Act, less than one-sixth of the African-American population resided in suburban areas. This compared to 40 percent of white population. By 1980, more than 22 percent of the African-American population resided in suburban communities. By 1995 the proportion of the African-American population living in suburban communities had risen to almost 32 percent. In actual numbers, seven million African Americans moved from inner-city areas to suburban communities between 1970 and 1995. To appreciate the magnitude of this transition, one must consider that this involved 2.4 million more individuals than the 4.4 million African Americans who participated in the historic migration from southern fields to northern factories between 1940 and 1970.[23]

The following chart shows the levels of African-American suburbanization in 1990 and 2000:

(see page 78)

Essay 4

Suburban regions ranked by % black in 2000
(50 largest suburban regions by total population)

RANK	SUBURBAN REGION	1990	2000
1	Atlanta, GA MSA	18.8	25.6
2	Washington, DC / MD / VA / WV PMSA	18.8	22.9
3	Richmond / Petersburg, VA MSA	17.9	21.3
4	New Orleans, LA MSA	17.7	21.0
5	Fort Lauderdale, FL PMSA	13.3	20.6
6	Miami, FL PMSA	18.8	20.4
7	Newark, NJ PMSA	15.7	17.8
8	Baltimore, MD PMSA	10.4	14.9
9	Greenville / Spartanburg / Anderson, SC MSA	13.6	14.6
10	West Palm Beach / Boca Raton, FL MSA	10.9	13.7
11	New York, NY PMSA	11.1	12.6
12	St. Louis, MO / IL MSA	9.5	12.5
13	Orlando, FL MSA	9.4	12.4
14	Charlotte / Gastonia / Rock Hill, NC / SC MSA	10.6	10.9
15	Houston, TX PMSA	8.9	10.7
16	Cleveland / Lorain / Elyria, OH PMSA	8.0	9.7
17	Philadelphia, PA / NJ PMSA	7.8	9.7
18	Dallas, TX PMSA	7.3	9.7
19	Chicago, IL PMSA	6.4	8.8
20	Nassau / Suffolk, NY PMSA	7.1	8.7
21	Oakland, CA PMSA	7.4	8.4
22	Los Angeles / Long Beach, CA PMSA	8.4	8.2
23	Bergen / Passaic, NJ PMSA	7.5	8.1
24	Middlesex / Somerset / Hunterdon, NJ PMSA	6.4	8.0
25	Riverside / San Bernardino, CA PMSA	6.1	7.9
26	Las Vegas, NV / AZ MSA	6.8	7.5
27	Detroit, MI PMSA	4.3	6.6
28	Monmouth / Ocean, NJ PMSA	6.2	6.3
29	Hartford, CT MSA	3.8	6.1
30	Tampa / St. Petersburg / Clearwater, FL MSA	4.0	5.8
31	Cincinnati, OH / KY / IN PMSA	4.5	5.7

Suburban regions ranked by % black in 2000 (continued)
(50 largest suburban regions by total population)

RANK	SUBURBAN REGION	1990	2000
32	Sacramento, CA PMSA	4.2	5.7
33	Pittsburgh, PA MSA	4.1	5.3
34	San Diego, CA MSA	3.8	4.6
35	Fort Worth / Arlington, TX PMSA	3.5	4.5
36	Seattle / Bellevue / Everett, WA PMSA	1.9	3.9
37	Denver, CO PMSA	2.9	3.9
38	San Francisco, CA PMSA	4.7	3.7
39	Kansas City, MO / KS MSA	2.2	3.7
40	Rochester, NY MSA	2.5	3.5
41	Grand Rapids / Muskegon / Holland, MI MSA	2.6	3.4
42	Phoenix / Mesa, AZ MSA	2.2	3.1
43	Minneapolis / St. Paul, MN / WI MSA	1.1	2.9
44	Boston, MA / NH PMSA	1.7	2.8
45	Buffalo / Niagara Falls, NY MSA	1.4	2.4
46	Indianapolis, IN MSA	13.0	2.2
47	Orange County, CA PMSA	1.4	1.7
48	Milwaukee / Waukesha, WI PMSA	0.7	1.6
49	Portland / Vancouver, OR / WA PMSA	0.6	1.3
50	Salt Lake City / Ogden, UT MSA	0.5	1.0

Source: Lewis Mumford Center

Most African Americans who move to the suburbs are relocating to predominantly white communities but many are choosing to reside in all-black suburban enclaves. African-American, middle-class suburbs are a growing phenomenon that can be found in the metropolitan areas of several cities. The residents range from middle- to upper-middle-income families. These neighborhoods often feature expensive luxury homes. Many of the residents choose these areas to avoid the racial isolation that is associated with predominantly white suburban communities. Ironically, the migration of middle- and upper-income African

Americans to the suburbs has led to a fragmentation of the African-American community.[24]

In *Middle-Class Black Suburbs and the State of Integration*, Sheryll Cashin, a professor at Georgetown University, examined the growth of African-American suburban enclaves.[25] Professor Cashin described a series of incidents in a suburb of Washington D.C., which reflected conflicts among African Americans from different economic backgrounds. Prince George's County, Maryland, is located just outside of Washington D.C. It contains a high concentration of middle- and upper-middle-income African Americans. The residents moved to suburban areas, in part, to escape the crime, poor schools, crumbling infrastructure and other adverse conditions that are prevalent in inner- city neighborhoods. Some suburban African Americans are not comfortable with living in close proximity to their less affluent counterparts. In some circumstances, African-American suburbanites can be as hostile to the interests of poor urban African Americans as their white neighbors.

One example of class conflict arose in the summer of 1996, in Perrywood, a suburban Prince George's community. Low-income African-American youths from nearby Washington, D.C. began to frequent recreational areas in Perrywood to play basketball. The middle-class African-American residents became apprehensive after repeated complaints about rising noise levels and incidents involving the young visitors. Eventually, the African-American suburbanites hired a private security service to prevent outsiders from entering the neighborhood. A similar dispute arose when the African-American residents of Lake Arbor, another affluent area in Prince George's County, objected to allowing low-income students from nearby Landover to attend a newly constructed high school.

Wayne Curry, Prince George's first African-American county executive, campaigned on a platform that included a promise to limit the construction of low-income housing units. Curry argued that too many low-income housing developments were being located in Prince George's County. He complained that an influx of tenants in publicly assisted housing would increase crime rates and cause other problems. After his election, Curry kept his promise and encouraged developers to construct upscale housing that low-income families could not afford. Curry also supported a successful effort to obtain a release from a court-ordered desegregation program in which African-American students from Washington were bussed to schools in Prince George's County. Curry's African-American, middle-class constituents applauded these actions.

Similar attitudes are displayed in other cities: Atlanta, Georgia, has a large and rapidly growing middle- and upper-middle income African-American community. For more than 100 years, the colleges in the Atlanta University system have produced generation after generation of highly educated African Americans. Economic institutions such as the Atlanta Life Insurance Company, African-American-owned banks and other business establishments have long been pillars of Atlanta's African-American community. Since the early 1970s, Atlanta's African-American mayors have insisted that minority entrepreneurs share in contracts for goods and services, worth millions of dollars annually, generated by the City. This has resulted in favorable climate for large numbers of African-American business owners and professionals who can afford luxury homes. In Cascade Heights, an affluent, all-African-American neighborhood in Atlanta, developers are constructing a gated community in which the price of homes will average $500,000. Gated communities have been an increasing presence on the American landscape. Access to these communities is typically controlled by a guard and limited to residents and their guests. The "undesirable element" is kept out. The Atlanta development may be the first time this concept has been employed in an all-African-American community. This is additional evidence of increasing divisions along class lines within the African-American community.

The demographic trends of Wilmington, Delaware, and the surrounding metropolitan region, reflect a trend toward similar divisions. A survey prepared by the Metropolitan Wilmington Urban League compared Delaware's African-Americans and Hispanic residents to the state's white residents in education, employment, income, homeownership and business ownership. The researchers found that Delaware's African-American and Hispanic residents earn, on average, 60 cents for each dollar earned by the average white family. The state's African Americans and Hispanics are severely under-represented in professional and upper-level management positions and over-represented in the lowest paying and least desirable occupations. The average levels of educational attainment for minorities in Delaware lags far below the average for whites. The rate of homeownership for African Americans is twenty percent lower than the level of white ownership. Even when family incomes are essentially the same, the levels of African-American homeownership are significantly lower than comparable whites. Delaware's minority-owned business enterprises are under-represented in every classification except the service industry, and they are virtually absent from banking and financial services, the fastest growing sectors in the state's economy.

The African-American population in the city of Wilmington has grown steadily over the last 40 years. By 1990, the city's population was nearly 50 percent African American. The 2000 census showed that African Americans constituted a majority of the city's population. The dissimilarity index showed high levels of residential segregation. However, when the suburban regions of Wilmington were disaggregated from the city, a noteworthy pattern emerged. From 1970 to 1990, the index of dissimilarity between African Americans and whites in the city of Wilmington decreased from 60, in 1970 to 53, in 1990. This was a slight improvement but it still reflected high levels of segregation within the city. However, the dissimilarity index for the surrounding suburbs fell dramatically, from 1970 to 1990, showing a steep decline, from 65 to 38. (A dissimilarity index of 30 or below is considered integrated.) The 2000 census also showed that for the first time, more African Americans resided in suburban areas of New Castle County than in the city of Wilmington. This shows a marked trend toward the suburbanization of African Americans in metropolitan Wilmington and a deepening isolation of the city's inner-city residents.

The geographic separation of African Americans along economic lines is a recent development. During the years of enforced segregation, African-American neighborhoods included a range of families, from doctors and lawyers to domestics and factory workers. In cities with large middle-class populations, there were enclaves where affluent African Americans resided. But the distances between neighborhoods were not great and there were regular interactions across class lines. African Americans attended the same schools, ate in the same restaurants and worshipped in the same churches. This gave segregated neighborhoods a considerable degree of cohesiveness and stability. This has changed; the families that remain in urban ghettoes tend to be the poorest, least educated, and most isolated individuals in the nation. In many ways, economic and social advancement is less likely for them than it was for their forbears during the segregation era.

Class distinctions have always existed within the African-American community. [26] In many important respects, however, the bonds of commonalty have endured. As the recent presidential election confirmed, African Americans tend to vote heavily for the same candidates for elective offices. Polls reflect shared ideological perspectives among African Americans with different income levels. The Pulitzer Prize winning playwright, August Wilson, explained, "Black Americans are a racial group which do not share the same sensibilities [as whites]. We have a different way of responding to the world. We have different ideas about religion, different manners of social intercourse. We have different ideas about style, about language. We have different esthetics. Someone who does not share the specifics of a culture remains an outsider, no matter how astute a student or how well-meaning their intentions."[27] As the connections linking inner-city residents to more affluent African Americans become increasingly attenuated, the larger African-American community is likely to become more fragmented.

The Adverse Affects of Extreme Isolation

The increasing isolation of inner-city African Americans and the profoundly negative, often irreparable, effect this trend has on them should be a considerable cause for concern. Researchers have documented the devastating impact of hypersegregation on African Americans.[28] Inner-city areas across the nation share the same attributes: high unemployment, insufficient health care, an inadequate supply of affordable housing and long waiting lists for subsidized units. Schools are neglected and under-funded, and dropout rates are high. Crime is prevalent, drug trafficking is rampant, and the streets are not safe.

The location in which a family resides has a critical affect on its opportunities for advancement. "In a market economy such as the United States, opportunities, resources, and benefits are not evenly distributed across the urban landscape."[29] Some communities are deemed to be more desirable than others. They tend to have more expensive homes, better amenities and safer streets. An improvement in a family's economic circumstances is typically accompanied by advancement in its residential status. This is the normal progression for individuals advancing in their careers. However, discriminatory housing practices interfere with this process.

The ideal of the single-family, detached home in a suburban setting has long been at the heart of the American dream. This was reflected in Norman Rockwell's sentimental illustrations for the *Saturday Evening Post*. It was inculcated by depictions of families on "Leave it to Beaver" and other popular television programs. During the 1940s and 1950s white families pursued the dream by moving in record numbers to suburban communities. This dramatic population shift was facilitated by a thriving post-war economy and federal financial assistance in the form of loans insured by the Veterans Administration (VA) and the Federal Housing Administration (FHA). The Federal Housing Administration and Veterans Administration programs insured mortgages against default. If a borrower failed to make payments and a property went into foreclosure, the federal government would pay the outstanding debt to the lender. This reduced the risk of loss to lending institutions. Under the FHA program, homebuyers could purchase homes with very low down payments. Under the VA program, eligible veterans received 100 percent financing, which meant that they could purchase homes with no down payment. Mortgage payments were spread over several years, which made them relatively affordable. Homeowners were allowed to deduct mortgage interest payments from their taxable incomes. These programs were immensely important to millions of white Americans who were able to buy single-family homes in America's newly forming suburbs.

Between 1933 and 1978, these governmental policies assisted thirty-five million families in home purchases. This allowed them not only to become homeowners, but also, given the appreciation housing values through the end of the 20th century, to be staked in a source of future wealth. Researchers estimate that billions of dollars were produced by the appreciation of home values in suburban communities during this period. However, while Ozzie and Harriet were moving to Scarsdale, African Americans—including World War II veterans who were ready, willing and able to purchase homes in suburban communities, were prevented from doing so by restrictive covenants and other discriminatory practices. And the federal government was as much to blame as a private market. African Americans were deliberately excluded from suburban homes financed by VA and FHA mortgage programs.[30]

That old saw about commercial real estate applies equally to the residential market. When it comes to residential living, everything is affected by location, including the quality of schools, property values, exposure to crime and the quality of public services. African-American families that are confined to segregated neighborhoods by discriminatory practices tend to reside in areas where schools are inferior, home values are lower, the incidence of crime is high and routine services such as grocery stores and pharmacies are scarce.

The African-American migration to urban industrial centers during the first half of the 20th century was based on the availability of employment opportunities in what was then a rapidly industrializing American economy. Jobs were plentiful in steel mills, automobile assembly plants, and several other industries even though discriminatory practices limited African Americans to the lowest paying, least desirable occupations. Recent technological advances eliminated many of the low-skilled occupations that employed African Americans.

Essay 4

Globalization has caused many assembly positions to be relocated to factories in Mexico, or the Pacific Rim, where labor and other production costs are far lower than those in the U.S. This has severely curtailed the employment options available to inner-city residents. The factory jobs that lured their forebears to cities have moved to the suburbs or disappeared altogether.[31]

The physical distance separating inner-city neighborhoods from other areas, both within and outside cities, is usually small but the psychological impact on those left behind can be enormous. The extreme isolation of inner-city residents is reflected in speech patterns. Social science researchers have concluded that it is no accident that the African-American dialect is essentially the same in Michigan as it is in Maryland while white speech patterns reflect distinct regional differences. Professor William Labov, a noted linguist, has conducted several studies analyzing African-American and white speech patterns. Professor Labov found that white speech patterns tend to reflect the region in which the speakers reside; hence, the familiar southern and northern accents are shared by most whites residing in those regions. African-American speech patterns, in contrast, are relatively uniform in urban areas in different parts of the country. Labov found that the speech patterns of African Americans in Boston, Chicago, Detroit, New York, and Philadelphia were increasingly similar in their rhythm, grammar and syntax. Labov concluded that the similarities in these speech patterns were the product of generations of segregation and isolation that has confined African Americans to a self-contained, linguistic community.[32]

The isolation of inner-city African Americans has produced, in some cases, a form of oppositional behavior; attitudes that reject traditional values and encourage individuals engage in behaviors that are self-destructive and pose a danger to others.[33] In *Code of the Streets: Decency, Violence, and the Moral Life of the Inner City,* Professor Elijah Anderson described the conditions of inner-city Philadelphia, but his observations would apply to most urban ghettoes. Professor Anderson concluded, among other things, that "of all the problems besetting the poor inner-city, African-American community, none is more pressing than that of interpersonal violence and aggression."[34] This tendency toward violence arises from the circumstances of life among the ghetto poor: the lack of jobs, limited health services, the stigma of race, and the dangers posed by drug trafficking. The resulting alienation and lack of hope for the future has engendered, what Anderson terms, a "code of the street," an underwritten set of rules based largely on an individual's ability to command respect in an environment in which the threat of violence is constant.

Analyzing similar conditions in Chicago, Illinois, Professor William Julius Wilson's research has shown that traditional notions of hard work, delayed gratification, and family stability are not reasonable expectations in an environment in which few adults are employed and those who do cannot earn enough to support a family. Wilson concluded that the decline of manufacturing, the suburbanization of employment and the rise of a low-wage service sector dramatically reduced the availability of jobs in inner-city areas that pay wages sufficient to support a family. This has led to high rates of joblessness among inner-city residents. African Americans were affected by structural changes in the economy more than other groups because generations of discriminatory practices confined them to inner-city neighborhoods that were disproportionately affected by these trends.[35] By placing them at a severe disadvantage in terms of education, employment, and other opportunities for advancement, the persistence of residential segregation makes it difficult for African-American families to escape the poverty and isolation of urban ghettoes.

This should not be interpreted to mean that African Americans believe that physical proximity to whites is necessary for them to have a complete and meaningful existence. As numerous scholars, including Maria Bey, among recent ones, have shown, African Americans survived state sponsored segregation that severely limited their contacts with whites throughout the first half of the 20th century, creating a rich communal life that not only nourished millions of ordinary individuals but also produced numerous "giants" of American culture. W.E.B. Du Bois' writings explored African-American separatism in the mid-1930s.[36]

Leaders such as Malcolm X and Kwame Ture articulated similar themes during the 1960s. Currently, many upper-income African Americans choose to live in upscale, African-American neighborhoods. African-American students, who could go elsewhere, choose to enroll in historically African-American colleges and universities. In short, African Americans do not need close contact with whites to live well and prosper. What African Americans have always felt they needed is the freedom to do whatever they choose and whatever their abilities can get for them. This would include, among other things, a choice of a neighborhood unfettered by the burdens of race.

The critical issue then is not the social desirability of integration or whether African Americans must live in close proximity to whites to enjoy full and meaningful lives, but how restrictions on individual liberty caused by hypersegregation undermine the social and economic stability of inner-city residents. This dynamic is not confined to low-income families. African Americans with middle-class incomes tend to reside in segregated areas where schools are inferior, crime is high, and services are marginal. Compared to whites with similar incomes, African Americans are less likely to be homeowners and the homes they own are of relatively poor quality, with lower value than homes in non-segregated areas. As professors Massey and Denton explained in *American Apartheid:*

> Among the northern metropolitan areas, for example blacks, no matter of what their income, remain very highly segregated from whites. In 1980, black families earning under $2,500 per year experienced an average segregation index 86, whereas those earning more than $50,000 had an average score of 83; blacks and the middle category display a score of 81. This pattern of constant, high segregation was replicated in virtually all northern areas. In Chicago, for example, the poorest blacks displayed an index of 91; the most affluent blacks had an index of 86. In New York, the respective figures were 86 and 79; and in Los Angeles they were 85 and 79. In no northern metropolitan area did blacks earning more than $50,000 per year display a dissimilarity index of lower than 72. [37]

Segregated housing patterns affect most African Americans directly or indirectly, but the burden weighs most heavily on inner-city residents. Despite these barriers, many African Americans have benefited from the opportunities created by the Civil Rights legislation of the 1960s. They took advantage of educational, employment and other opportunities that were not available during the first half of the 20th century. The success of middle- and upper-income African Americans and the growth in their numbers over the last thirty years was an extraordinary accomplishment. For these groups, the Civil Rights Movement cleared a path to unparalleled advancement. However, the one-third of the African-American population residing in the nation's inner cities was not equipped to participate in the opportunities created by the Civil Rights Movement.

These individuals wrestle with conditions that are as bad, if not worse, than those African Americans endured during the depths of the segregation era. Unemployment is higher, there are more single-parent households, their educational opportunities have not improved, and the threat of violence is an ominous presence in their communities. Not only is there isolation from whites, there is also a growing separation of inner-city residents from middle- and upper-middle-income African Americans. This threatens to break the bonds of commonality that have unified African Americans and could lead to a balkanization of the African-American community. Over the last thirty years, much of the attention of Civil Rights organizations has focused on efforts to achieve equal educational opportunities. A broader focus is needed. Community leaders, elected officials, and Civil Rights organizations should develop new strategies that devote more attention to the geography of discrimination.

Notes

[1] Leland Ware, Louis L. Redding Professor of Law & Public Policy, University of Delaware and Antoine Allen Ph.D., Metropolitan Wilmington Urban League.

[2] *Ethnic Diversity Grows, Neighborhood Integration at a Standstill* (Lewis

Essay 4

Mumford Center, April 3, 2001). For a detailed discussion of this trend and an in-depth examination of the development of hypersegregation in urban communities see, Douglas Massey and Nancy Denton, *American Apartheid: Segregation And The Making of the Underclass* (1993).

[3] *American Apartheid*, supra, note 2.

[4] John Yinger, *Closed Doors, Opportunities Lost: The Continuing Costs of Housing Discrimination* (1995).

[5] *Plessy v. Ferguson*, 163 U.S. 537 (1896).

[6] Leon F. Litwak, *Trouble in Mind* (1998); Gunnar Myrdal, *An American Dilemma* (1944)

[7] Id.

[8] *Buchanan v. Warley*, 245 U.S. 60 (1917). See also, David Delaney, *Race Place & the Law*, 1836-1948 (1998)

[9] Clement E. Vose, *Caucasians Only: The Supreme Court, The NAACP and the Restrictive Covenant Cases* (1959).

[10] *Corrigan v. Buckley*, 271 U.S. 323 (1926).

[11] Vose, *Caucasians Only*, supra, note 12.

[12] This was a long-range, carefully orchestrated approach involving several cases handled by the nationwide network of lawyers associated with the NAACP. Limited successes were won in cases such as *Hansberry v. Lee*, in which the Supreme Court refused to enforce a restrictive covenant on procedural grounds. Beginning in 1945, however, the NAACP convened a series of conferences to discuss the pending covenant cases and to develop an overall strategy for securing a victory in the Supreme Court. The first meeting was held in Chicago in July 1945. Others were held in New York City and Washington, D.C. Mark Tushnet, *Making Civil Rights Law: Thurgood Marshall and the Supreme Court* 1936-1961(1994).

[13] *Shelley v. Kraemer*, 334 U.S. 1 (1948.)

[14] 42 U.S.C. 3601- 3619, 3631.

[15] *American Apartheid,* supra. note 2 at 77

[16] Yinger, supra, note 5.

[17] Margalynne Armstrong, *Race and Property Values in Entrenched Segregation,* 52 U. Miami L. Rev.1051 (1998); Sheryll D.Cashin, *Middle Class Black Suburbs and The State Of Integration: A Post Integrationist Vision For Metropolitan America,* 85 Cornell L. Rev. 729 (2001).

[18] *What We Know About Mortgage Lending Discrimination In America* (September, 1999).

[19] The Department of Housing and Urban Development analysis showed that: "1) From 1993 to 1998, the number of subprime refinancing loans increased ten-fold. 2) Subprime loans are three times more likely in low income neighborhoods than in high-income neighborhoods. 3) Subprime loans are five times more likely in black neighborhoods than in white neighborhoods. 4) Homeowners in high-income black areas are twice as likely as homeowners in low-income white areas to have subprime loans." *Unequal Burden Income and Racial Disparities In Subprime Lending In America* (April 2000); See, also, *Curbing Predatory Home Mortgage Lending* (June 2000).

[20] Id.

[21] "Insurer Settles Bias Suits Filed By Black Homeowners," *Los Angeles Times,* p.1. March 31,1995. (American Family Mutual Insurance Co. paid $16 million dollar settlement in case alleging company sold insurance policies to black customers in inferior terms to similarly situated white homeowners.)

[22] "Housing Bias Case Settled," *Milwaukee Journal Sentinel,* p. 1D (April 25, 2000). (Nationwide Insurance Company settled case alleging insurance red lining for $17. million dollars.)

[23] Stephen Thernstrom & Abigail Thernstrom, *America in Black and White: One Nation, Indivisible* (1997).

[24] Some African Americans are relocating to predominantly white communities but others are choosing to reside in black suburban enclaves. Despite the relative affluence of the residents, however, black suburban communities often lack high quality public schools, restaurants, shopping centers and other amenities that are associated with upscale suburban communities. Sheryll D. Cashin, Middle Class Black Suburbs, supra, note 25.

Essay 4

[25] Cashin, *Black Middle Class Suburbs*, supra, note 17.

[26] E. Franklin Frazier, *Black Bourgeoisie* (1957).

[27] August Wilson, Why I Want a Black Director, *N.Y. Times*, Sept. 1990, at A25.

[28] *American Apartheid*, supra, note 2.

[29] Douglas S. Massey and Nancy Denton, *America Apartheid*, supra note 2

[30] Melvin L. Oliver and Thomas M. Shapiro, *Black Wealth/White Wealth* (1995).

[31] William Julius Wilson, *When Work Disappears: The World of the New Urban Poor* (1996).

[32] William Labov and Wendell A. Harris, "De Facto Segregation and Black of White Vernaculars" in David Sankoff, ed. *Current Issues in Linguistic Theory* (1986);

[33] Elijah Anderson, *Code of the Street: Decency, Violence and the Moral Life of the Inner City.* (1999).

[34] Id at p. 32.

[35] William Julius Wilson, *The Truly Disadvantaged: The Inner City, The Underclass and Public Policy* (1987).

[36] David Levering Lewis, W.E.B. DuBois: *A Biography of A Race* (1993).

[37] *American Apartheid*, supra, note 2. (This was based on 1980 census data.)

Military Organizations: Best Practices and the Status of Black Americans

By John Sibley Butler

The purpose of this paper is to discuss the status of Black Americans, of African, European and Asian descent, within the military and identify the "best practices" which have enhanced the capacity of both the military as a whole and the people of color within it to perform to the best of their ability. My focusing on best practices, in addition to summary statistics, is a return to the literature on African Americans that developed systematically from the late 1800s and continued until about the middle of the 1960s. Best practices discussions are designed to enhance a person or an organization's ability to perform more efficiently.

Because this paper is driven by the notion of best practices, and military organizations must be seen in that light, I recall some of the early literature on best practices that relate to Black Americans. I then turn to the state of blacks within the military.

I

The exploration of "best practices" that would aid African Americans in their struggle for full citizenship stood at the very center of early research that examined the state of Black America, and celebrated the success of the group in a hostile legal and non-legal racial environment.[1] Henry Minton (1913), W.E.B. Du Bois (1898, 1907), Booker T. Washington (1911), Abraham Harris (1936) and Joseph Pierce (1947) wrote works that explored and suggested models for successful business enterprises.[2] Winold Reiss in *The New Negro* (1925) identified the best practices in art, literature, building educational institutions, and music. That work dove-

Essay 5

tailed with John Chamberlain's "The Negro as a Writer," published in 1930, and the later celebration of Gwendolyn Brooks, the first African American to win a Pulitzer Prize, for *Annie Allen*. Benjamin Brawley, in "The Negro Genius" celebrated the best practices of literature and culture. The scholar Carter G. Woodson established Negro History Week in the 1920s in order to publicize the achievements of African Americans in all fields of endeavor, so that black individuals and organizations, and the race as a whole would be inspired to strive to do their best. One can easily see, then, from just these few references, that the celebration of best practices, and lessons from those best practices for Black America, dominated the literature on African Americans between the late 1800s and the middle 1960s.

Although best practices for Black Americans have now almost been buried in the literature (replaced with a literature which put an emphasis on what blacks cannot do, or what whites keep them from doing), the military in the era after World War II has slowly at first, and then with great vigor constructed a best-practice method of enabling African Americans to take advantage of opportunity. Although not perfect when it come to opportunities for Black Americans, it has provided an opportunity structure that is unmatched by other institutions. The state of Black America within the military is the result of the need to defend the country and the extraordinary patriotism of black Americans. Unlike English-Americans, Italian-Americans, Japanese-Americans, Pre-Columbia Americans (sometimes called Native Americans) and Mexican Americans, African Americans have never, historically, fought against the United States.

II

Today, we examine the status of black Americans in the military in the context of America at War. Since September 11, 2001, President Bush, as Commander-in-Chief of the military, has been developing strategy for a war on terror, and Secretary of State Colin Powell, the former Army General and member of the Joint Chiefs of Staff, stands in the center of the Administration's diplomatic efforts to thwart terrorism. Born in Harlem of Jamaican immigrants, he is cut out of the same cloth that the best practice scholarship on Black Americans published during an earlier time period. His father was a merchant, involved heavily with a Presbyterian college. Education runs deep in his family. His wife graduated from Fisk University, and her father graduated from Talladega College and holds a master's degree from Fisk. Historically Black Colleges and Universities, the foundation for workhorse for Black America's success in the past, continue to play a crucial role in providing individuals who can take advantage of the best practices of the present.[3]

It is also no coincidence that Condoleezza Rice, who as the president's national security advisor is also instrumental in important military deployment issues, is cut out of this same best-practice cloth. Born in Birmingham, Alabama her mother was a teacher and her father a dean at Historically Black, Stillman College, a combination which fueled her own outstanding educational achievements. While Colin Powell and Condoleeza Rice connect the black presence to the highest office in the land, Black Americans of African, Asian and European descent continue a tradition of military participation that started with the inception of the country.

The status of Black Americans in the military begins with an analysis of the rank structure. The rank structure also represents pay grades, thus when we control for rank structure we also have a notion of income. This structure is divided into officers (officially called Commissioned Officers) and enlisted categories. One can think of the officer's crop as the executive group and enlisted as the workers. This is what the old enlisted saying, "Don't call me Sir, I work for a living," means. Traditionally, because an officer might have to order an enlisted person to his or her death, all social contact, or fraternization, between the groups were prohibited. Pay grades also correspond to the categories of Private, Master Sergeant, and so on-on up to the various ranks of General.

Table 1 presents the percentage of blacks by service and rank, with the name corresponding to the grade in parenthesis. For comparative purposes, the years 1980, 1990, and 1998 are presented.[4] The first thing to notice is that there are great differences between services.

Starting with the Army, we see that the number of Commissioned

Essay 5

Officers (including Warrant Officers) increased, between 1980 and 1998, from 7.1 percent to 12.7 percent. It is especially noteworthy that the percentages of Generals, the most senior rank, and the one with the highest pay, increased from 5.3 percent to almost 9 percent. We should also note that for the ranks 0-3 to 0-6 show an increase in the percentage of black officers. For example, the percentage of Captains (03) increased from 7.5 percent to 11.9 percent, and the percentage of 0-5s (Lt. Colonel) increased from 4.9 percent to 10.0 percent. As has been noted in other analysis, this kind of promotion of black leadership would be hard to match in any civilian organization.[5] Indeed, if officers are the executives of the military, the military boast more black executives than any other organization or institution in the country. This trend is most pronounced in the Army.

The branch's more than 8,000 African-American officers emerge from a number of places, with the most prestigious place being the U.S. Military Academy at West Point. Blacks have made up about seven percent of graduating classes from West Point during the last several years. Of course ROTC at civilian colleges is the workhorse for the production of both black and non-black officers, producing about six times more officers than West Point.[6]

The root of the growth of the number of black officers is the Historically Black Colleges and Universities. The same colleges that produced people such as Oprah Winfrey (Tennessee State), Martin Luther King and Spike Lee (Morehouse College), have been busy producing the value structure of black military officers. Twenty-one of these institutions produce about half of all black Army ROTC commissions. Indeed, the first national scholarship for black students was an ROTC scholarship. This best practice of these schools persisted through the tumult of anti-war sentiment during the Vietnamese Conflict in the 1960s to play an ever-increasing role in providing leaders for the military.

Two trends are evident from examining the Army's enlisted ranks. While the total percentage of blacks in the ranks has declined from 29.2 percent to 26.6 percent, the significance of the percentage change within the structure is significant. The drop in the percentage, of course, is related to the numbers who are enlisting within the ranks. This fell to 27 percent from 29.6 percent for E-1, Private first class. On the other hand, those in the two highest ranks (E-9, or Sergeant Major, and E-8, or Master Sergeant), increased from 20.5 percent to 33.5 percent, and from 25.3 percent to 36.6 percent, respectively, during this period. Thus, the rank structure of blacks within the Army has been clearly increasing. Indeed, since the 1950s, the Army has had a significant black enlisted corps, including those who are above E-5 and make up the noncommissioned officer (NCO) ranks.

From the data it is obvious that the Army, with its strong tradition of black participation, is the best practice for black opportunity. The percentage of Navy officers increased from 2.5 percent in 1980 to 6.3 percent in 1998. For the same time period, the Air Force's percentage increased from 5.7 to 6.0; for the Marine Corps the number was 3.9 percent to 6.9 percent. The percentage of enlisted personnel in the Navy, Air Force, and Marine Corps is also less than the Army. The most important thing is that all services have significant numbers of blacks at the enlisted level. Overall, the enlisted percentage of enlisted members of the military services is 19.9 percent.

During the last twenty years or so all analysis of the rank structure points have shown that African Americans have the highest re-enlistment rate, particularly for the Army, of all groups.[7] That includes African-American women. In 1980 black women made up 37 percent of its female members, while white women comprised 56 percent. By 1998, however, the composition was 47 percent black and 39 percent white.[8] This is largely due to the fact that black women have a much lower attrition rate (at the standard three-year mark) than white women. In all four services black women have significantly lower attrition rates than their white counterparts: in the army, the attrition rate for white women is 54 percent, compared to 35 percent for black women; in the Navy it's 39 percent compared to 30 percent; in the Marine Corps, 51 percent compared to 38 percent; and in the Air Force, 31 percent compared to 24 percent.[9]

Table 2 displays enlisted ranks for all services by race and ethnicity for broad occupational areas. Black Americans make up 13.2 percent of those in the infantry, gun crews and Seamanship areas. Other significant areas are functional support and administration (26.6 percent) and electrical mechanical equipment repairs (15.2 percent).

As can be seen from the above data, the numbers of Black Americans make up a significant, if not large, percentage of military personnel, especially in the area of combat arms. Whenever this is assessed there is attention paid to the possibility of causalities in the event of war. This brings together issues of economics, patriotism, and the impact of parent's occupation on their children. The present status of Black Americans shows a decrease in their numbers in the combat arms. At the same time, there has been an increased concentration in support and logistics services branches, and a lower concentration in the infantry.[10]

For decades scholars have examined data that asked soldiers to make comparisons between civilian and military life, with a focus on perceived discrimination. Indeed, the present status of African Americans in the Military cannot be understood without referring to that scholarship. It was Samuel Stouffer and his associates who first began to examine the interaction of race, opportunities in the military and general race relations.

Stouffer and his associates used the military as a natural laboratory to study race relations in its classical forms.[11] During this time, "race relations" exclusively meant relations between people of African descent and those of non-African descent. In a work entitled *The American Soldier*, Stouffer came up with perhaps the most significant sociological proposition on race relations—the contact hypothesis.[12] His basic point was that, under certain conditions, the more contact people from different races have with each other, the more positive their attitudes toward each other. The conditions necessary to make the contact work were, first, an authority that strongly promotes those interactions; secondly, a shared sense of common goals between the parties; third, that the contacts be between those of roughly equal status; and fourth, that the interactions be cooperative, prolonged, and cover a wide range of activities.

The military proved an excellent laboratory to test this proposition. The overall finding of *The American Soldier* was that soldiers who were white and in a company containing a black platoon were more favorable toward that arrangement than those in large units with no black platoons.

In other words, the more experience white soldiers had with an integrated work environment, the more they favored serving in a racially-mixed organization.[13]

In 1967, William Brink and Louis Harris noted that in terms of organizational acceptability, Black Americans had found a home in the military. Their findings showed that black soldiers considered the military as being more egalitarian than the civilian work sector.[14] This finding, which also noted the military's imperfections in regard to race relations, would be repeated in later decades as the opportunities the military provided African Americans and other Americans of color.

By the early 1970s, under the direction of Human Sciences Research and Peter Nordlie, the military developed a systematic survey to measure its racial progress, which developed into The Equal Opportunity Survey, an instrument designed to measure the perceived treatment of personnel within its ranks.[15] Originally designed for black/white measures, the survey now contains issues related to all military personnel, including groups who have been designated as "minorities."[16] One of its findings was that a significant population of blacks, 34 percent, still believe that African Americans had greater freedom from discrimination in the military than in civilian life; 61 percent, however, said that military and civilian life were the same in regard to racial freedom and opportunities.[17]

Given the changing opportunity structure for Black Americans within the civilian sector, one should expect that this question would show significant change. But what is significant about the military is that the organization has a significant number of blacks to fill out questionnaires, and they are represented throughout the ranks. Within the civilian sector, it is still difficult to find an organization with significant numbers of Black Americans to fill out a questionnaire.

III

The status of Black Americans in the military, the highest form of civic participation, must be seen as the product of a best-practice organization that other organizations can learn from when it comes to developing opportunities for African Americans. In *All That We Can Be: Black*

Essay 5

Leadership and Integration the Army Way, Charles C. Moskos and myself looked at best practices or lessons from military organizations for civilian organizations. One of our major points is that, despite daunting racial discrimination, Black Americans have a long tradition of achievement. Another is that many black families have connections with military service that spans generations. A third is that children from military families have a strong tradition of college matriculation. In fact, we asserted that black Military families have replaced the small black middle-class family cohort of the early 1900s—Black America's major force for the education and achievement of children.[18]

Also in that work, we set out best practices of lessons for the larger society. Those best practices have anchored the experience of Black Americans within the military, where race relations are, not perfect, but nonetheless quite admirable. Following are some of the best practices that emerge from the military:

First, although blacks and whites do not view opportunities and race relations in the same way, the military experience has shown that blacks and whites do not have to hold identical views of America's racial situation in order to jointly defend the country.

Second, organizations should focus on their opportunity structure, and not on prohibiting racist expression. Somewhere along the line, in this free country, people became concerned with who "liked" Black Americans and the racist comments that some people make. We should remember that the history of Black America is one of success, even in the face of racism. It would be ridiculous to argue that blacks cannot achieve until racist ideas and behaviors are completely overcome. Universities have switched from providing opportunities to worrying about racist expression. The point is to concentrate on opportunities and stop worrying about what racists say.

The third best practice is to be ruthless against all forms of discrimination. This means placing an emphasis on what people can do, and how they are rewarded. The legal means to fight discrimination are there, and should be utilized by organizations in order to insure equal opportunity.

The fourth best practice is to prepare individuals to be as successful as possible. This means that families, as well as other organizations, should strive to introduce people to the best practices in America. The sad thing about too much of the current literature is that it stresses black failure rather than black success. This started to happen when the best practices of Black Americans (in terms of building institutions, taking responsibility for the education of their children, and creating safe communities) was replaced by concentrating on failures so that grants could be generated from sources to "take care of people within communities." The military, with all of its emphasis on the defense of the country and the possibility of being placed in harms way, contradicts the prevalent failure paradigm.

This realization does not mean that Black Americans do not have choices. It simply means that for those who do choose the military, the possibility of opportunity exists, and has always existed. It is not an organization where people speak of increasing the number of African Americans, but rather an organization that has set the best practices for the large numbers who are members.

(see tables 1 and 2 on pages 102–105)

TABLE 1: Blacks as a Percentage of Total Personnel by Grade and Service 1980, 1990, 1998

1980

GRADE	ARMY	NAVY	AIR FORCE	MARINE CORPS	DOD TOTAL
Total Commissioned Officers	7.2	2.4	4.5	3.7	4.8
O-7 and above (Generals)	5.3	0.1	0.2	0.3	0.3
O-6 (Colonel)	4.5	0.7	1.8	N/A	2.3
O-5 (Lt. Colonel)	4.9	0.5	2.0	0.5	2.6
O-4 (Major)	4.4	1.2	2.4	1.6	2.7
O-3 (Captain)	7.5	3.0	4.3	4.4	5.1
O-2 (1st Lieutenant)	10.2	3.8	8.0	5.4	7.1
O-1 (2nd Lieutenant)	10.4	3.3	8.3	4.4	7.6
Warrant Officers	5.9	4.6	N/A	6.8	5.7
All Officers	7.1	2.5	5.7	3.9	4.9
Enlisted					
E-9 (Sergeant Major)	20.5	5.7	9.0	13.3	11.9
E-8 (Master Sergeant)	25.3	5.7	17.7	15.2	15.8
E-7 (Sergeant 1st Class)	24.7	5.5	13.6	14.8	15.9
E-6 (Staff Sergeant)	23.9	6.0	14.8	18.6	15.5
E-5 (Sergeant)	31.2	8.2	18.3	18.4	20.5
E-4 (Specialist)	37.2	11.4	16.1	17.8	24.2
E-3 (Private 1st Class)	39.0	14.9	15.9	25.1	24.1
E-2 (Private)	37.0	16.6	17.7	27.5	26.5
E-1 (Private Recruit)	27.0	15.7	13.5	23.6	21.0
Subtotal	32.5	11.2	16.0	22.0	21.6
Total	29.2	10.1	14.0	20.5	19.3

TABLE 1 continued: Blacks as a Percentage of Total Personnel by Grade and Service 1980, 1990, 1998

1990

GRADE	ARMY	NAVY	AIR FORCE	MARINE CORPS	DOD TOTAL
Total Commissioned Officers	11.2	3.9	5.6	4.6	6.8
0-7 and above (Generals)	6.4	1.1	1.2	N/A	3.0
0-6 (Colonel)	4.6	0.8	2.1	1.4	2.5
0-5 (Lt. Colonel)	5.3	2.1	2.6	2.3	3.3
0-4 (Major)	9.5	3.3	6.0	4.3	6.2
0-3 (Captain)	14.0	4.2	6.6	4.9	8.1
0-2 (1st Lieutenant)	12.9	4.6	6.0	5.2	7.7
0-1 (2nd Lieutenant)	11.8	5.8	5.5	5.6	7.8
Warrant Officers	11.0	7.5	N/A	9.9	8.9
All Officers	11.0	4.0	5.6	5.1	6.9
Enlisted					
E-9 (Sergeant Major)	30.5	5.7	17.5	13.3	16.0
E-8 (Master Sergeant)	24.8	5.7	20.1	15.2	16.5
E-7 (Sergeant 1st Class)	30.7	7.5	20.9	18.7	20.0
E-6 (Staff Sergeant)	37.6	12.3	25.9	18.2	23.2
E-5 (Sergeant)	36.7	16.1	24.3	19.0	24.1
E-4 (Specialist)	32.5	17.8	19.5	19.2	23.7
E-3 (Private 1st Class)	28.3	23.6	19.2	14.5	21.9
E-2 (Private)	25.6	21.6	19.9	12.5	21.3
E-1 (Private Recruit)	25.2	24.9	20.4	14.2	24.0
Subtotal	29.1	17.3	20.8	17.6	22.7
Total	26.8	15.6	19.2	15.4	20.4

TABLE 1 continued: Blacks as a Percentage of Total Personnel by Grade and Service 1980, 1990, 1998

1998

GRADE	ARMY	NAVY	AIR FORCE	MARINE CORPS	DOD TOTAL
Total Commissioned Officers	11.0	6.0	6.0	6.1	7.6
0-7 and above (Generals)	8.8	3.2	3.3	4.8	5.3
0-6 (Colonel)	6.7	2.9	3.5	4.0	4.4
0-5 (Lt. Colonel)	10.0	3.4	6.7	4.3	6.8
0-4 (Major)	12.4	5.0	5.9	4.5	7.6
0-3 (Captain)	11.9	6.7	5.9	5.3	7.9
0-2 (1St Lieutenant)	10.5	8.3	6.4	7.7	8.4
0-1 (2nd Lieutenant)	10.7	7.9	6.9	9.9	8.8
Warrant Officers	15.3	14.8	N/A	14.1	15.1
All Officers	12.7	6.3	6.0	6.9	8.1

TABLE 2: FY 1998 Occupational Areas of Active Component Enlisted Personnel by Race/Ethnicity (Percent)

OCCUPATIONAL CODE AND AREA	WHITE	BLACK	HISPANIC	OTHER
0 Infantry, Gun Crews, and Seamanship Specialists	18.2	13.2	17.9	15.4
1 Electronic Equipment Repairers	10.7	6.7	7.2	6.4
2 Communications and Intelligence Specialists	9.4	8	7.4	6.2
3 Medical and Dental Specialists	6.3	8.3	7.7	10.6
4 Other Allied Specialists	3.3	2.5	2.5	2.6
5 Functional Support and Administration	12.2	25.6	17.2	18.3
6 Electrical/Mechanical Equipment Repairers	21.9	15.2	19	20.4
7 Craftsmen	3.9	3	3.2	3.4
8 Service and Supply Handlers	7.2	12.1	8.7	9.3
9 Non-occupational*	6.9	5.5	9.2	7.5
Total	**100.0**	**100.0**	**100.0**	**100.0**

Notes: Columns may not add to total due to rounding. * Non-occupational includes patients, students, those with unassigned duties, and unknowns.

Also see Appendix Tables B-29 (Occupational Area by Service and Gender) and B-30 (Occupational Area by Service and Race/Ethnicity).

Essay **5**

Notes

¹ For an excellent listing, and summary review of this literature, see James M. McPherson et al (1971), *Blacks In America: Bibliographical Essays* (Garden City, New York: Doubleday)

² Minton, Henry M. (1913) "Early History of Negroes in Business in Philadelphia," Read before the American Historical Society, March; Du Bois, W.E.B. (1898) *The Negro in Business* (Atlanta, Ga.: Atlanta University Press).

Du Bois, W.E.B. (1907) *Economic Co-Cooperation Among Negro Americans* (Atlanta, Ga., Atlanta University Press, 1907).

³ For a review see Charles C. Moskos and John Sibley Butler. 1966. *All That We Can Be: Black Leadership and Racial Integration the Army Way* (New York: Basic Books)

⁴ Also see John Sibley Butler and Charles C. Moskos, "Labor Force Trends: The Military as Data," in Neil J. Smelser, William Julius Wilson and Faith Mitchell (editors) *America Becoming: Racial Trends and Their Consequences Volume II* (National Academy Press, Washington, D.C.) pp. 174-189.

⁵ *Ibid.*, p. 178.

⁶ Charles C. Moskos and John Sibley Butler. 1966. *All That We Can Be: Black Leadership and Racial Integration the Army Way* (New York: Basic Books), p. 47.

⁷ See for example John Sibley Butler. "Assessing Black Enlisted Participation in the Army," in *Social Problems 23* (June): 558-566. 1976.

⁸ John Sibley Butler and Charles C. Moskos, "Labor Force Trends: The Military as Data," in Neil J. Smelser, William Julius Wilson and Faith Mitchell (editors) *America Becoming: Racial Trends and Their Consequences Volume II* (National Academy Press, Washington, D.C.) p. 179.

⁹ *Ibid.*, pp. 183-184.

¹⁰ *Ibid.*, p. 179. For a general discussion of this issue see Charles C. Moskos and John Sibley Butler. 1966. *All That We Can Be: Black Leadership and Racial Integration the Army Way* (New York: Basic Books). As noted in this work, and Butler and Moskos (Ibid), for decades critics have argued that the United States uses Blacks as

cannon fodder-a charge that is untrue. During Vietnam, Black fatalities amounted to 12.1 percent of all Americans killed during that conflict (DoD does not keep statistics for other white ethnic groups in this so-called multi-cultural society)., a figure proportionate to the percentage in the general population and lower than the percentage of Blacks in the military during that time period. Also, the racial data on combat deaths of soldiers during campaigns in Mayaguez, Lebanon, Grenada, Panama, the Persian Gulf and Somalia show that Blacks accounted for 14 percent of all combat deaths. Butler and Moskos have concluded that no case can be made that Blacks suffer disproportionate during conflicts in which America has been involved.

[11] Samuel Stouffer, et al, *The American Soldier* (Princeton, N.J.: Princeton University Press, 1949), vol. 1, p. 54.

[12] This discussion follows John Sibley Butler's "Race Relations in the Military," in Charles C. Moskos and Frank Wood (editors), *The Military: More Than Just a Job* (New York: Pergamon-Brasseye's, 1988).

[13] *Ob. Cit.* Stouffer et al, p. 594.

[14] William J. Brink and Louis Harris, *Black and White: A Study of U.S. Racial Attitudes Today* (New York: Simon & Schuster, 1967).

[15] See Robert L. Hiett, Robin S. McBride, Bryon G. Fiman, *Measuring the Impact of Race Relations Programs in the Military.* Human Sciences Research, 1974. Final report to DoD, report HSR-RR-74/5-Tr. Washington, D.C.

[16] For the latest survey results see Jacquelyn Searville, Scott B. Button, Jack E. Edwards, Anita R. Lancaster, and Timothy W. Elig, *Armed Forces Equal Opportunity Survey.* Defense Manpower Data Center, Survey & Program Evaluation Division, Arlington, Va.

[17] *Ibid.*

[18] Charles C. Moskos and John Sibley Butler. 1966. *All That We Can Be: Black Leadership and Racial Integration the Army Way* (New York: Basic Books).

6

Holding the Accountants Accountable: Why Are There So Few African-American CPAs?

By Theresa A. Hammond

Until the Enron debacle of 2002, Americans had paid little attention to the public accounting profession. That changed, however, after the story broke and the media soon recognized the key role played by Enron's auditor, Arthur Andersen. Andersen now finds itself deeply mired in legal trouble and fighting for its corporate life.

There are nearly half a million certified public accountants (CPAs) in the United States. Although historically the profession has garnered relatively little media coverage, it wields substantial power over the nation's most consequential financial transactions. Every publicly traded company and most major governmental entities must have their financial records audited by a CPA. The "Big Five" firms that dominate the industry—Andersen, PriceWaterhouseCoopers, KPMG, Deloitte & Touche, and Ernst & Young—audit over 95 percent of the Fortune 500, and earn revenues in excess of $40 billion.

None of these firms employed African Americans until the 1960s. Today, less than one percent of CPAs are African American. This woeful underrepresentation contributes significantly to the shortage of African Americans in leadership positions in corporate America and compares unfavorably with other professions. The current heightened attention to the role of CPA firms provides an unusual timely window of opportunity to examine the racial composition of these important American businesses.

Essay 6

African-American Representation in Three Professions[1]

	LAWYERS	DOCTORS	CPAS
1930	0.8%	2.5%	0.03%
1960	1.0%	2.0%	0.1%
1997	2.7%	4.2%	Less than 1%

African-American CPAs Since 1921

Only a fraction of those who major in accounting in college become CPAs, which requires passing a demanding examination and, in most states, serving an apprenticeship under a CPA. Before the Civil Rights Movement, many talented African-American men and women earned accounting degrees and passed the examination, but meeting the experience requirement proved extremely difficult because for the first two-thirds of the 20th century, rarely would white CPAs hire and train an African American. By 1965 there were only 100 African-American CPAs in the United States, less than one in one thousand CPAs.

Because finding employment with a white-owned CPA firm was nearly impossible, African Americans helped each other. In 1923, before the State of Illinois adopted an apprenticeship requirement, Chicagoan Arthur Wilson became the second African-American CPA in the United States. Certification in hand, he trained Mary T. Washington, with whom he worked at a black-owned bank. She in turn opened a CPA firm (now Washington, Pittman, and McKeever) that provided training to others, so that by 1965 one-quarter of all the African-American CPAs in the country worked in Chicago. Chicago's large and diverse black population and its, relatively speaking, sizeable black business community could support that tiny band. But in other cities African American CPAs had a difficult time finding clients because of the scarcity of wealth in the African-American community. In contrast, Washington's firm provided services to some of the largest black-owned businesses in the country, and African Americans from around the nation moved to

Chicago in order to work for her and earn their credentials.

Those aspiring CPAs who were outside of Chicago displayed remarkable tenacity. Some applied fruitlessly for dozens of jobs, even in ostensibly liberal cities such as New York and Los Angeles. The experiences of Bernadine Gines and Talmadge Tillman are characteristic of those trailblazers who entered the profession prior to the Civil Rights Movement.

Bernadine Coles Gines

Bernadine Coles Gines grew up in Virginia, and was encouraged by one of her professors at Virginia State College to pursue a graduate degree in accounting. Because the University of Virginia, only a mile from her home, did not admit African Americans, in 1946 Gines headed for New York University. Her tuition was funded by an out-of-state scholarship program that the state of Virginia had developed in order to defend its "separate but equal" educational system. Gines moved to New York with great hope for increased opportunities in her adopted home.

Two years later, when Gines completed her master's degree at NYU, she had intense difficulty finding a position with a CPA firm. She worked as a bookkeeper for an African-American newspaper, the *New York Age*, but wanted to get experience working for a CPA so that she could earn her certificate. From her residence at the YWCA in Harlem, she sent many letters of application but did not get a single positive response.

Gines moved from Harlem to Queens, and suddenly, because her address no longer revealed her race, she was invited for several interviews. Nevertheless, when she appeared for interviews, she received no offers. A partner at the first firm with which she interviewed told her that he could not hire her as an accountant. Instead, he asked if she could help him find a maid for his wife.

After two years of searching, Gines was interviewed by two young Jewish men who quickly overcame their surprise that she was African American. To her delight, they offered her a position. In 1954, while working for the firm, she became the first African-American woman in New York State to earn her CPA.

Essay 6

Talmadge Tillman

Like Bernadine Gines, Talmadge Tillman grew up in the South but moved in the hope of finding better opportunities. Born in North Carolina, Tillman attended Morehouse College and Indiana University as an undergraduate, and became the first black graduate of Syracuse University's MBA program in 1948. In 1951 he moved to California, where he hoped to find a firm that would provide the requisite experience so he could become a CPA.

Immediately upon arrival in Los Angeles, Tillman registered his resume with the California CPA Society. Based on his exceptional educational credentials, a CPA telephoned him and offered him the job over the phone. "I went to his office the next morning and he stated, 'Boy, what can I do for you?' I told him I was Tillman and that he had given me a job and told me to come to work. He placed his head on the desk and just shook it. He then said, 'You are a Negro; I cannot give you the job.'"

Tillman bought a detailed map of Los Angeles. Using a phonebook, he mapped out all the CPA firms in the city, spending six weeks walking different neighborhoods and applying for jobs. He knew he was ahead of his time, but he was convinced that "somewhere out there someone was going to give me a job." At the end of the six weeks, his conviction proved to be true, and he accepted a position as an auditor with a Jewish-owned CPA firm.

Tillman worked for the firm for almost a year. During this period, the managing partner of the office had been serving in the Korean War. As Tillman describes it, "[A]fter he came back from fighting for democracy, he walked in the office and saw me and a [black] girl named Linda ... [H]e told me, 'It doesn't look good to have Negroes in the office.'" Within days, both Tillman and Linda had been fired by mail.

Tillman persevered. Still in need of more experience to meet the requirement, one of Tillman's professors arranged an interview with a firm that had four open positions. The firm recruiters gave him a written test, an unusual, if not unheard of, approach when interviewing someone with an MBA for an entry-level job in accounting. Tillman passed the test, but was told he would not be hired. Tillman asked them why they had given him the test if they knew they were not going to hire him. He was told, "We wanted to see what a Negro could know about accounting."

Tillman turned to teaching high school math. He ultimately earned his +CPA in 1965 and his doctorate in accounting in 1968, when he became the 8th African American to hold both. He became a professor at California State University at Long Beach.

The 1960s and 1970s

The Civil Rights Movement improved in opportunities for African-American CPAs both by expanding the demand for black accountants and by opening opportunities in the white-owned firms. Burgeoning donations to civil rights organizations required greater financial expertise. Georgia's first African-American CPA, Jesse Blayton, worked for the Southern Christian Leadership Conference as its donations mushroomed. And when the State of Alabama charged Martin Luther King, Jr. with felony tax evasion, it was Blayton who developed the accounting evidence that resulted in King's acquittal. (Later, King joked that perhaps the all-white jury's antipathy towards the tax authorities outweighed their prejudice against African Americans.) [2]

In 1965 the National Urban League hired its first CPA, Audley Coulthurst. Coulthurst reports, "I worked for the Urban League [because] I liked what they were doing. I figured that the students were sitting in at the lunch counters, getting their heads whipped and getting dogs sicced on them ... but the skills I had as a CPA [meant that] I could contribute to the movement by working for the League, and helping the League raise the funds that would [support] these activities."

The Civil Rights Act of 1964, which forbade employment discrimination on the basis of race, brought an end to the most intransigent barriers to African Americans' entry into many professions, including accounting. Between 1968 and 1971, the number of African Americans employed in the major CPA firms in New York quintupled. The big firms began recruiting at black colleges and the American Institute of CPAs initiated programs to encourage African Americans to major in accounting. In 1969 the National Association of Black Accountants was founded, and its membership mushroomed over the ensuing years.

President Lyndon B. Johnson's War on Poverty provided much-needed funds to urban community organizations, which in turn required the services of CPAs. Black-owned CPA firms grew, and the National Association of Minority CPA Firms was created in 1971 with funding from Richard Nixon's Commerce Department. Later in the 1970s, set-aside programs played a key role in the continued expansion of African-American CPA firms. Jimmy Carter as well as newly elected African-American mayors in several major cities required that government contracts include the participation of minority-owned firms. For African-American CPAs, this led to many joint-venture audits, including the audit for the City of Chicago, with major public accounting firms.

Nevertheless, many African Americans continued to find it difficult to

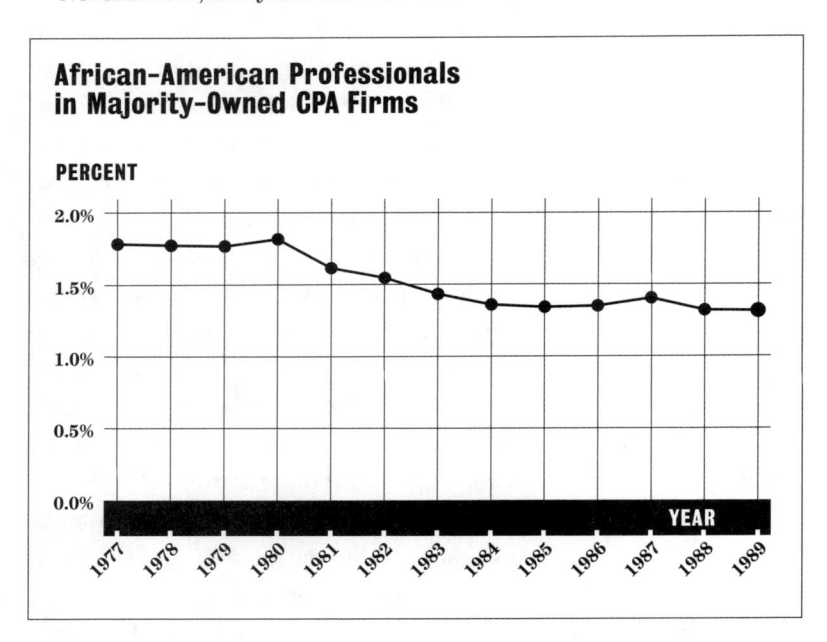

African-American Professionals in Majority-Owned CPA Firms

obtain positions with CPA firms. Although the major firms recruited at the historically black colleges in the South, they typically made job offers only for their offices in northern cities. By 1976, the number of

African-American CPAs had grown to 450, but still fewer than 3 in one thousand CPAs were black. [3]

The Reagan Era

The era of progress that followed the Civil Rights Movement was short-lived. Growth in the employment of African Americans in CPA firms came to a halt in the 1980s. Ronald Reagan's attacks on affirmative action and on set asides were swiftly felt in the profession. Every measure of African-American progress in public accounting firms declined in the 1980s: percentage of African Americans hired, percentage of African Americans remaining with the firms, percentage of African Americans promoted, and percentage of historically black college graduates hired. [4] The decline in the 1980s led into a decade of stagnation in the 1990s, and CPAs currently have the lowest representation of African Americans of any major profession.

A Homogeneous Profession

While African Americans are most severely under-represented in the profession, other groups also experience exclusion. Virtually all of the few African Americans who worked for white firms prior to the 1960s worked for Jewish CPAs. In the mid-1950s in Los Angeles, aspiring CPA William Collins entered an interview with a recruiter from one of the nation's largest firms. The recruiter interrupted the interview before Collins could sit down, saying, "Mr. Collins, [this interview] is just a waste of my time and yours, too. We do not hire Negroes. ... Now we have not had Jews in our firm until recently, and we haven't had Orientals in our firm until recently, but we have not come around to having blacks on our staff, not even in the clerical field." Collins ultimately met his experience requirement in a Jewish-owned firm.

Decades later, the profession continued to consider many groups "outsiders." In 1976, during an investigation of the CPA profession prompted by several failed audits, the U.S. Senate asked the major accounting firms to provide data on black partners. Coopers & Lybrand defended its poor record on African-American advancement by stating,

Essay **6**

in part, "However we have large numbers of Jewish and Roman Catholic people at all levels." [5]

A 1981 book on the profession told of a white, recently retired CPA firm partner's reaction to visiting his old firm:

> In my day lunchtime was a relaxed affair. A good meal and good conversations with men of your own ilk. Now if you want to tell a joke, you have to look around the table first. One of your partners may be Negro, Spanish, a Jew, or a woman. You know how sensitive they are. [6]

Although the profession remains homogeneous on many dimensions, the exclusion of African Americans has proven to be more intransigent than that of other groups. While the proportion of African-American professionals in CPA firms was declining in the 1980s, the proportions of white women, Latinos, and Asian Americans were rising. [7] These increases have provided cover for a profession that is losing ground in African-American participation; typically firms will refer to their records on "minorities" or "diversity" and thus obscure the lack of progress for African Americans.

Corporate America

As crucial as it is to diversify the CPA profession itself, the exclusion of African Americans from the profession has a direct and damaging impact on the composition of the finance and accounting divisions of corporate America. Most new accounting graduates who enter the Big Five stay only a few years, meet the experience requirement and earn their CPAs, and then join corporate America—frequently one of the companies whose audits they conducted. Thus, the CPA degree and experience is a pathway into and escalator up the ladder of corporate America because it gives one the responsibility of handing the "hard assets" of the nation's business community.

As seen in the Enron case, it is not atypical for the internal financial management of a corporation to include former external auditors of that company. Articles in the accounting industry's main journal underscore the fact that being a CPA is great preparation for becoming a Chief Financial Officer or even a Chief Executive Officer. [8] The lack of African-American CPAs thus perpetuates the under-representation of African Americans in corporate accounting departments.

The absence of African Americans in finance divisions was at issue in the two largest race discrimination lawsuits in U.S. History. In 1990, Bari-Ellen Roberts became the first African-American woman to be hired into a professional position in Texaco's finance division. [9] Her treatment in the division led to a discrimination suit against Texaco that was settled for $176 million in 1996. Coca Cola settled a similar suit for $192.5 million in 2000. The major complaint was that African Americans only advanced in certain areas of the companies, such as human resources, and were excluded from more powerful divisions that could lead to greater career advancement, especially international marketing and finance. [10]

Though none of them are CPAs, there are now three African-American Chief Executive Officers at Fortune 500 companies. Since 1999, when Franklin Raines of Fannie Mae became the only such African-American CEO, Kenneth Chenault has become CEO of American Express and Richard Parsons has become CEO of AOL Time Warner. One of the highest ranking African Americans in corporate America, Thomas Jones, Chairman and CEO of Citigroup's global asset management division, is a CPA who began his career with one of the major public accounting firms. [11]

Other Professions

While the CPA profession has a direct impact on the composition of corporate America, in terms of their internal structure, they have the same type of hierarchical structure as law firms. While African

Percentage of African Americans in Major Professional Firms 1996 [12]

	LAW FIRMS	CPA FIRMS
Professionals	3.7%	1.4%
Partners	1.2%	0.1%

Essay 6

Americans are severely under-represented in law firms at both the professional and partnership levels, comparable statistics for CPA firms are even more dire.

One major reason for the differences is historical. There has been more demand for lawyers in the black community than for accountants, because African Americans were kept on the margins of capitalism. [13] Another important reason is that the Big Five accounting firms have an oligopoly unparalleled in other professions. This handful of firms has over 150,000 professional employees in the U.S. alone, and they recruit from hundreds of schools. In contrast, in the legal profession there are many law firms and relatively few top schools from which to recruit. The students in these desirable schools put pressure on the law firms to report their success in hiring and promoting African Americans and other under-represented groups. Each year this information is published in a recruiting guide, and the few firms that refuse to provide numbers risk alienating those they would like to employ. In CPA firms, the employment situation is reversed. It is impossible to get firm-specific employment data on race from the Big Five firms, and currently there is no meaningful pressure for them to provide this information.

Holding the Accountants Accountable

Throughout its history, the CPA profession has been loath to change except when it has faced direct government pressure. Only in the late 1960s and early 1970s were significant efforts undertaken to increase the participation of African Americans in the profession. In the 1980s, when pressure from the federal government waned, the impact on CPA firms was immediate: the meager participation of African Americans declined.

The public understands that it is important to have African-American leadership in the visible professions of law and medicine, but the abysmal numbers of African-American CPAs has not caused much concern. The severe under-representation must be rectified so that the certified public accounting profession truly represents the public. By adding new viewpoints and perspectives, a more diverse profession may help prevent excessively cozy relationships between CPA firms and their clients.

The Enron scandal has resulted in a closer look at the accounting profession, and the current scrutiny provides an opportunity to bring about change in its composition. Accountants know best that if something is important, it should be measured and reported. In corporations, success is a result of accountability: a recent study revealed that three-quarters of the best companies for minorities rewarded managers for meeting diversity targets, whereas only one quarter of all Fortune 500 companies do so. [14]

From 1976 until 1989, and only intermittently in the 1990s, the American Institute of CPAs provided aggregate data on the composition of CPA firm employees. Except for the one time it was requested by the Senate in 1976, firm-specific data has been unavailable. That has to change. Congress and the SEC should require each firm to report annually its success in recruiting, retaining, and promoting African Americans. If the numbers are public, the Big Five and other firms will compete with each other to improve their profiles.

Given the profession's history of glacial movement in integrating its ranks, it is clear that only proactive efforts will result in significant increases in the proportion of African Americans at all levels of CPA firms. Without intervention, I fear that the participation of African Americans will remain at abysmal levels. Even in law and medicine, fields in which African-American participation continued to grow for the thirty years following the Civil Rights Movement, parity for African Americans has not been achieved. CPAs lag far behind these two professions, and the current system perpetuates indifference. It is time to hold the accountants accountable.

Notes

[1] This data and most of this essay are based on my book, *A White-Collar Profession: African American CPAs Since 1921* (Chapel Hill: University of North Carolina Press, 2002).

[2] Taylor Branch, *Parting the Waters: America in the King Years 1954-1963* (New York: Simon & Schuster, 1988).

Essay **6**

³ Bert Mitchell, "The Status of the Black CPA—An Update," *Journal of Accountancy* (1976): pp. 52-58.

⁴ Report on Minority Accounting Graduates, *Enrollment and Public Accounting Professionals* (New York: American Institute of Certified Public Accountants, 1976-1989).

⁵ Senate Committee on Government Operations, *The Accounting Establishment: A Staff Study*, pp. 845-875.

⁶ Mark Stevens, *The Big Eight* (New York: Macmillan, 1981), p. 22.

⁷ Nevertheless, though not as low as the African American hiring rates, Latino and Asian American hiring rates were below their representation in graduating accounting classes throughout the period for which data is available. The numbers for Native Americans are so low that patterns are impossible to interpret.

⁸ E.g. Carol Lippert Gray, "What does it Take to Become a CFO?" *Journal of Accountancy*, December 2000; NYSSCPA Special Advisory Task Force to Study Blacks in the CPA Profession, Report on the Status of Blacks in the CPA Profession (New York State Society of CPAs, 1990), p. 4.

⁹ Bari-Ellen Roberts with Jack White, *Roberts vs. Texaco: A True Story of Race and Corporate America* (New York: Avon Books, 1998), p. 109.

¹⁰ Davan Maharaj, "Coca-Cola to Settle Racial Bias Lawsuit," *Los Angeles Times* November 17, 2000, p. 1.

¹¹ Karen Jacobs, "More companies seek diversity as internal bias suits increase," *Houston Chronicle* 2/10/02 p. 2; Ellis Cose, "Rethinking Black Leadership" *Newsweek* 1/28/02, p. 42; Garth Alexander, "From Wood Shack to Wall Street," *Sunday Times* (London) July 29, 2001. For an excellent discussion of minority executives in corporations, see David Thomas and John Gabarro, *Breaking Through: The Making of Minority Executives in Corporate America* (Boston: Harvard Business School Press, 1999). For coverage of investment banking, see Gregory S. Bell, *In the Black: A History of African Americans on Wall Street* (New York: John Wiley, 2002).

¹² Elizabeth Chambliss, *Miles to Go 2000: Progress of Minorities in the Legal Profession* (American Bar Association Commission on Racial and Ethnic Diversity in the Profession, 2000); and Gregory Johnson, *Report on Minority Accounting Graduates*,

Enrollment and Public Accounting Professionals-1997 (American Institute of CPAs, Minority Initiatives Committee, 1997).

[13] For analysis of African Americans' long history of success in business, see Juliet E. K. Walker *The History of Black Business in America: Capitalism, Race, Entrepreneurship* (New York: Macmillan, 1998).

[14] Stephanie Mehta, "What Minority Employees Really Want," *Fortune* July 10, 2000.

African Americans Confront a Pandemic: Assessing Community Impact, Organization, and Advocacy in the Second Decade of AIDS

By Maya Rockeymoore

Abstract

Last year marked the twentieth anniversary of the recognition of a new pandemic called Acquired Immunodeficiency Syndrome. Over time, the landscape of AIDS policy, politics, research, and epidemiology have shifted dramatically to engulf individuals, communities, states and nations in a battle to ward off mass destruction resulting from the spread of AIDS. Despite growing attention to the issue, solutions for curbing the spread of AIDS have largely been elusive.

The progression of the disease in the U.S. is similar to its evolution in the world: Black and brown people are disproportionately the sufferers of the AIDS epidemic. While an analysis of the global implications of AIDS on poor nations of color is an important and necessary undertaking, this essay will maintain a narrow analytical lens in considering the plight of people of African descent living in the United States of America. It is the hope that this will illuminate community processes that could prove useful in efforts to mobilize individuals and communities elsewhere.

Introduction

Since the beginning of the epidemic, the politics and policies that developed in reaction to the AIDS scourge have been rooted in the unique experiences of America's gay community. Overwhelmingly white and male, the vocal gay community responded to the early threat of AIDS by mobilizing and using political muscle to marshal federal, state, and local resources. Their remarkable achievements in battling the ravages of a mystifying disease should not be minimized-the more so because they simultaneously had to fight a widespread social stigma and blatant discrimination in order to bring the devastation of AIDS in their communities to national and international attention. Their early dominance and success, however, have influenced the content and shape of the political processes surrounding the distribution of AIDS resources to such an extent that it has had a crowding-out effect on other groups who have also been severely affected by the epidemic.

Unbeknownst to many, African Americans have been disproportionately affected by HIV/AIDS since the beginning of the epidemic. Early surveillance data issued by the Centers for Disease Control and Prevention (CDC) revealed that black Americans were among the first cases of AIDS in America and that their rate of infection was disproportionate to their representation in the general population. Unlike the white gay community, however, the black community failed to formulate a coordinated early response to the epidemic for a variety of reasons that were rooted in the campaign of misinformation about risk categories and transmission that surrounded AIDS in its early years, and in socio-cultural biases that colored attitudes toward people affected by the disease, as well as in depressed socio-economic conditions that made it difficult to discern the gravity of a new threat amidst other pressing concerns.[1] The salience of this last point cannot be ignored. In the 1980s, the crack-cocaine epidemic, a dramatic spike in drug-related crime activity, massive unemployment, and the hostile posture and punitive policies of the Reagan/Bush administration consumed African-American communities. The impact of these and other factors diminished their capacity to recognize the spread of AIDS and to formulate an appropriate response.

The second decade of AIDS would bring new concerns to the fore as epidemiologists and the mainstream news media brought heightened attention to the growing devastation created by HIV and AIDS in communities of color. Since 1994, African Americans have outpaced other groups in new cases of HIV/AIDS. Although only 12 percent of the population, African Americans represent 38 percent of all AIDS cases reported in the United States. In 2000, more African Americans were reported with AIDS than any other racial and ethnic group. Indeed, 63 percent of all women and 65 percent of all children reported with AIDS in 2000 were African American. The rate of reported cases for African Americans was two times greater than the rate for Hispanics and more than eight times greater than the rate for whites.[2]

Contrary to the malaise in the first decade of AIDS, however, the second decade of AIDS was very different in terms of impact, organization, and advocacy in the African-American community. By the second decade it became clear that the institutions created by the AIDS epidemic were a micro-version of the racialized institutions and processes of the larger U.S. health care system and society-at-large. The fact that African Americans were contracting HIV and dying from AIDS in record numbers provided an indicator that AIDS service organizations, research entities, and treatment and prevention models-formed to meet the needs of white men of means-were inadequate to address the unique circumstances of African Americans and other racial and ethnic minorities. These stark socio-political realities would serve as a catalyst for a new era of black political activism.

The "Changing Face" of AIDS

Changed realities and perceptions in the second decade of AIDS resulted in more attention to the epidemic's impact in communities of color both in the mainstream and in the African American community. Many have argued that the early depiction of AIDS as a disease primarily affecting white homosexual men distorted the reality of AIDS transmission and contributed to the rise of AIDS among other groups who believed that they were not at risk for the disease (Cohen 1999; Schiller 1992; Shilts 1987).

Yet a series of events in the 1990s, all of which involved prominent African Americans, served to heighten awareness and combat old stereotypes about HIV/AIDS and its transmission in the African-American community. Star athlete Earvin "Magic" Johnson's November

1991 announcement that he had tested positive for HIV during a routine physical exam was a shock to the black community (and many in White America as well). As a result, more news stories focused on AIDS in the black community and more African Americans were made aware of their risk. Another critical moment influencing African-American perceptions of AIDS came in April 1992 when famed tennis champion Arthur Ashe announced that he had contracted AIDS from a 1983 blood transfusion during open-heart surgery. Ashe died of AIDS-related pneumonia in February of 1993. His struggle served to further educate the community about the epidemic. Finally, the sudden death of popular rap star Eric "Eazy-E" Wright at the age of 31 from AIDS in March of 1995 served as a wake up call to younger African Americans who admired Wright and his music. For many younger African Americans, Wright's death smashed the long-held myth that heterosexuals were immune from contracting HIV and AIDS.

The rapidly escalating numbers of African Americans and Hispanics contracting HIV and AIDS would be another factor that heightened attention to what some in the popular media referred to as the "changing face" of AIDS. The proportional distribution of African-American AIDS cases reported by the CDC increased dramatically throughout much of the '90s with the proportion of blacks with AIDS surpassing that of whites by mid-decade. By the end of the decade, African Americans and Hispanics made up more than half—56 percent—of the total number of AIDS cases reported in the U.S. In 2000 alone, African Americans represented almost half (47 percent) of all reported AIDS cases even though they made up just 12 percent of the population.

African Americans' growing concerns were reflected in a 1998 survey conducted by the Kaiser Family Foundation. Their report, based on telephone interviews with 811 African-American adults, found that a majority, 52 percent, considered AIDS the most urgent health problem facing the nation. Forty-nine percent of the respondents indicated that they personally knew someone with HIV/AIDS or who has died from the disease. A majority, 58 percent, also indicated that they believed the situation was a more urgent health problem than it was a few years ago.

Their responses lent qualitative weight to the CDC data on black infection rates and provided a clear indication that the African-American community had finally awakened to the growing devastation wrought by AIDS.

The increased impact of the epidemic in black and brown communities would prove a challenge for traditional community-based AIDS organizations unfamiliar with the unique needs of their newer clientele.

AIDS and Community Mobilization

As the disease spread and more people gained first hand experience with AIDS, segments of the African-American community began to organize in an effort to heighten awareness about the threat presented by the epidemic. By the 1990s, a small but growing cadre of activists, minority community-based organizations, and AIDS bureaucrats emerged and began to agitate for additional resources for AIDS prevention, treatment and research geared toward halting the spread of the disease in African-American communities.

In Boundaries of Blackness, Cathy Cohen identifies two stages of AIDS activism.[3] In the first stage, she documents how black gays and lesbians were the first to organize around AIDS in the mid-80s. Their early involvement was in tandem with the response of the larger gay community and demonstrated their quick realization of the threat that AIDS posed. Their activism resulted in some of the earliest minority community based AIDS organizations such as the Minority Task Force on AIDS in New York, the Black Coalition on AIDS in San Francisco, the Minority AIDS Project in Los Angeles and Blacks Educating Blacks About Sexual Health Issues in Philadelphia (Cohen 1999).

It is important to note that Minister Louis Farrakhan and the Nation of Islam were also prominent on this issue in the early years. Under the direction of Dr. Alim Abdul Mohammad, the Nation of Islam spoke out about the inadequacy of treatment options for poor people of color. They established the Abundant Life Clinic in Washington, DC in 1986 in an effort to provide alternative community-based treatment options for African Americans.

Essay 7

This early activism was followed by limited engagement on the part of black leaders and traditional institutions within the African-American community in the second stage of the black community's response. From 1987 to the early '90s, this phase was characterized by more involvement from leaders and organizations that clearly saw the impact of the disease in their communities. Their involvement, however, was tempered by limited resources and, for some, old beliefs about the transmission of AIDS and the types of people who contract the disease. During the 1990 debate surrounding the creation of the Ryan White Care Act, the National Urban League applied pressure on Congress to protect the 15 percent set-aside for services to infants, children, women and families with HIV. The Urban League was also an early recipient of CDC funds to conduct HIV prevention and education activities in African-American communities. This stage also saw the expansion of national minority AIDS organizations like the Black Leadership Commission on AIDS, People of Color in Crisis, Housing Works, and the National Minority AIDS Council. These community-based organizations (CBO's) specialized in providing HIV/AIDS treatment, education and prevention services in communities of color.

The growth of these indigenous AIDS service organizations occurred alongside the development of federal legislation requiring culturally sensitive local programs and community representatives from diverse populations to serve on the local boards set up by the Ryan White CARE Act. The legislative objective was to create a policy and political environment more inclusive of minority populations who were increasingly affected by AIDS. Although more money became available to establish education and outreach programs in communities of color, an unfortunate side effect was that the minority AIDS organizations found themselves competing with the longer established organizations rooted in the gay community.

Central to the problems faced by minority community-based organizations in cities across the country was a lack of access to funds that would enhance their ability to provide critical services. In many cases the story was the same: longer established, resource rich AIDS organizations based in the white gay community continued to win grants and obtain other vital resources, to the detriment of growing needs within minority communities. Traditional CBO's had become adept at obtaining funds, and their members served in key positions on local AIDS boards that were influential in overseeing the distribution of local resources and delivery services. Newer minority AIDS organizations claimed that they found it difficult to influence processes determining the allocation of AIDS resources in the community.

Much of the discussion of inequitable funding centers on the question of racism in the white gay community. Charges of racism in the gay community are nothing new (Cohen 1999; Shilts 1986). What was different in this case was the charge that the allocation of AIDS funds favored white gay communities despite the fact that African Americans outpaced whites in terms of the number of new AIDS cases diagnosed. Thus, many believed that the cultural bias of existing institutions would be a factor that contributed to skyrocketing infection rates in African-American and Hispanic communities.

It was also obvious that hard-hit black and Latino communities experienced a unique set of circumstances unfamiliar to traditional AIDS service organizations. First, African Americans and Hispanics shared a history of oppression and exclusion that kept them outside of the social and economic mainstream of America. Unlike the high socio-economic status of gay white men, minority populations remained disproportionately represented among lower-income families. Their economic condition also dictated their relationship with the U.S. health care infrastructure. It is telling that in 1999, African Americans, Hispanics and Asian/Pacific Islanders comprised 75 percent of all uninsured individuals in the United States-a disenfranchisement that exacerbated health disparities and created a climate conducive to the spread of disease.

Second, the primary mode of transmission among minorities proved to be different than that of gay white men. While men having sex with men would continue to influence transmission of HIV/AIDS among African Americans, substance abuse would prove to be the primary factor fueling its spread. Specifically, injection drug users and individuals engaging in sex with injection drug users were at risk because of their habit of sharing used needles and other contaminated drug paraphernalia. Again, poverty related issues often accompanied substance abusers and these factors would serve as a barrier for providing culturally competent care at traditional AIDS service organizations.

Frustrated with these dynamics and seeking to increase service capacity in black and brown communities, minority AIDS organizations took their complaints to Capitol Hill where they found a receptive audience in the Congressional Black Caucus.

Leaning on the 'Conscience of the Congress' [4]

As the decade wore on, it became increasingly evident that a third stage, extending from the early to late 1990s, had evolved. This stage was marked by the increased professionalization and expansion of minority community-based AIDS organizations. The strongest of the organizations created in the first and second phases extended their reach among the populations they served, became more polished in their public relations efforts, and, perhaps most significantly, became adept at placing political pressure on government officials at the local, state and federal levels.

Community organizations that were created in earlier stages began to push for legislative remedies addressing the challenges of providing education and care services to the African-American community. The Black Leadership Commission on AIDS, the National Minority AIDS Council, Balm in Gilead, and Gay Men of African Descent were just a few of the organizations that came together to lobby members of Congress. As active participants in the Congressional Black Caucus Health Brain Trust, representatives from these organizations were also involved in working with Congressional Black Caucus members to develop an AIDS plan of action.

The minority organizations and CBC members believed that AIDS dollars should follow the course of the epidemic to reduce the incidence of HIV/AIDS and provide quality services for those already infected. Representatives from the African-American CBOs eventually worked with the CBC to formulate an initiative designed to circumvent their funding difficulties by creating a new funding pool dedicated to capacity building in minority communities. The political response of the gay community in the 1980s demonstrated that government resources were the key to saving lives because they were vital to supporting and promoting AIDS research, treatment and prevention measures.

Thus, by pursuing more resources, community activists, AIDS bureaucrats and politicians in the black community were following a previous mobilization model that directed critical resources to support and validate the lives of people with AIDS and HIV infection.

For years, Representative Louis Stokes of Ohio, serving as chair of the Congressional Black Caucus Health Brain Trust, brought together experts, bureaucrats, and constituents from all over the country to discuss health issues facing the community. From diabetes to glaucoma and health insurance coverage, his Brain Trust provided a forum to bring attention to pressing health matters in need of a legislative remedy. AIDS activists and professionals from many of the organizations discussed previously participated in these Brain Trusts and in 1994, the CBC held it's first hearing on HIV/AIDS in the African-American community. Since that time, the CBC has dedicated a segment of its bi-annual Health Brain Trust to the issue. The networking facilitated by the brain trust helped set the stage for CBC political action on AIDS.

It would not be until 1997 that AIDS was placed on the formal legislative agenda of the CBC. Under the leadership of newly elected Chairwoman Maxine Waters, the CBC issued a document called "The Agenda" that outlined the organization's legislative priorities for the 105th Congress. Encompassing a host of issues from drugs to education, computer literacy and employment, The Agenda listed HIV/AIDS as a legislative priority for the first time in the organization's history. While previous Brain Trusts and a special CBC hearing provided crucial information and attention to the issue, its inclusion on the formal agenda meant that HIV/AIDS was now a legislative priority that the organization could officially pursue as a collective.

The AIDS language in "The Agenda" reflected the no-nonsense style

Essay 7

of the new CBC chair. It acknowledged that many African Americans considered HIV/AIDS to be "taboo" and challenged the perception of AIDS as a "gay disease." The document's frank approach marked a significant departure from the largely conservative response of many in the community and directly challenged the way the disease had been framed by black leaders-particularly among faith-based leaders. The document also underscored the serious nature of the epidemic and assured that "immediate action" would be taken to reduce the spread of the disease through the pursuit of additional resources for education, research, treatment and prevention directed towards communities of color "at risk" for HIV/AIDS.

The CBC began to act on the promises set forth in The Agenda the following spring. On Friday, April 24, 1998, the CBC held its annual spring Health Brain Trust in a half-day forum held in the Rayburn House Office Building on Capitol Hill. In the presence of Rep. Waters and others assembled, Dr. Beny Primm, Executive Director of the Addiction Research and Treatment Corporation, outlined the growing severity of AIDS in the African-American community and urged the CBC to ask the Clinton Administration to declare a "State of Emergency" with the intent of stemming the spread of AIDS in the African-American community. CBC Chairwoman Maxine Waters wasted no time springing into action. One week after the Brain Trust meeting, the chairwoman issued a memorandum to CBC members informing them that an emergency CBC meeting would be held the following week with AIDS activists and professionals from across the country and with representatives from the Department of Health and Human Services in attendance. The memo also announced a press conference following the meeting "to release the findings of our discussion and a resolution to be delivered to the President."

On Monday, May 11, 1998 CBC members met with AIDS activists from cities across the country-San Francisco, Los Angeles, New York, Atlanta-in a jam-packed room in the bowels of the U.S. Capitol. Representatives from the Department of Health and Human Services participated as "silent observers." Led by Waters, the session allowed AIDS activists and representatives from minority AIDS CBO's to share their experiences from the field. Many of the participants spoke out about issues related to the dearth of funding opportunities, the difficulties encountered treating persons with substance abuse problems, the need for more prevention efforts, and the stigma associated with AIDS-particularly the need to address the issue of homophobia in the black community. The activities of May 11th became the springboard for subsequent political action. Merging Primm's blueprint for action with the recommendations resulting from the meeting with grassroots activists, CBC leaders, particularly Reps. Maxine Waters, Donna Christian Christensen, and Louis Stokes, worked with CBO representatives and Clinton Administration officials to create the foundation of what would become known as the CBC AIDS Initiative.

Later that year, the Clinton Administration announced its support for an AIDS state of emergency in minority communities. The Administration framed the situation as a threat to national security and dispatched the National Security Agency (NSA) to look into the matter. The involvement of the NSA was a curious response to a matter that had been traditionally viewed as falling solely within the jurisdiction of the Department of Health and Human Services. The Administration's response demonstrated, however, the severity of the epidemic and the power of the CBC Chair who had established a close working relationship with a receptive White House weakened by political scandals. In addition to declaring a state of emergency, framing the crisis as a threat to national security served to provide the administration with a justification for dedicating additional federal resources toward the CBC AIDS Initiative.

Ironically, the success of the initiative was ultimately furthered by the actions of House Speaker Newt Gingrich (R-GA). This highly ideological and controversial leader of the Republican majority and author of its Contract With America was at the helm of a rocky House budget process during the 105th Congress. After stalling on spending measures for much of the year for political purposes, Gingrich was forced to negotiate with Administration officials to complete an omnibus spending bill containing all of the spending measures for the next fiscal year.

Essay 7

Completed behind closed doors with only a few players from the White House and Congress, the Omnibus Appropriations Bill of 1998 stood 16 inches tall and contained over 4,000 pages. In the chaotic atmosphere surrounding its completion, Clinton negotiators were able to insert an authorization for $165.7 million in new AIDS dollars to be dedicated to the CBC AIDS initiative in fiscal year 1999.[5]

The CBC AIDS initiative broke new ground for minority communities in their fight against AIDS. It directed critical resources toward minority populations severely impacted by the epidemic. It also ensured that funds would go toward minority AIDS CBO's who had been previously left out of the funding process, by stipulating that organizations eligible for the funds had to have a governing board comprised of a majority of its members representative of racial and ethnic minority groups. This controversial measure had the effect of excluding traditional AIDS service organizations based in the white gay community.

The substance of the initiative was a conglomeration of new and expanded grants and programs spanning the various HHS agencies including the National Institutes of Health, the Substance Abuse and Mental Health Agency, the Centers for Disease Control, the Office of Minority Health, the Health Services and Resources Administration, and the Agency for Health Care Policy and Research. These "targeted investments" sought to provide more technical assistance and infrastructure support for minority community-based organizations, better access to prevention and care for communities of color, and stronger linkages between government resources and local systems of care. Examples of new or expanded programs targeting minorities included research on prevention interventions for gay men of color, support for faith-based initiatives that focused on integrated HIV and substance abuse prevention, grants for increasing access to bilingual HIV/AIDS and prevention services, new pilot programs in prisons to promote effective treatment and prevention methods, and special grants to directly fund programs in minority community-based organizations.

Working with grassroots activists and organizations, the CBC directly confronted issues of stigma and access in its effort to prevent the spread of the epidemic in the African-American community. The end result was a community initiated policy effort that utilized input from individuals and organizations close to the epidemic to shape the final product. By working with informed activists, the CBC pursued policy goals that represented a realistic response to the challenges of AIDS in the black community. Inclusive of populations traditionally referred to as deviant, the CBC initiative spoke to AIDS issues involving gays, women, prisoners, and substance abusers and demonstrated that the African-American political leaders were indeed capable of prioritizing the needs of all within the community.

Continued Challenges in the Third Decade

Among states with HIV reporting, the CDC has shown a continued rise in HIV infection rates among African Americans. Cognizant of this threat, the CBC has remained attentive to the need to protect and expand the CBC AIDS Initiative. Under the leadership of Rep. Donna Christian Christiansen (D-VI), the CBC Health Brain Trust continues to work with grassroots activists and representatives of community-based organizations to identify continuing challenges of access, treatment, research and prevention in an effort to formulate and implement a legislative response. With the development of advanced drugs that prolong life, many in the public have been lulled into believing that the problem of HIV/AIDS has been largely addressed. Unfortunately, glaring holes remain in terms of access to medical treatment, housing, and prevention services.

The Housing Opportunities for Persons With AIDS program (HOPWA), administered by the U.S. Department of Housing and Urban Development (HUD), is intended to provide temporary and permanent housing assistance to people living with AIDS (PLWA) whose illness places them at risk for homelessness due to the loss of income accompanying the inability to work. Unfortunately, while the ideal of the HOPWA program is laudable, its scope of services falls far short of the need. Only 49,000 people living with HIV/AIDS were served by HOPWA in 1999.[6] This is a small fraction of the 800,000 to 900,000 estimated persons living with HIV and the 300,000 estimated persons living with AIDS

Essay 7

in the U.S. Out of the total number assisted in 1999, 50 percent were white, 44 percent were African American, 12 percent were of Hispanic origin, and 6 percent were American Indian/Alaskan native. The limited scope of HOPWA means that housing slots are in limited supply and that many are left on waiting lists or shut out entirely. The program's limitations complicates the lives of those it's supposed to help, many of whom face rising housing costs and limited affordable housing options in the areas where they live. Further, HUD does not have an adequate tracking mechanism to determine what happens to those who do receive temporary payment assistance after their 27 weeks of assistance has expired.[7] This limited and haphazard approach to providing housing assistance increases the chances that those who the program is supposed to help, particularly people of color, will fall through the cracks.

Because of their exclusion from private health insurance and increased likelihood of living in poverty, African Americans with AIDS are more likely to rely on the Medicaid program for health care assistance. Indeed, Medicaid serves about 55 percent of all people living with AIDS and up to 90 percent of all children with AIDS in the U.S.[8] Yet, the assistance Medicaid provides is deeply problematic because it does not provide funding that would enable recipients to gain access to the lifesaving treatment and drugs that prevent full-blown AIDS until an individual can show financial need and prove that he or she has already developed full-blown AIDS.

The problem with this backward approach is illustrated by a 1995 study in the New England Journal of Medicine.[9] The study found that an HIV-infected individual's likelihood of progressing to full-blown status and dying from AIDS is not related to demographic factors like race, income, or gender but is instead a function of age, whether they had a low CD4 cell count (CD4 or t-cell counts measure the weakness of the immune system. A count below 200 means that an individual has developed full-blown AIDS) and were showing symptoms upon enrollment in the study. The study concluded that higher AIDS death rates among African Americans and women could more credibly be attributed to inadequate medical care than to biological differences among groups.

In essence this study illustrates that when African Americans are finally eligible for Medicaid, they have little chance of surviving the disease for long. In essence, while providing services only when a person living with AIDS is near death may prove a cost-saving measure for federal and state Medicaid coffers, the institutional biases it represents drive down the survival rates of those African Americans forced to rely on Medicaid services.

Two additional studies illustrate the discriminatory nature of the health care available to people of color. A study published in the Archives of Internal Medicine found that Medicaid patients treated for AIDS-related Pneumocystis Carinii Pneumonia (PCP) were 75 percent more likely to die than those with private insurance.[10] In addition, Medicaid patients, who are more likely to be African American and injection drug users, were dramatically less likely to receive the proper treatment for PCP or even to have their complication diagnosed. Those Medicaid patients who did receive proper treatment, received it later in their hospital stay than those PLWA who were privately insured. Findings from this study, have been corroborated by a more recent study, conducted by the Institute of Medicine, which found that African Americans had higher death rates due to pervasive discrimination that made them less likely to receive appropriate AIDS treatments.[11]

The AIDS Drug Assistance Program is another public program designed to help PLWA purchase expensive drug treatments that are the key to disease management and prolonging life. In 1999, 40 percent of individuals receiving assistance from this program were white, 31 percent were black and 24 percent were of Hispanic origin. ADAP is a critical program but access to its services varies from state to state. Because of the high costs of AIDS drugs, many states cap enrollment in the program creating waiting lists for drug assistance. There is also significant differences in formulary coverage with six states cap or restrict access to lifesaving protease inhibitors and antiretroviral therapies.[12]

In addition to the services provided by the Ryan White CARE Act, HOPWA, Medicaid, and ADAP comprise the components of America's system of care for PLWA. Evidence from a variety of sources show that, for minorities with HIV and AIDS, this system is a substandard "danger net" that denies them access to early treatment and care and provides them with a poor quality of care once they do receive assistance. The disparate outcomes are indicative of larger systemic problems in the U.S. health care system that grossly deny a majority of racial and ethnic minorities access and it illustrates the disconnect between the unique circumstances of minorities with HIV/AIDS and the culturally biased policies that shape the HIV/AIDS infrastructure.

Since a diagnosis of HIV means a certain early death for African Americans as compared to diagnosed whites, the only way to stem higher mortality rates under the current system is by preventing HIV infection in the first place. Prevention efforts, however, have been hampered by a ban on federal funding for needle exchange programs, by limited resources made available for substance abuse treatment, and by the absence of a coordinated and comprehensive national prevention program. Absent universal health coverage, the U.S. should at least establish a national system of care for people diagnosed with HIV/AIDS that standardizes treatment options and enables all persons living with HIV and AIDS to access care early, thereby increasing their chances for survival.

Obstacles to prevention are also presented by factors internal to the African-American community.

Despite advances in understanding about HIV transmission, many African Americans continue to engage in risky behaviors and many black leaders—particularly faith based and traditional leaders—maintain biased attitudes about the epidemic and the people affected by it.[13] It is important to note that resistance to behavioral changes and negative attitudes toward the disease are also widespread among other racial and ethnic groups in the U.S. and abroad. The continued prevalence of these factors, however, will hamper efforts to address the AIDS epidemic in a constructive fashion. While transformative leaders in the African-American community have done much to erase the stigma of AIDS, [14] increased involvement of pastors and other traditional leaders are still needed. Indeed, it will take nothing less than mass mobilization including widespread dissemination of prevention information and individual empowerment to attain the level of awareness that is needed to effectively combat the spread of AIDS.

Conclusion

Just as the historic struggle for equal access and equal opportunities for minorities in the U.S. has been influenced by the early dominance of white men of means, so has the modern fight for equal opportunity in AIDS treatment, service, and prevention. Early advocates for minority communities hard hit by the epidemic confronted the inadequacy of policy models designed to assist white gay men of means. These models would prove to be inappropriate for helping communities of color curb the spread of AIDS. Combined with a host of complicating factors like poverty, substance abuse problems, and exclusion from social insurance programs, African-American and Hispanic communities have been placed at a distinct disadvantage in their efforts to ward off the spread of AIDS.

Despite these challenges, a nascent AIDS lobby indigenous to the African-American community organized in the 1990s to combat the challenges presented by the epidemic. Their mobilization and activism served as a catalyst for engaging political leaders on Capitol Hill and their expertise on the issues faced by African Americans with AIDS formed the basis for the CBC AIDS Initiative.

Ironically, the political maturity of minority AIDS community-based organizations comes at a time when mainstream media, political leaders, business leaders, and other opinion leaders have become increasingly focused on the international AIDS crisis. With an estimated 40 million people infected with the HIV worldwide, the challenges presented by AIDS abroad are enormous.[15] The egregious infection rates in African countries illustrate a global disenfranchisement of poor people of color. In order to prevent mass annihilation of Africans throughout the Diaspora, it is probable that the next phase of political activity will focus on developing a global agenda that links the issues faced by black and brown people in the U.S. with those faced by black and brown people in the international arena.

Essay 7

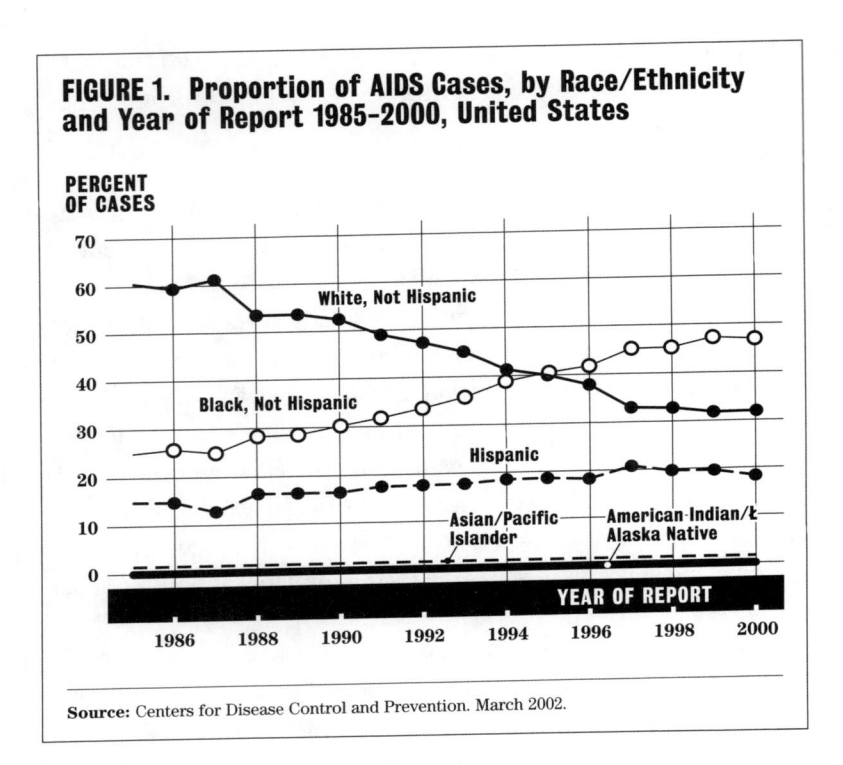

FIGURE 1. Proportion of AIDS Cases, by Race/Ethnicity and Year of Report 1985–2000, United States

Source: Centers for Disease Control and Prevention. March 2002.

TABLE 1. AIDS Cases in Adults and Adolescents by Exposure Category and Race/Ethnicity, Reported through 2000, United States

EXPOSURE TOTAL	WHITE NOT HISPANIC		BLACK NOT HISPANIC		HISPANIC	
	NUMBER	%	NUMBER	%	NUMBER	%
Men Who Have Sex with Men (MSM)	223,470	68%	78,651	27%	48,287	35%
Injection Drug Use (IDU)	39,764	12%	102,492	36%	50,196	36%
MSM and IDU	24,958	8%	15,848	6%	7,673	5%
Heterosexual Contact	16,866	5%	45,601	16%	18,683	13%
Other/Not Identified*	24,551	7%	44,699	16%	14,823	11%
TOTAL	329,609		287,291		139,662	

Source: Centers for Disease Control and Prevention, March 2002. *Includes patients with hemophilia or transfusion-related exposures and those whose medical record review is pending; patients who died, were lost to follow-up, or declined interview; and those with other or undetermined modes of exposure.

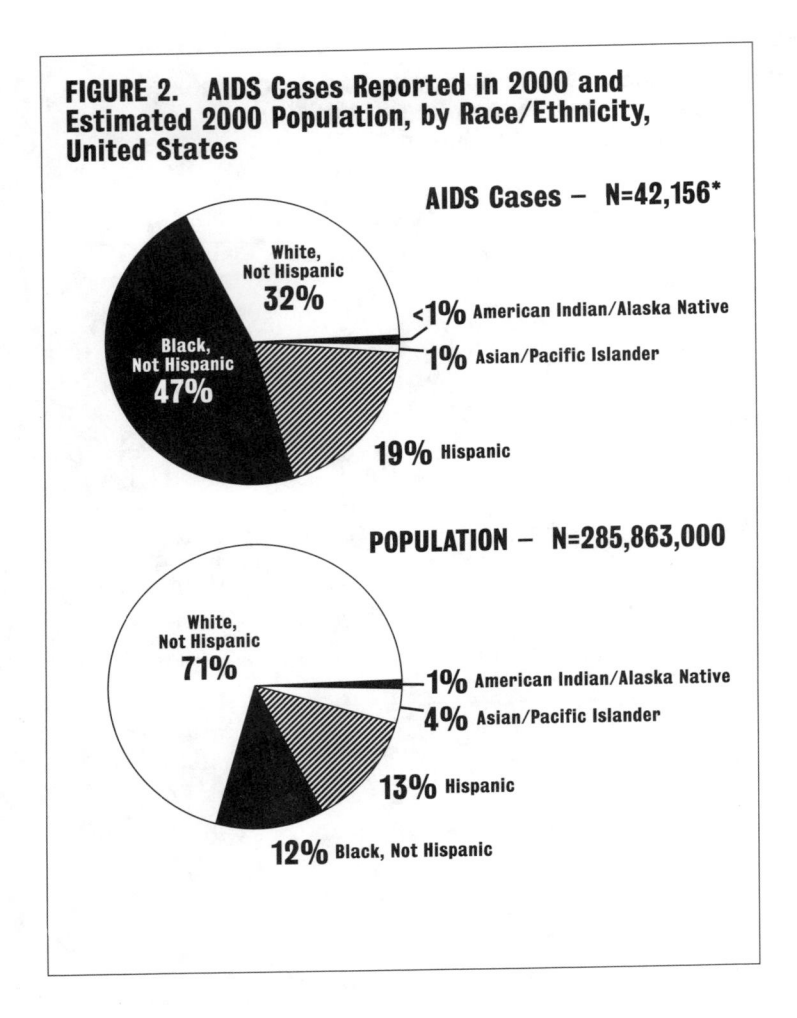

FIGURE 2. AIDS Cases Reported in 2000 and Estimated 2000 Population, by Race/Ethnicity, United States

AIDS Cases – N=42,156*

- White, Not Hispanic 32%
- <1% American Indian/Alaska Native
- 1% Asian/Pacific Islander
- 19% Hispanic
- Black, Not Hispanic 47%

POPULATION – N=285,863,000

- White, Not Hispanic 71%
- 1% American Indian/Alaska Native
- 4% Asian/Pacific Islander
- 13% Hispanic
- 12% Black, Not Hispanic

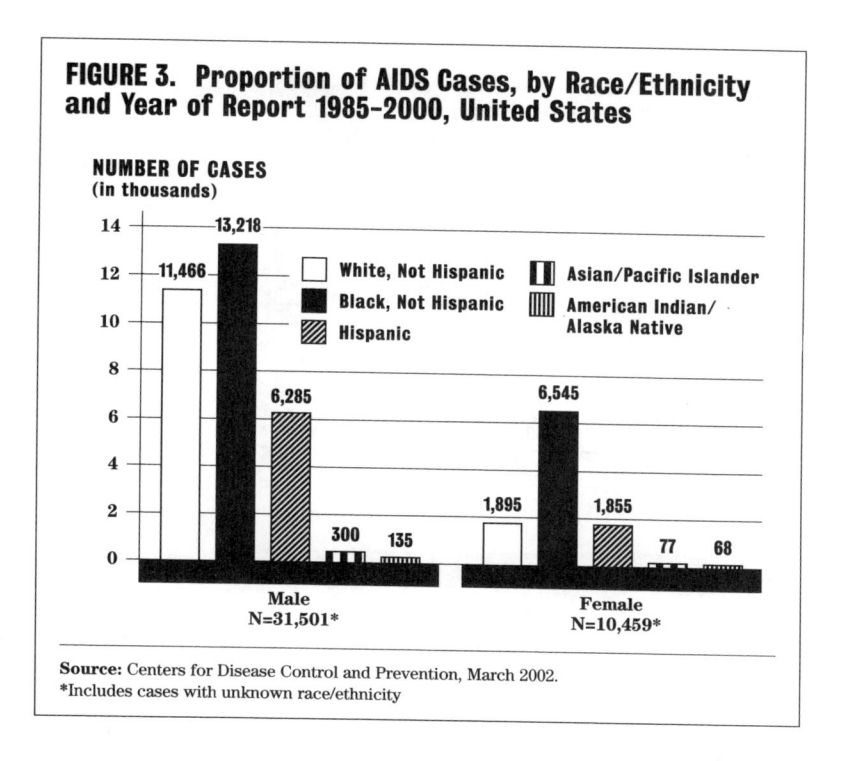

FIGURE 3. Proportion of AIDS Cases, by Race/Ethnicity and Year of Report 1985-2000, United States

NUMBER OF CASES (in thousands)

Male N=31,501*
- White, Not Hispanic: 11,466
- Black, Not Hispanic: 13,218
- Hispanic: 6,285
- Asian/Pacific Islander: 300
- American Indian/Alaska Native: 135

Female N=10,459*
- White, Not Hispanic: 1,895
- Black, Not Hispanic: 6,545
- Hispanic: 1,855
- Asian/Pacific Islander: 77
- American Indian/Alaska Native: 68

Source: Centers for Disease Control and Prevention, March 2002.
*Includes cases with unknown race/ethnicity

TABLE 2. Percent Who View AIDS as the Most Urgent Health Problem Facing the Nation by Race/Ethnicity[9,10,11,12]

Percent who view AIDS as the most urgent health problem

	1995	1997	2000
African American	56%	52%	41%
White	42%	35%	23%
Latino	51%	50%	40%
Total	44%	38%	26%

	RANKING		
	1995	1997	2000
African American	1st	1st	1st*
White	1st	2nd*	2nd
Latino	1st	1st	1st*
Total	1st	1st*	2nd

Source: Kaiser Family Foundation, 2001.
*Responses not statistically different from cancer.

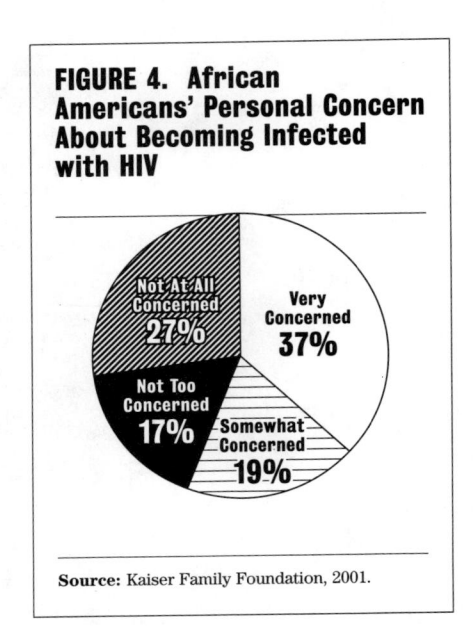

FIGURE 4. African Americans' Personal Concern About Becoming Infected with HIV

- Very Concerned: 37%
- Somewhat Concerned: 19%
- Not Too Concerned: 17%
- Not At All Concerned: 27%

Source: Kaiser Family Foundation, 2001.

FIGURE 5. Percent of African Americans Who...

Legend: 2000, 1997±, 1995

- ...say AIDS is a more urgent problem for local community**: 41% (2000), 44% (1997±)
- ...know someone living with HIV/AIDS or who has died of AIDS: 57% (2000), 49% (1997±), 56% (1995)
- ...believe AIDS is a serious* problem for people they know: 52% (2000), 72% (1997±), 73% (1995)

Source: Kaiser Family Foundation, 2001. *Combines "very" and "somewhat" response.
**No data for 1995

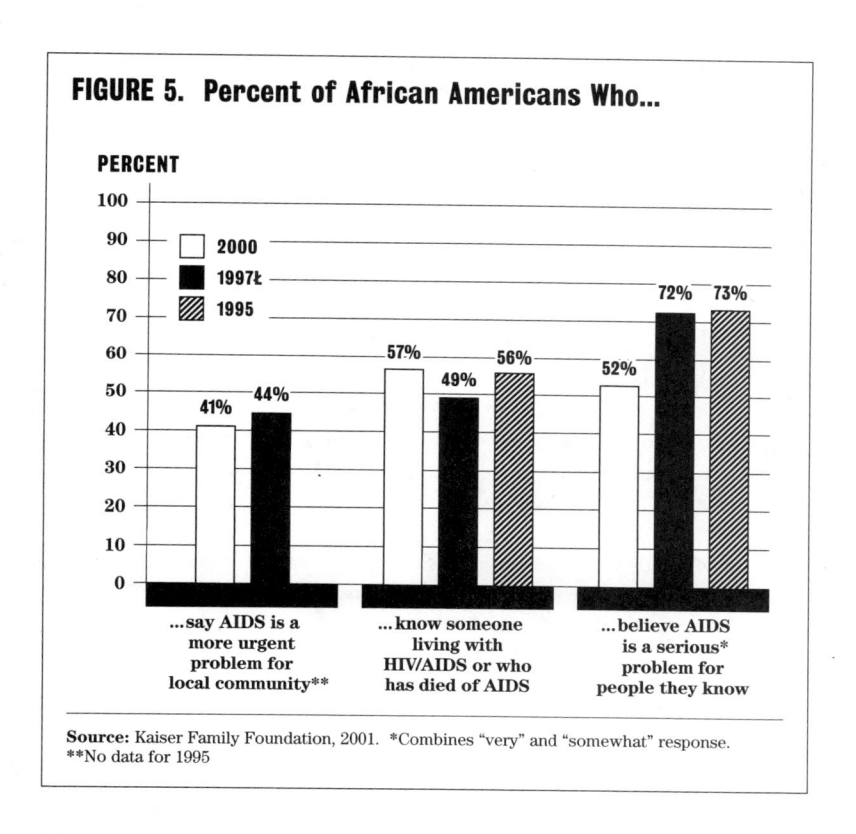

Notes

[1] Cathy Cohen, 1999. *Boundaries of Blackness*.

[2] Centers for Disease Control. "HIV/AIDS Among African Americans," March 15, 2002.

[3] Cohen, Cathy. 1999. *The Boundaries of Blackness: AIDS and the Breakdown of Black Politics.* Chicago: The University of Chicago Press.

[4] Much of the information in this section is synthesized from primary data that the author collected first-hand while studying the CBC as a Congressional Black Caucus Fellow in the 105th Congress. The results of her study are documented in: Maya Rockeymoore. *The African American Political Response to HIV and AIDS: A Study of the Congressional Black Caucus in the 105th Congress.* Dissertation, Purdue University, 2000.

Essay 7

⁵ While subject to the vagaries of changing political times, this appropriation would increase in subsequent years to its current level of $381 million in FY 2002.

⁶ Dave Pollack, et al. *National Evaluation of HOPWA Program*. Washington, DC: The Office of Policy Development and Research, Department of Housing and Urban Development, 2000.

⁷ Ibid.

⁸ Centers for Medicaid and Medicare Services. Medicaid and AIDS and HIV Infection, Jan. 2002.

⁹ "Race, sex, drug use, and progression of human immunodeficiency virus disease," by Dr. Chaisson, Jeanne C. Keruly, B.S.N., and Richard D. Moore, M.D., M.Sc., in the September 21, 1995 *New England Journal of Medicine* 333(12), pp. 751-756.

¹⁰ "Racial differences in care among hospitalized patients with Pneumocystis carinii pneumonia in Chicago, New York, Los Angeles, Miami, and Raleigh-Durham," by Drs. Bennett and Cohn, Ronnie D. Horner, Ph.D., and others, in the August 7/21, 1995 issue of the *Archives of Internal Medicine* 155, pp. 1586-1592.

¹¹ Brian D. Smedley, Adrienne Y. Stith, and Alan R. Nelson, Eds. *Unequal Treatment: Confronting Racial and Ethnic Disparities in Health Care*. National Academy of Sciences Institute of Medicine, 2002.

¹² Arnold Doyle and Richard Jefferys, *National ADAP Monitoring Project Annual Report*, March 2000.

¹³ Cohen, 1999.

¹⁴ Rockeymoore, 2000.

¹⁵ Joint United Nations Programme on HIV/AIDS, "AIDS Epidemic Update." December 2001.

African Americans and American Politics 2002: The Maturation Phase

By Martin L. Kilson

There is no better point of departure for portraying the maturation phase of the political status of African Americans in the overall American political process than examining this year's 30th Annual Report on Black Elected Officials by the Washington-based think tank, the Joint Center for Political and Economic Studies, and written by its senior political analyst, Dr. David Bositis. Under the deft leadership of Eddie Williams, the Joint Center has provided the indispensable service of tracking both the growth and overall comparative systemic attributes of African Americans holding the several kinds of political office in the United States since 1970. All Americans genuinely interested in the growth of equality and diversity in political officeholding in our American democracy are greatly in its debt for having skillfully performed this function for a generation and a half.

An Overview of Black Elected Officials

As the militant phase of the Civil Rights Movement began to gain a favorable public policy and legislative response from the United States federal government by, say, 1964, there were around 350 black elected officials. When those halcyon days ended and the Joint Center conducted its first census of black elected officials (BEOs) in 1970, that number had reached 1,469. The steady shift in the politics of African-American life between 1970 and today—from full-fledged civil rights activism to a mixed-politics of both civil rights activism and sophisticated black electoral mobilization—has produced the unprecedented number of 9,040 BEOs the Joint Center found for the year 2000. This figure amounts to between two percent and three percent of all United States elected officials. [See Table I for an aggregate portrait of BEOs in the United States from 1970 to 2000]

Viewed in regional terms, some 869 BEOs, or 9.7 percent of the total represent Northeast states; 1,636, or 18.2 percent, represent Midwest states; and 326, or 3.6 percent represent Western states. Not surprisingly, the South recorded the largest 30-year growth in BEOs, with 6,170, or 68.5 percent of the total. The reasons for this are plain enough. First, about 55 percent of all African Americans live in the South. Secondly, local, state, city, and federal officeholding jurisdictions include large concentrations of African Americans. And thirdly, the necessity of ethnic-bloc political and electoral mobilization is still a reality of African-American life today—just as Irish-American, Jewish-American, Polish-American, Italian-American, Latino-American, Chinese-American, WASP-American, etc., ethnic-bloc political and electoral mobilization are still realities in overall American life.

Keep in mind that ever since the rise of an ethnically pluralistic American political culture in the post-Civil War era, when Irish-Catholic Americans became a major force in the urban industrial working class-and were joined from the 1890s onward by Italian-Americans, Polish-Americans, Jewish-Americans, Chinese-Americans, Japanese-Americans, etc.—the American political culture has allowed democratic space for ethnic-bloc political and electoral mobilization. The WASP host cultural group in our American democracy first designed and utilized electoral methods based on ethnic patterns. WASPs did this initially in the pre-Civil War era with political exclusion purposes in mind; they manipulated voting boundaries or districts to keep down the votes of competing religious groups among the WASP sector. Then, from the post-Civil War era onward, competing WASP politicians also manipulated electoral districts for political inclusion purposes, recruiting Irish Catholic voters who might favor Republican Party candidates in industrial cities or states over Democratic Party candidates. This WASP-initiated manipulation of electoral mobilization through the design and redesign of voting districts became known as "gerrymandering," after Elbridge Gerry, the 18th-century WASP highborn Massachusetts merchant who had an extraordinary but deeply checkered career in the political life of the young nation. As governor of Massachusetts in 1811 (Gerry would become James Madison's vice president in 1813, before dying in 1814), it was his party's re-drawing of voting districts—one of which had the shape of a salamander—to ensure their continued power that his opponents seized upon to produce the eternal pun.

From the 1890s on, as Irish-Americans learned to employ ethnic-bloc activism in the electoral process, such ethnic-bloc patterns in the electoral process became a key element in expanding the political incorporation of weak and marginal white groups. It was through such democratic ethnic-bloc electoral space that the first Irish-American city councilmen, mayors, state assemblymen, congressmen, and governors gained office in great states and cities like New York and New York City, Illinois and Chicago, etc. The names of James Michael Curley (an early Irish Mayor in Boston and also Governor in Massachusetts), Timothy Sullivan (an early Irish Mayor in New York City), Alfred Smith (first Irish governor of New York and in 1928 the first Irish candidate for president of the United States), and even John Fitzgerald Kennedy (the first victorious Irish candidate for president in 1960) reflect the long-standing pragmatic weaving of ethnic-bloc modalities into the electoral fabric of American political culture.

Thus, in our contemporary American society this ethnic-bloc pattern of electoral mobilization is legitimately applicable to African Americans, Latino Americans, Asian Americans, etc.

Curiously enough, however, beginning in the conservative Reagan and Bush Republican Administrations in the 1980s onward, conservative analysts and pundits have pejoratively labeled this very American mode of political organizing as "identity politics" and declared that it violates the very traditions of American social and political conduct. In fact, just the opposite is true. The historical record on the role of ethnic-bloc modalities among WASPs and white ethnic groups alike makes it unmistakably clear that their use has qualitatively advanced the nature of democratic space in American political culture. So, too, now for African Americans: Their use of ethnic-bloc patterns since the late 1960s has made possible a steady-state growth of BEOs to the 9,000-officeholder level and beyond. I have no doubt that the invention of the "identity politics" rhetorical maneuver among conservative analysts and pundits—put forth often in such organs as *The New Republic*, *The National Review*, *Commentary*, and so on, and by such conservative black analysts as Thomas Sowell, Shelby Steele, K. A. Appiah, Randall Kennedy, and John McWhorter—emerged as a racist response to this hard-wrought African-American political achievement.

Of course, even as black voters have voted heavily for BEOs, they have also voted for white candidates who have supported blacks' civil rights agenda. Recently, black voters have elected two white mayors in two large black-majority cities—Gary and Baltimore. In a similar vein among whites, the past decade has seen a growth in electoral liberalism among white Americans in regard to their voting for African-American candidates. As I will discuss below, this has been the case especially for BEOs representing statewide offices, and even some county and city offices. On the other hand, since the 1960s, only a few African-American Congressional officeholders have gained office through majority support from white voters—namely, Senator Edward Brooke (Republican, 1967-1979) in Massachusetts, Senator Carol Moseley-Braun (Democrat-1993-1996) in Illinois, and Congressman J. C. Watts (Republican, first elected in 1994) in Oklahoma. Currently, there are 39 African-American members of Congress (compared to 10 in 1970), all in the House of Representatives; Watts is the only Republican. Nevertheless, it is reasonable to expect that a growing number of African-American candidates will contest statewide and House of Representatives offices in white-majority districts. Indeed, it seems clear now that even the White House is within reach of a uniquely appealing African-American political personality, such as General Colin Powell, America's first African-American Secretary of State.

Looking at it in broad strokes, then, since 1970 the African-American political class has acquired and put to use some important new political status attributes that have led to a distinctive maturation of its position at city, state and federal levels. Because I will end this essay focusing on municipal politics, I'll begin this part of the discussion considering black political advancement at the state level.

Attributes of Black State Officials

In the early 1960s, there were no more than 40 black state officials (BSOs) across the country. Now, this category of African-American political officeholders totals 606 and includes 571 state legislators and 35 statewide administrators. Further, it should be noted that nearly a third of the 35 statewide administrator posts held by African Americans are major decision-making offices. They are: Colorado: Lieutenant Governor (Joe Rogers); Connecticut: State Treasurer (Denise L. Nappier); Georgia: Attorney General (Thurber E. Baker); Georgia: Public Service Commissioner (David L. Burgess); Georgia: Chief Justice-State Supreme Court (Robert Benham); New York: State Comptroller (H. Carl McCall); North Carolina: State Auditor (Ralph Campbell); Oregon: State Treasurer (Jim Hill); Tennessee: Chief Justice-State Supreme Court (Adolpho A. Birch); and Texas: Chair-State Railroad Commission (Michael L. Williams).

Again, the African-American electorate in the South has generated the largest number of black state legislators, Mississippi has 45; Georgia, 43; Alabama, 35; South Carolina, 33; Louisiana, 31; North Carolina, 24; Florida, 20; Tennessee and Texas, 16 each; Arkansas and Virginia, 15 each; and Kentucky and West Virginia, 4 each. The rising status of African-American women in black leadership councils is seen in the fact that the percentage of black women state legislators now stands at 31.7 percent of black state representatives and 33.8 percent of black state legislators. Moreover, as Bositis observes in the document, "Of the states with a significant number of black state legislators, black women constitute the largest proportions of state representatives in Tennessee (53.8 percent), Illinois (46.7 percent), Texas (42.9 percent), Georgia (40.6 percent), and Florida (40 percent). Georgia (54.5 percent), Ohio (50 percent), and Virginia (50 percent) have the largest pro-

Essay 8

portions of black women among state senators.¹ Finally, it's important to take note of the expanding appetite among the African-American political class for contesting top decision-making statewide offices, and especially the pinnacle state office of governor. Currently, six African-American politicians, all Democrats, have come forth as serious gubernatorial candidates: Roland Burris, in Illinois; Gary George, in Wisconsin; Jim Hill, in Oregon; Daryl Jones, in Florida; H. Carl McCall, in New York; and Alma Wheeler Smith, in Michigan.²

Changing Attributes of Black Mayoralties

The black political class' qualitative advances in municipal politics have paralleled their advances at the state-level. When the Joint Center launched its annual census in 1970, there were barely a dozen black mayors holding office in cities whose population was 100,000 or more. The most important of these cities then were Cleveland (Mayor Carl Stokes), Gary (Mayor Richard Hatcher), Newark, NJ (Mayor Kenneth Gibson), and New Orleans (Mayor Ernest Morial). More than with the election of blacks to state offices or to the U.S. Congress, the election of the first cadre of black mayors in the late 1960s and early 1970s epitomized the post-Civil Rights Movement electoral ethnic-bloc mobilization of Black Americans. The election of black mayors among the early cadre from 1967 through the 1970s—which later included such mayors as Maynard Jackson and Andrew Young in Atlanta, Coleman Young in Detroit, Wilson Goode in Philadelphia, and Marion Barry in Washington D.C.—produced political leaders who became household names among millions of African Americans in a way statewide officials among the African-American political class never have.

This was so mainly because the smashing of white racist barriers to viable black electoral participation and governance parity in American society required fashioning at the level of urban politics a special activist chemistry that was publicly "pro-black," on the one hand, and sharply anti-white-supremacist, on the other. After all, it was in American cities where a fierce alliance of several entrenched negative forces of American political culture dominated the urban civic life from the mid-19th century well into the mid-1960s. That fierce and roguish political alliance involved a culture of governmental corruption, electoral chicanery, and the Northern urban variant of the overall American white-supremacist patterns of behavior: It fomented, among other things, massive and violent job discrimination, massive and violent housing-market discrimination, massive discrimination in access by blacks to public education resources, racist criminal justice practices, and an all but official tolerance of some significant level of anti-black (and Latino) police brutality. Keep in mind especially that as the weak and poor white-ethnic working classes mounted their own electoral mobilization challenge of the WASP power class' hold over American politics in general, they started that process in the cities and with the structures of municipal government.

From these structures, the white-ethnic working classes and their middle-class politicians forged a sharply politicized access to county offices, state legislatures, governors' offices, state bureaucracies, federal offices in Congress and the powerful federal bureaucracies, and the presidency itself. In a very real sense, then, city-level structures are the foundation of the American political system. And just as white-ethnic groups learned this and conquered city-level structures from the post-Civil War era through the first half of the 20th century, so, too, the African-American working class and its middle-class leadership had to learn this.

Thus, in the past 30-odd years African Americans have fashioned-against the grain of the white majority's anti-black bigotry—their own special use of democratic space to achieve governance parity in running city-level structures. The numbers compiled by the Joint Center in Table 1 tell the story in dramatic fashion: In 1970 there were 623 municipal officeholders across the country. Today there are 4,465—nearly half the total of all African-American officeholders. Although this aspect of black Americans' struggle for equality is still in progress, the quantitative and qualitative status of black Mayoralties today represents a veritable sea-change from the late 1960s. For example, there are today some forty-seven black mayors in cities 50,000 and above. These cities range from the large ones—Houston (1,953,631), Philadelphia

Essay 8

(1,517,550), Dallas (1,188,580), Detroit (951,270), San Francisco (776,733), Columbus, OH (711,470), Denver (554,636), Cleveland (478,403), Minneapolis (382,618) and Arlington, TX (332,969); to medium- and near-medium-sized cities—Newark (273,545), Birmingham (242,820), Rochester (219,773), Richmond (197,790), Paterson, NJ (149,222), Savannah (131,510), Flint, MI (124,943), Portsmouth, VA (100,565), Trenton, NJ (85,403), Wilmington, DE (72,664), Mount Vernon, NY (68,381), Saginaw, MI (61,799), and Monroe, LA (53,107).

Perhaps the most interesting new development on this front has been the growth of black mayors in white-voter majority cities. This important development is shown in Table 2, which is based on cities whose population is less than 40 percent black. These white-voter majority black Mayoralties also range across the population spectrum of cities— from large ones: Houston (24.3 percent black), Dallas (25.9 percent black), San Francisco (7.8 percent black), Denver (11.1 percent black), and Minneapolis (18 percent black); to those of medium size: Jersey City (28.3 percent black), Chesapeake, VA (28.5 percent black), Des Moines (8.1 percent black), and Oceanside, CA (6.3 percent black); to smaller municipalities: Carson, CA (25.4 percent black), Kalamazoo, MI (20.6 percent black), Evanston, IL (22.5 percent black), Hempstead Village, NY (25.7 percent black), and Sarasota, FL (16 percent black).

Changing Attitudes Among Second Generation BEOs

Because their electoral success was a product of the successes and lessons of the Civil Rights Movement, the 1960s "generation" of black elected officials held and acted on broadly uniform attitudes regarding the main public-policy issues of primary concern to African Americans. Between the middle 1960s and the middle 1980s, there was a broad consensus among BEOs on issues relating to school desegregation, criminal justice practices and police practices, abortion, affirmative action, etc. (The same high level of consensus on key issues existed between black elected officials and the black electorate.) During the 1990s and first two years of the 21st century, however, some measure of conflict has surfaced between the 1960s generation of the black political class and second-generation cohort of post-Civil Rights era BEOs. A 1999 poll conducted by the Joint Center was the first to uncover the signs of attitudinal fissures along generational lines within the African-American cadre of black elected officeholders; and this poll also discovered competing perceptions about public schools' performance between the officials and average African-American voters. The findings revealed that the black general public is more inclined to rank public schools as "fair" and "poor" than are black elected officials. As shown in Table 3, 65 percent of those in the 18 to 25 age group ranked public schools as "fair" and "poor' (33 percent rated them fair; 32 percent, poor), compared to 51 percent of the 18 to 40 age group of elected officials (31 percent rated the schools as fair; 20 percent, poor). The elected officials were much stronger in ranking public schools "excellent" and "good" in all age categories—50 percent in the 18 to 40 age group, 61 percent in the 41 to 49 age group. But, among the black general public, only a plurality rate the public schools as "excellent" and "good"—35 percent of the 18 to 25 age cohort viewed them that way, while 44 percent and 41 percent among the 26 to 35 age group and the 36 to 50 age group, respectively, did so. Perusing this data, the Joint Center's David Bositis observed that a "significant part of this difference is attributable to school board members, who seem to hold unusually high opinions of their local public schools, with 71 percent rating them as excellent or good and only 6 percent rating them as poor.[3] In other words, to put it in the most charitable terms, many black school board members around the country lack an evaluative understanding of their own policy roles. Perhaps local chapters of the NAACP and the National Urban League can help these myopic and ideologically self-serving black school board members and other black education personnel become more aware of the terrible record of performance, generally speaking, of public schools—which 95 percent of African-American children attend. The issue of school vouchers highlights a particularly sharp rift in perceptions as between younger and older generation black officeholders. In the Joint Center's 1999 poll, the attitude of older-generation BEOs toward school vouchers contrasted sharply with that of the black general public. Some 60 percent of the latter favor school vouchers while, according to Bositis, "opposition to school vouchers averages more than 70 percent" among BEOs in the middle and older age groups, which constitute the vast majority of the nation's black officeholders. Thus, as shown in Table 4, only 27 percent of BEOs in the 41 to 49 age group favor school vouchers and only 23 percent in the 50-64 age group favor school vouchers. Only in the minority sector of BEOs—in 18 to 40 age group—can a 49-percent plurality of support for school vouchers be found. This situation contrasts sharply with the attitude toward school vouchers among the black general public. Some 71 percent of its 18 to 25 age group, 76 percent in the 26 to 35 age group, 67 percent in the 36 to 50 age group, and a plurality of 49 percent in the 51 to 64 age group support school vouchers.

Reflections on Newark's 2002 Mayoral Campaign

As African Americans enter the second year of the 21st century, there has so far been little serious indication of changes in black electoral behavior stemming from the small shifts in political attitudes among generationally-defined sectors of black officeholders, or between BEOs and the black general public. For example, black Republican Party candidates—and conservative candidates, black or white, in general—have not demonstrated any significant capacity to advance electorally among African-American voters by exploiting the evolving attitude differences among BEOs or between BEOs and the black general public. According to the Joint Center's 2000 data, only seven black Republicans hold office in black-majority districts nationally—a record which, it must be said, indicates a stunning lack of interest by both the white and the black politicos of the GOP in sincerely pressing their case with black voters. Despite more than two decades of rhetoric that Republican conservatism offers African Americans a viable avenue for inclusion, the GOP has yet to mount a substantive real-life effort to address what poll after poll shows African Americans consider major core issues—such as racist practices in housing, job markets, income/wealth patterns, educational opportunities, health patterns, and the criminal justice system. Instead, the Republicans have seemed content to play appointive politics with the black electorate. The 2000 presidential campaign and its aftermath saw the Bush Administration and its allies in the mainstream media temporarily shelve two decades' worth of a hard-line rhetorical advocacy of "color-blindness" in order to vigorously trumpet its high-profile black appointments. Make no mistake: this development is progress of some significance, and not only in comparative terms with the paucity of black appointments in the Reagan and Bush (1) administrations. In fact, these black appointments were an historic acknowledgement from the conservative political establishment that its heretofore sacred whites-only at the top rule is an unacceptable way to conduct politics now even to those it considers its core constituency. In short, the conservatives have been forced by the power of African-American political activity since the 1960s, the emergence of Asian Americans and Latino Americans as political forces in their own right, and by white Americans' move toward greater tolerance to realize that to be considered modern and legitimate in American politics now, one has to have—to use that once-verboten word—diversity at the top of the administrative structure.

Nonetheless, the high-level appointments cannot obscure the GOP's abysmal electoral record. In the 2000 election campaign, there were 24 blacks running for Congress on the GOP ticket—incumbent J.C. Watts, of Oklahoma, and 23 first-time candidates. Of the 24, only Watts won: all the 23 others lost. As Lee A. Daniels put it in the February 2001 issue of *Opportunity Journal*, "What does it say about the Grand Old Party that it could capture the White House, but not get a single new black Republican elected to Congress. ... Imagine the impact if 20 of those 23 black candidates had won office. Or if 15 had. Or 10, or even 5. We'd have been bombarded with declarations that the GOP was now making serious inroads into the Democratic stranglehold on the black vote ..."

Daniels' particular point was that, the individual strengths or weaknesses of the black GOP candidates aside, the fact that all 23 lost bespoke a lack of commitment from the national party itself. And that lack of commitment to include blacks among its ranks of elected officeholders continues:

Essay 8

Note, first, that the Republicans are assiduously courting Latino voters, trying to cut into the 69-percent support the Democrats garnered in 2000. A June 3, 2002 article in *The New York Times* ("Bilingual, So to Speak, but Halting") underscored this point when it recalled that the President last year made the first-ever radio address in Spanish by a U.S. President. "He doesn't try very hard to get the pronunciation the way native speakers speak," the *Times* quoted Otto Santa Ana, a Chicano studies professor at the University of California as saying. "But Latinos were very encouraged by him. Here is the president of the United States speaking Spanish, however haltingly. He's simply legitimizing what is so obvious to us that people cheer him. And they cheer him because he's acknowledging them as Americans." The article declared that Bush will make significant use of his Spanish-speaking skills in 2004, when Latinos are likely to be as much as 10 percent of the electorate, up from their 7 percent in 2000. "So by necessity," said Matthew Dowd, one of the President's pollsters, "Republicans have to win a larger share of them. Speaking Spanish can only help with Latinos who as a group are inclined to vote Democratic."

No such obvious ethnically-targeted effort is being mounted to enlarge the GOP's small slice of the black electorate, however. Recall that all six of the African Americans who've mounted serious challenges for their states' gubernatorial chairs this year are Democratic. In others words, when it comes to electoral politics, the Grand Old Party, America's mainstream conservative party, is still the same old party—it considers black voters invisible men and women.

However, one important exception to the absence of a substantive conservative attempt to corral black votes has now occurred in Newark, New Jersey, during the bid this past spring by the incumbent four-term mayor, Sharpe James, for a final term in office. James was challenged not by an openly conservative black Republican candidate, but rather by what might be called "a covert black Republican candidate"—a conservative black Democratic Newark city councilman, Cory Booker. Booker, 33, had stellar "public" credentials: He was young, good looking, highly articulate and charismatic, with degrees from Stanford, Yale

Law School, and Oxford University via a Rhodes Scholarship. He mounted a major challenge to the 66-year-old James, who during his 16 years in office had transformed the majority black voter base in Newark (whose population is 53 percent black and 30 percent Latino) into a major New Jersey statewide swing vote, as was demonstrated in the Democratic electoral victory in 2000 of U.S. Senator Jon Corzine and in 2001 of New Jersey's current Governor James McGreevey.

What sparked the ostensibly surprising capacity of Booker, a one-term city councilman, to mount a major challenge to a longstanding incumbent was, first, Booker's skill at appealing to a segment of black voters disenchanted over what they viewed as the poor performance record of Newark's public schools. Booker took up the advocacy of school vouchers as his policy response to the schools-performance issue.

There's no question that, although there's nothing genuinely "liberal-reform" about school vouchers, the idea, as the Joint Center's data has shown, understandably, has great appeal to many working-class black voters who've become disenchanted with the general (and specific) poor performance of public schools. Furthermore, during the Newark campaign Booker was adept at fashioning a liberal-reform appeal to both black and white middle-class voters (whites comprise some 15 percent of Newark's population). He lambasted the longstanding role of patronage in Newark politics and the perks available to patronage appointees in order to paint James as the "Old Guard Black Leadership" and himself, by contrast, as leading a "New Guard Black Leadership." His seemingly liberal-reform appeal caught many Newark voters' imaginations, and, as the election approached, polls showed James leading by only 4 to 6 percentage points—which meant that the contest was, statistically speaking, virtually dead even.

The Newark race generated an enormous amount of coverage from the national mainstream media—and the quality of that coverage, both in news stories and in opinion columns raised profound questions. James, who once simultaneously held a state senate seat along with the mayoralty, is widely acknowledged, as Kean University political science professor Merle Treusch told the *New York Times*, as "probably the most powerful African-American political figure in the history of New Jersey." Yet, with few exceptions, the mainstream media devoted little space to discussing the significance of that achievement or to presenting any but the most superficial accounts of Newark's struggle over the past three decades. Instead, the media coverage was so one-sided in Booker's favor as to be nothing short of astonishing. There's no doubt that Booker's candidacy was buoyed by vigorous—one might say, swooning-endorsements from conservative, centrist and liberal columnists in *Newsweek*, *The Wall Street Journal*, *U.S. News and World Report*, and the *Newark Star-Ledger*, among other media outlets publications; and ultimately by editorial endorsements from *The Star-Ledger*, and *The New York Times*. Booker was also endorsed by a host of national luminaries, including New Jersey Senator Bill Bradley and scholar-activist Cornel West; many of them contributed to the nearly $3-million war chest he raised for the campaign—a figure substantially larger than what James raised.

But the endorsements and the out-sized war chest weren't enough on Election Day, May 14th, to counter James' support by the entire state Democratic political establishment, from McGreevy to the entire Newark City Council (excepting Booker, of course) and the mayor's superb voter-mobilization skills. James won with 53 percent of the vote, to Booker's 47 percent. Despite Booker's claim that James did not represent the city's black masses, James won all of the city's black-majority districts, including the one Booker represents, while Booker won the Latino-majority and white-majority districts.

James had said before the election that this would be his last term in office. Booker declared after the final results were in that he fully intended to run for the top post the next time around.

As I said, the Newark contest was important in several respects—but its greatest importance is revealed by the coverage it drew. Indeed, the quality of that coverage, especially the opinion columns, provides a very big clue that, despite the liberal-reform aura projected onto Booker's campaign, what-voters-saw-is-not-necessarily-what-they-would-have-gotten from a Cory Booker mayoralty. In fact, my view is that Booker, while nominally a Democratic councilman, is substantively "a covert conservative Republican candidate." Why do I say this?

First, the initial public evidence of Booker's conservative leanings was revealed by the ultra-conservative columnist, George F. Will, in his March 17, 2000, weekly syndicated column, when Booker had already made clear his plans to challenge James. Will wrote that "Booker's plans for Newark's renaissance are drawn from thinkers at ... the Manhattan Institute think tank, and from the experiences of others such as Stephen Goldsmith, former Republican mayor of Indianapolis, a pioneer of privatization [of public institutions] and faith-based delivery of some government services. ... " Will's reference to Booker's connection to the Manhattan Institute was particularly telling. After all, it is at the Manhattan Institute where longstanding conservative opponents of the mainline black leadership's civil rights agenda—in regard to housing, jobs, education, criminal justice, and an overall pro-active federal role in ending racism's impact in these areas through affirmative action and related policies—hang their hats, or have significant links. That list includes such white conservatives as Abigail Thernstrom, William Bennett, Nathan Glazer, and such black ones as Shelby Steele, Alan Keyes, and John McWhorter.

Will's column also revealed another dimension of the de facto conservative operational dimension of Booker's mayoral candidacy: Namely, that it was a stealth affair in regard to its campaign funding. For, although nominally a Democrat, Booker's funding came mainly from conservative Republican sources—whom Will euphemistically described as "reform-minded supporters [of Booker]." Will noted that by March 2000 Booker had "raised $1.5 million through reform-minded supporters in New York financial circles." This May, as the election drew near, the one-term councilman was reported to have raised a total of $2.8 million for his campaign, exceeding the $2.3 million raised by James—a four-term incumbent! Whence Councilman Booker's resources? That important question was plumbed by a skillful African-American journalist in nearby Jersey City, New Jersey, Glenn Ford. Ford's April 5, 2002 article on his "The Black Commentator" website

Essay 8

traced the strong ties between Booker and, via conservative black Republicans, such Republican-linked rightwing foundations as the Bradley Foundation and the Walton Foundation. At the center of the relationship stood the Black Alliance for Educational Options (BAEO), which declares vouchers are the answer to the lack of quality education available to many black children in public schools. Established in the late 1990s by Dr. Howard Fuller, a conservative black school superintendent in Milwaukee, BAEO organized its own activist mechanism, coalesced with Alan Keyes' political action committee called Black America's Political Action Committee (BAMPAC), and fashioned ties with such conservative white organizations as the Free Congress Foundation. The Bradley Foundation, the Walton Foundation, and other deeply conservative foundations heavily supported these latter groups. In turn, as Ford found, "BAEO has received $1.7 million from [the] Bradley [Foundation] since June of 2001 ... [and the] Walton Foundation came up with $900,000 in seed money."

Thus, as Ford declares, neither the BAEO nor BAMPAC has a "life independent of Bradley [Foundation] and ... the Walton Foundation. ... In a December 2001 report, the liberal People for the American Way asked rhetorically whether the BAEO was a 'Community Voice or Captive of the Right?' Transparency in Media, which keeps track of rightwing foundations, describes the BAEO as 'a project' of the Bradley Foundation." Ford concludes "that Cory Booker's [Newark mayoral campaign] organization is a wholly-owned subsidiary of Bradley and Walton [foundations]."

Considering Glenn Ford's research and insight in the broader context of American politics and African-American politics, his findings offer the first systematic description of an emergent conservative and Republican Party strategy of using black conservative activists in "stealth" fashion to corral the votes of a segment of the African-American electorate. Ford's words are worth citing in full:

> It is the BAEO [on whose board Cory Booker sits] and its patrons that have propelled a one-term [Newark] councilman into places of honor at the

tables of the rightwing rich. The Free Congress Foundation proclaimed Booker among the nation's top four 'New Black Leaders,' along with J.C. Watts, the Republican congressman from Oklahoma; Deborah Walden-Ford, a professional Right operative who also sits on the BAEO board, and Star Parker, a former welfare mother turned ultra-conservative speaking circuit maven. The Free Congress Foundation gets a fat check every year from Bradley—$425,000 in 2000. Parker sits on the board of Black America's Political Action Committee (BAMPAC), the political toy of ... Alan Keyes, 1996 GOP presidential candidate and MSNBC talk-show host. White Republicans get most of BAMPAC's campaign contributions, but Cory Booker certainly qualifies for access to some of Keyes' more than $2 million treasury. Last year, Booker won the first BAMPAC Leader of Tomorrow Award, bestowed on those under 40 who promote the BAMPAC mission and are seen as rising stars on the political landscape. Another BAMPAC board member, Phyllis Meyers Berry, is president of the Center for New Black Leadership, created ... with $215,000 from the Olin, Scaife and VCJ Foundations—and Bradley. ... Booker's stock soared in the circles of selfish wealth.

The Manhattan Institute ... recipient of $250,000 in Bradley money in 2000, invited Booker to one of its power lunches [seminars], where [in an address] he effortlessly dropped Right-speak code words.

This constellation of conservative forces that constituted the soul of Councilman Cory Booker's mayoral campaign in Newark is just the opposite—ideologically and politically—of the genuine liberal wing of the Republican Party, the one that produced such national black figures as Arthur Fletcher, an important Labor Department official in the Nixon

Administration, and William T. Coleman, the former longstanding chair of the NAACP Legal Defense Fund who was Secretary of Transportation in the Ford Administration; and, which in the administration of New Jersey Governor Thomas Kean two decades ago fostered the careers at the cabinet level of such black Republicans as Leonard Coleman, who later became National Urban League Board Member and President of the National Baseball League.

Conclusion: Lessons of the Booker Campaign

The campaign of Cory Booker for the mayor's chair in Newark thus illustrates one new facet of what I call the maturation phase of African-American politics. Namely, that the national Republican Party—articulated at its pinnacle through a deeply conservative but politically savvy Republican White House under President George W. Bush—is seeking to penetrate the fissures in political attitudes and policy issues that, understandably, have now emerged among the expanded segments of Black America. So, it should be, in contemporary parlance, a wake-up call to Black America's national civil rights leadership in the NAACP, the National Urban League, the National Council of Negro Women, the Southern Christian Leadership Council, and a variety of national professional associations among African Americans, as well as the Congressional Black Caucus and related organizations of BEOs. They must sharpen their political antenna for the long-haul task of detecting the next round of what I call "Black Stealth Candidacies" for mayoral, congressional, state legislator, and other offices around the country— that is, black candidacies packaged ostensibly along black liberal-reform views, but which their true funding sources and ideological objectives are conservative. Ostensibly black-run conservative machinery (the BAEO, the BAMPAC, and the Center for New Black Leadership, fueled by conservative funding sources linked to the Republican Party, are now equipped to initiate more of these "black "stealth candidacies"—and they surely will.

One ingredient black progressive forces will find useful in dealing with this latest effort to block black political progress is to remember one of the attributes that contributed mightily to black political development in the century just ended: an understanding of how to transfer leadership from one generation to the next.

One notion continually trumpeted by the pro-Booker columnists and the pro-Booker news stories was that the Newark campaign represented a "generational conflict" between the "old" (and, by implication, no longer viable) civil rights-oriented and progressive leadership out of which James emerged, and the "new" African American, under-35 cohort. However, this isn't the first time the generation-conflict gambit has been substituted for honest analysis of black political behavior. It was trotted out in the 1980s, too, when the Reagan Administration was trying to declare black progressive politics dead by fiat. Then, the media also anointed a small group of black conservative ideologues, such as Steele, and young black political wannabes as the "new generation" of leaders of Black America. While Steele and several of his fellow ideologues are now ensconced in conservative think tanks or academia, the political wannabes quickly faded from sight. A second revealing fact about the "generational-conflict" notion is that it is only applied to black politics—not to the powerful currents re-shaping the political activity of Latino and Asian Americans, and never, of course, to the dynamics of political activity among white Americans.

In fact, the notions put forward in this fashion are hostile as well as politically tendentious interpretations of the generational factor—not conflict—in African-American politics, not liberal and black-friendly interpretations. They are motivated by a desire to divide and conquer.

In fact, the maturation phase of African-American politics has shown how skillfully the first-generation cohort of black elected politicians have transferred leadership to a second-generation cohort, on the one hand, and on the other hand sustained solid commitment among the second-generation cohort to the core policy features of the longstanding African-American leadership's civil rights agenda. This occurred, for instance, as Carl Stokes and Louis Stokes transferred black mayoral leadership to Michael White in Cleveland; as Maynard Jackson and Andrew Young transferred black mayoral leadership to Bill Campbell in

Essay 8

Table 1: Black Elected Officials in the U.S. by Category of Office 1970-2000: Number and Percent Change From Preceding Year

YEAR	TOTAL BEOs		FEDERAL		STATE		SUBSTATE REGIONAL	
	NO.	% CHANGE	NO.	% CHANGE	NO.	% CHANGE	NO.	% CHANGE
1970	1,469	–	10	–	169	–	–	–
1971	1,860	26.6	14	40.0	202	19.5	–	–
1972	2,264	21.7	14	0.0	210	4.0	–	–
1973	2,621	15.8	16	14.3	240	14.3	–	–
1974	2,991	14.1	17	6.3	239	-0.4	–	–
1975	3,503	17.1	18	5.9	281	17.6	–	–
1976	3,979	13.6	18	0.0	281	0.0	30	–
1977	4,311	8.3	17	-5.6	299	6.4	33	10.0
1978	4,503	4.5	17	0.0	299	0.0	26	-21.2
1979	4,607	2.3	17	0.0	313	4.7	25	-3.8
1980	4,912	6.6	17	0.0	323	3.2	25	0.0
1981	5,038	2.6	18	5.9	341	5.6	30	20.0
1982	5,160	2.4	18	0.0	336	-1.5	35	16.7
1983	5,606	8.6	21	16.7	379	12.8	29	-17.1
1984	5,700	1.7	21	0.0	389	2.6	30	3.4
1985	6,056	6.2	20	-4.8	396	1.8	32	6.7
1986	6,424	6.1	20	0.0	400	1.0	31	-3.1
1987	6,681	4.0	23	15.0	417	4.3	23	-25.8
1988	6,829	2.2	23	0.0	413	-1.0	22	-4.3
1989	7,226	5.8	24	4.3	424	2.7	18	-18.2
1990	7,370	2.0	24	0.0	423	-0.2	18	0.0
1991	7,480	1.5	26	8.3	458	8.3	15	-16.7
1992*	7,552	1.0	26	0.0	484	5.7	15	0.0
1993*	8,015	6.1	39	0.5	533	10.1	13	-13.3
1994*	8,162	1.8	39	0.0	539	1.1	10	-23.1
1995*	8,419	3.1	41	5.1	576	6.9	7	-30.0
1996*	8,579	1.9	41	0.0	578	0.3	7	0.0
1997*	8,656	0.9	40	-2.4	586	1.4	18	157.1
1998*	8,868	2.4	40	0	587	0.2	17	-5.6
1999*	8,936	0.8	39	-2.5	595	1.4	18	5.9
2000*	9,040	1.2	39	0	598	0.5	17	-5.6

* Includes District of Columbia Statehood offices

COUNTY		MUNICIPAL		JUDICIAL & LAW ENFORCEMENT		EDUCATION	
NO.	% CHANGE	NO.	% CHANGE	NO.	% CHANGE	NO.	% CHANGE
92	–	623	–	213	–	362	–
120	30.4	785	26.0	274	28.6	465	28.5
176	46.7	932	18.7	263	-4.0	669	43.9
211	19.9	1,053	13.0	334	27.0	767	14.6
242	14.7	1,360	29.2	340	1.8	793	3.4
305	26.0	1,573	15.7	387	13.8	939	18.4
355	16.4	1,889	20.1	412	6.5	994	5.9
381	7.3	2,083	10.3	447	8.5	1,051	5.7
410	7.6	2,159	3.6	454	1.6	1,138	8.3
398	-2.9	2,224	3.0	486	7.0	1,144	0.5
451	13.3	2,356	5.9	526	8.2	1,214	6.1
449	-0.4	2,384	1.2	549	4.4	1,267	4.4
465	3.6	2,477	3.9	563	2.6	1,266	-0.1
496	6.7	2,697	8.9	607	7.8	1,377	8.8
518	4.4	2,735	1.4	636	4.8	1,371	-0.4
611	18.0	2,898	6.0	661	3.9	1,438	4.9
681	11.5	3,112	7.4	676	2.3	1,504	4.6
724	6.3	3,219	3.4	728	7.7	1,547	2.9
742	2.5	3,341	3.8	738	1.4	1,550	0.2
793	6.9	3,595	7.6	760	3.0	1,612	4.0
810	2.1	3,671	2.1	769	1.2	1,655	2.7
810	0.0	3,683	0.3	847	10.1	1,638	-1.0
857	5.8	3,697	0.4	847	0.0	1,623	-0.9
913	6.5	3,903	5.6	922	8.9	1,689	4.1
925	1.3	3,960	1.5	979	6.2	1,707	1.1
912	-1.4	4,042	2.1	986	0.7	1,853	8.6
924	1.3	4,099	1.4	993	0.7	1,935	4.4
937	1.4	4,115	0.4	996	0.3	1,962	1.4
930	-0.7	4,277	3.9	998	0.2	2,017	2.8
921	-1.0	4,430	3.6	997	-0.1	1,935	-4.1
953	3.5	4,465	0.8	1,037	4.0	1,930	-0.3

Table 2: Number of Black Elected Officials in the United States, by State and Office, January 2000

STATE	Total	Net Change Since 1/31/02	Senators	Representatives	Governors	Administrators	Senators	Representatives
			FEDERAL			**STATE**		
Alabama	731	6		1			8	27
Alaska	3	0						
Arizona	14	1						2
Arkansas	502	-2					3	12
California	238	1		4			2	4
Colorado	19	-2				1	1	2
Connecticut	71	3				1	3	11
Delaware	24	0					1	3
District of Columbia	204	5		1				
Florida	226	10		3			5	15
Georgia	582	-2		3		3	11	32
Hawaii	0	0						
Idaho	0	0						
Illinois	621	-6		3		1	8	15
Indiana	83	-1		1			6	7
Iowa	13	-1						1
Kansas	19	0					2	5
Kentucky	62	0					1	3
Louisiana	701	-13		1			9	22
Maine	0	0						
Maryland	176	-9		2			9	29
Massachusetts	31	0					1	5
Michigan	340	2		2			5	15
Minnesota	18	2						1
Mississippi	897	47		1			10	35
Missouri	196	-5		1			4	13
Montana	0	0						

Members, Regional Bodies	Other Regional Officials	County Executives	Members, County Governing Bodies	Members, Other County Bodies	Other County Officials
SUBSTATE REGIONAL		COUNTY			
			82		18
					5
1			4		1
			1		
			2		
			23	2	
			91		5
			39	1	2
			8		
			4		
			1		
			2		
1			130		
		1	8		
			24		2
			106	67	21
			2		

continued

Essay 8

Table 2 (cont'd): Number of Black Elected Officials in the United States by State and Office, January 2000 (continued)

STATE	Total	Net Change Since 1/31/99	Senators	Representatives	Governors	Administrators	Senators	Representatives
				FEDERAL			STATE	
Nebraska	6	2					1	
Nevada	14	1					3	2
New Hampshire	3	0						3
New Jersey	247	8		1			4	11
New Mexico	4	0						1
New York	320	15		4		1	6	21
North Carolina	498	-8		2		1	7	17
North Dakota	0	0						
Ohio	309	25		1		1	4	13
Oklahoma	104	-1		1			2	3
Oregon	7	0				1	1	2
Pennsylvania	186	22		1			3	15
Rhode Island	10	0					1	8
South Carolina	540	-2		1			7	26
South Dakota	0	0						
Tennessee	177	5		1			3	13
Texas	475	-4		2		1	2	14
Utah	3	2						
Vermont	1	0						1
Virgin Islands	39	-1		1	1	1	14	
Virginia	250	-1		1			5	10
Washington	24	3					1	1
West Virginia	21	2					1	3
Wisconsin	31	0					2	6
Wyoming	0	0						
TOTAL	9,040*	104	0	39	1	12	156	429

* Total Includes statehood senator from MC District Of Columbia. Data compiled by Alfred Baltimore, Jr., Roger Clark, and tabulated by Richard Hart. Database Administrator

Members, Regional Bodies	Other Regional Officials	County Executives	Members, County Governing Bodies	Members, Other County Bodies	Other County Officials
SUBSTATE REGIONAL			COUNTY		
			1		
			1		
			14		1
		1	18		
			58	3	1
			1		
			1		
			1		
			1		
			66	2	6
			47		
			17		1
	15				
			48		3
		1	2		
			5		
2	15	3	809	75	66

Essay 8

Table 2 (cont'd): Number of Black Elected Officials in the United States by State and Office, January 2000 (continued)

STATE	Mayors	Members, Municipal Governing Bodies	Members, Municipal Boards	Members, Neighborhood Advisory Commissions	Other Municipal Officials	Judges, State Courts of Last Resort	Judges, Statewide Courts
			MUNICIPAL			JUDICIAL AND >	
Alabama	40	403	2			2	
Alaska	1	1					
Arizona		1					
Arkansas	31	235			27		
California	8	42	8		5	1	
Colorado	1	3				1	1
Connecticut		33	9		3		
Delaware	2	12					
District of Columbia	1	6		185			
Florida	14	116				2	
Georgia	36	259	2		1	2	1
Hawaii							
Idaho							
Illinois	23	174	50		30	1	
Indiana		32		8	2	1	
Iowa	1	3					
Kansas		4					
Kentucky	3	42					
Louisiana	31	222			4	1	
Maine							
Maryland	10	73			1		
Massachusetts		12	8				
Michigan	17	86	6		15	1	
Minnesota	2	2				1	
Mississippi	52	358				1	
Missouri	21	111			4	1	
Montana							

The State of Black America 2002

Judges, Other Courts	Magistrates, Justices of the Peace, Constables	Other Judicial Officials	Police Chiefs, Sheriffs, and Marshals	Members, State Education Agencies	Members, Univ. & College Boards	Members, Local School Boards	Other Education Officials
LAW ENFORCEMENT				**EDUCATION**			
20	19	7	7	2		92	1
					1		
3	2				1	5	
8	55	2	2			122	
73		1	1		16	67	
7						1	
3						8	
1						3	
						10	
31						15	
30	1	4	3		2	102	
55						219	
8		1	1			8	
			1		1	2	
4						3	
3	2					6	
45	48	4	23	2		158	
28		3	1			11	
		1	1			3	
51	2	1		5	11	97	
7						5	
52	35	14	10			129	6
15		1			3	20	

continued

Table 2 (cont'd): Number of Black Elected Officials in the United States by State and Office, January 2000 (continued)

STATE	Mayors	Members, Municipal Governing Bodies	Members, Municipal Boards	Members, Neighborhood Advisory Commissions	Other Municipal Officials	Judges, State Courts of Last Resort	Judges, Statewide Courts
			MUNICIPAL			JUDICIAL AND >	
Nebraska		2					
Nevada		4					
New Hampshire							
New Jersey	15	107					
New Mexico							
New York	5	48	7		4		
North Carolina	30	258				1	2
North Dakota							
Ohio	12	118	4	75	5		
Oklahoma	15	51			10		
Oregon							
Pennsylvania	5	67			1		
Rhode Island		1					
South Carolina	29	227	4				
South Dakota							
Tennessee	3	58				1	
Texas	41	253	1				
Utah		2					
Vermont							
Virgin Islands							
Virginia	7	77			2		
Washington		9				1	
West Virginia	1	12					
Wisconsin		7					
Wyoming							
TOTAL	451	3,531	101	268	114	18	4

* Total Includes statehood senator from MC District Of Columbia. Data compiled by Alfred Baltimore, Jr., Roger Clark, and tabulated by Richard Hart. Database Administrator

Judges, Other Courts	Magistrates, Justices of Peace, Constables	Other Judicial Officials	Police Chiefs, Sheriffs, and Marshalls	Members, State Education Agencies	Members, Univ. & College Boards	Members, Local School Boards	Other Education Officials
		LAW ENFORCEMENT			EDUCATION		
						2	
2					1	1	
			1			93	
2						1	
79		1				125	
21		2	3			92	
24		3				48	
3						18	
2							
44	20	1	1			27	
2		1	5		1	163	
15	4	6				26	
8	33		2	2	6	92	
1							
				7			
1		9	5			82	
8						1	
3	1						
5						5	
664	222	62	67	18	42	1,863	7

Essay 8

Table 3: Black Elected Officials by State — 2000 Totals and Net Change Since 1999

STATE	BLACKS AS PERCENT OF 2000 VOTING AGE POPULATION**	ELECTED OFFICIALS ALL RACES	BLACK NUMBER	BLACK PERCENT OF TOTAL	NET CHANGE 1999-2000
Alabama	24.0	4,385	731	16.7	6
Alaska	3.3	1,929	3	0.2	0
Arizona	2.9	3,289	14	0.4	1
Arkansas	13.9	8,408	502	6.0	-2
California	6.4	18,925	238	1.3	1
Colorado	3.6	8,605	19	0.2	-2
Connecticut	8.2	9,147	71	0.8	3
Delaware	17.6	1,171	24	2.0	0
District of Columbia	56.2	348	204	58.6	5
Florida	12.7	5,588	226	4.0	10
Georgia	26.6	6,529	582	8.9	-2
Hawaii	1.8	183	0	0.0	0
Idaho	0.4	4,775	0	0.0	0
Illinois	13.8	42,336	621	1.5	-6
Indiana	7.7	11,624	83	0.7	-1
Iowa	1.8	16,479	13	0.1	-1
Kansas	5.3	18,895	19	0.1	0
Kentucky	6.8	7,060	62	0.9	0
Louisiana	29.7	5,051	701	13.9	-13
Maine	0.4	6,556	0	0.0	0
Maryland	26.4	2,123	176	8.3	-9
Massachusetts	4.9	22,173	31	0.1	0
Michigan	13.1	18,704	340	1.8	2
Minnesota	3.0	18,870	18	0.1	2
Mississippi	33.1	4,754	897	18.9	47
Missouri	10.2	17,281	196	1.1	-5
Montana	0.3	5,106	0	0.0	0

Table 3 (cont'd): Black Elected Cited Officials by State — 2000 Totals and Net Change Since 1999

STATE	BLACKS AS PERCENT OF 2000 VOTING AGE POPULATION**	ALL RACES	ELECTED OFFICIALS		
			BLACK		
			NUMBER	PERCENT OF TOTAL	NET CHANGE 1999-2000
Nebraska	3.5	13,899	6	0.0	2
Nevada	6.3	1,218	14	1.1	1
New Hampshire	0.7	7,347	3	0.0	0
New Jersey	12.6	9,042	247	2.7	8
New Mexico	1.8	2,201	4	0.2	0
New York	14.8	25,932	320	1.2	15
North Carolina	20.0	5,820	498	8.5	-8
North Dakota	0.5	15,482	0	0.0	0
Ohio	10.5	19,366	309	1.6	25
Oklahoma	6.9	8,989	104	1.2	-1
Oregon	1.5	7,833	7	0.1	0
Pennsylvania	9.0	30,476	186	0.6	22
Rhode Island	3.9	1,138	10	0.9	0
South Carolina	27.2	3,943	540	13.7	-2
South Dakota	0.6	9,684	0	0.0	0
Tennessee	14.8	6,950	177	2.5	5
Texas	11.0	27,628	475	1.7	-4
Utah	0.8	2,711	3	0.1	2
Vermont	0.4	8,534	1	0.0	0
Virgin Islands	NA	41	39	95.1	-1
Virginia	18.4	3,104	250	8.1	-1
Washington	3.0	7,724	24	0.3	3
West Virginia	3.0	2,772	21	0.8	2
Wisconsin	4.7	17,829	31	0.2	0
Wyoming	0.7	2,742	0	0	0
TOTAL	11.4	512,699	9,040*	1.8	104*

* Total includes one statehood senator from the District of Columbia. ** From the 2000 U.S. Census figures which include all persons age 18 and over who identified themselves as Black or African American (as their only race).

Table 4: Black Elected Officials, by Year and Gender, 1970-2000

YEAR	TOTAL	MALE	FEMALE NUMBER	FEMALE PERCENT OF TOTAL
1970	1,469	1,309	160	10.9
1971	1,860	1,635	225	12.1
1972	2,264	2,111	153	6.8
1973	2,621	2,276	345	13.2
1974	2,991	2,575	416	13.9
1975	3,503	2,973	530	15.1
1976	3,979	3,295	684	17.2
1977	4,311	3,529	782	18.1
1978	4,503	3,660	843	18.7
1979	4,607	3,725	882	19.1
1980	4,912	3,936	975	19.9
1981	5,038	4,017	1,021	20.3
1982	5,160	4,079	1,081	20.9
1983	5,606	4,383	1,223	21.8
1984	5,700	4,441	1,259	22.1
1985	6,056	4,697	1,359	22.4
1986	6,424	4,942	1,482	23.1
1987	6,681	5,117	1,564	23.4
1988	6,829	5,204	1,625	23.8
1989	7,226	5,412	1,814	25.1
1990	7,370	5,420	1,950	26.5
1991	7,480	5,427	2,053	27.4
1992	7,552	5,431	2,121	28.1
1993	8,015	5,683	2,332	29.1
1994	8,162	5,694	2,468	30.2
1995	8,419	5,782	2,637	31.3
1996	8,579	5,830	2,749	32.0
1997	8,656	5,847	2,809	32.5
1998	8,868	5,944	2,924	33.0
1999	8,936	5,939	2,997	33.5
2000	9,040	5,921	3,119	34.5

Source: Joint Center for Political and Economic Studies

Atlanta; as Coleman Young transferred black mayoral leadership to Dennis Archer in Detroit; and similarly in New Orleans, Birmingham, Richmond, Philadelphia, and so on. This dynamic generational change is quite clear in the numbers the Joint Center has compiled, as David Bositis points out in noting that most of the black politicos elected to office in the 1970s have since retired from office, moved on to other pursuits, or died—and then succeeded by younger generations. In 2001, [Michigan] State Representative Kwame Kilpatrick, who was born the year the first [JCPES] roster was published, was elected mayor of Detroit. The dynamics of this generational change of leadership are often overlooked, or else their significance is obscured ... between 1999 and 2000 765 newly elected BEOs were added to the list. In the preceding year (1998-1999) 851 were added, and in 1997-1998, 666 were added. Thus, between 1997 and 2000, there were 2,282 newly elected BEOs. Throughout this three-year period, the total number of BEOs was about 9,000, so the 2,282 represented a turnover of 25.4 percent.

Despite some understandably significant experiential differences between the older and younger BEOs, that natural transition has by and large gone smoothly and with minimal change in the long-held mainstream "Black Agenda." It is the continuing responsibility of the older generation of black civic leaders and politicians—now exemplified by a primary task of Mayor Sharpe James—to transmit their leadership skills to a succeeding younger generation cohort who exhibit genuine commitment to the mainline African-American leadership's civil rights agenda. That agenda is represented not only by the NAACP, the National Urban League, the National Council of Negro Women, the Southern Christian Leadership Conference, and the Congressional Black Caucus, but also by the sundry African-American professional associations, trade unions, and voluntary organizations. We need look no further than the black electorate of Newark to see the importance of this task. For when it became clear in the 2002 Newark mayoral campaign that the genuine African-American civil rights agenda was not the political agenda of Cory Booker's candidacy, the vast majority of Newark's African-American voters voted accordingly.

Essay **8**

Notes

[1] See tables 1-7B, Black Elected Officials, A Statistical Summary 2000, Joint Center for Political and Economic Studies, Washington, DC, 2002.

[2] See article on Black gubernatorial candidates in *Black Enterprise* (May 2002): pp. 21-22.

[3] David A. Bositis, "Generational Shift Among Black Elected Officials," *Focus: Monthly Magazine of Joint Center for Political and Economic Studies* (July/August 2001): p.5.

Afterword

Praising the Mutilated World

By Lee A. Daniels

As one who's made his living by writing, I've long considered putting titles to what I write central to the entire undertaking because titles express the essence of what it is one is writing—or, to put it more precisely, what it is one is thinking.

This is obvious if you think of other products of a creative intelligence: Fiction—Toni Morrison's The Bluest Eye; The plastic arts—Picasso's Guernica; Poetry—T.S. Eliot's The Waste Land; Playwrighting—David Merrick's 42nd Street, or John Guare's Six Degrees of Separation; Popular Music—Aretha Franklin's Respect, or James Brown's Cold Sweat (I'm dating myself, I know, but it's deliberate).

So, in thinking about this essay, I riffed through a bunch of titles. I began with: Is the Glass Half Empty—or Half Full? This was the question we posed in the foreword to the 2000 volume of *The State of Black America*, provoked by thinking about the significant economic and political progress African Americans had made as a group because of the Long Boom of the 1990s.

Then, I came up with another title: Is This a Measure of the Progress-or a Measure of the Resistance? What produced that suggestion was the appointment of Tyrone Willingham, the former head football coach at Stanford University, as the head football coach at Notre Dame, a place whose collegiate football legends make it in fact an icon of America itself. Willingham became the first black head coach at Notre Dame in any sport, which many people found surprising, given the number of "Black Irish" on the university's football and basketball teams in particular. But what really caught my eye was the statistic Willingham's appointment brought out of the woodwork: There are four black head coaches in the National

Afterword

Collegiate Athletic Association's Division 1-A, which comprises the major collegiate football programs.

How many schools are there in Division 1-A, you ask? I've seen two numbers. One is 115; the second is 124. Either way, I found the number 4 stunning.

Now, I'm no fool. I knew the situation of black head coaches in every sport—at every level—is atrocious. And I had what I thought were very low expectations about Division 1-A. I figured there were ... eight.

But four? After three decades when the participation of black players has made, and makes, college football what it is? After three decades when the volume of black players should have produced a whole slew of black head coaches?

I said to myself: That number 4 is not a measure of progress. It's a measure of the resistance to giving individuals who are black what they've earned, and to putting more blacks in the positions that are the ladder upward to head coaching slots.

If you apply that question to other arenas of American society—Is this a measure of the progress, or of the resistance?—What would we come up with?

But then I decided to choose the title which would most precisely declare what I'm thinking: Praising the Mutilated World.

Of course, this comes from the brilliant poem by Adam Zagajewski, translated from the Polish by Clare Cavanaugh, that closed the September 24th edition of *The New Yorker*, the edition which was devoted to the attacks of September 11, and whose cover was completely black and, seemingly at first glance, empty—until you could see in the blackness of the general cover the twin towers of the World Trade Center sketched in a deeper blackness.

Zagajewski wrote:

Try To Praise The Mutilated World
Try to praise the mutilated world.
Remember June's long days,
and wild strawberries, drops of wine, the dew.

*The nettles that methodically overgrow
the abandoned homesteads of exiles.
You must praise the mutilated world.
You watched the stylish yachts and ships;
one of them had had a long trip ahead of it,
while salty oblivion awaited others.
You've seen the refugees heading nowhere,
you've heard the executioners sing joyfully.
You should praise the mutilated world.
Remember the moments when we were together
in a white room and the curtain fluttered.
Return in thought to the concert where the music flared.
You gathered across the park in autumn
and leaves eddied over the earth's scars.
Praise the mutilated world
and the gray feather a thrush lost,
and the gentle light that strays and vanishes
and returns.*

What, some may be asking, does this poem have to do with the immediate future of Black America?

It has everything to do with it.

History—and our future—demand that we black Americans praise the mutilated world. That is, after all, our legacy. African Americans, like many other peoples around the world, have always had to accept the reality that they must learn how to praise a mutilated world. It is the only recourse to keep body and soul together, for example, when you endure the imprisonment of Slavery and you do the back-breaking work that allows Mr. Thomas Jefferson and his confreres to assuage their unbridled egotism by playing the English country squire. It is the only recourse, to cite another example, when you give your life for the defense of this country, as Lt. John Fox, of the U.S. Army's 92nd Infantry Division did in Sommocolonia, Italy on December, 26, 1944, [Frank Vivano, "Almost Forgotten Heroes: Italian Town Honors black GIs who were shunned by their own country," San Francisco

Afterword

Chronicle, July 13, 2000] even though you are not respected by your country or your army command, and your people will not gain full citizenship in that country for another two decades, and your action will not receive its deserved Congressional Medal of Honor for another 53 years.[1] It is the only recourse when you, as a working man or woman, live decently and honorably but are insulted in every possible way by the forces of government because you are African American.

Praising a mutilated world—learning how to keep one's eyes on the prize and one's humanity even while enduring a pervasive and often violent injustice—is a skill African Americans practiced very well in this land. They learned to praise a mutilated world, and they gave to this nation an unswerving loyalty that enabled it to come to freedom, and to a hope, as King said in the revolutionary speech he gave at the March on Washington in August 1963, that it would be able to live out the true meaning of the words of the Constitution.

Black people have made enormous strides since the 1960s, when more than two-thirds of blacks were poor or working class. Now, two-thirds are working class, middle class and even upper class. Back in the 1960s, blacks seeking higher education were still significantly limited to the Negro Colleges. Most colleges in the North and West, for all their rhetorical commitment to that great buzzword "merit" and integration, practiced, at best, a rigid tokenism when it came to including blacks as students or faculty. Now, for all the problems, for all of the *resistance*, that is different. One thing the recent tempest at Harvard over the Afro-American Studies Department and its leading faculty has made clear is the commitment of a significant patch of American institutions, in the corporate world as well as higher education, to the inclusion of all of those who make up America into their particular community. That this struggle between the progress and the resistance is the reality should not be surprising, and certainly not discouraging. It is the history of the experience of racial difference in America. And it, the discussion about our racial differences and our racial similarities and our racial kinship, is going to continue to be at the center of the discussion of what it means to be an American for a very long time to come.

African Americans have continued to show, as they always have, that grace under pressure which has made our existence in this land not only possible, but, when all is said and done, enjoyable. I'm thinking of such things as the continuing push of many of our youth toward achievement in higher education and other fields. I'm thinking, as these notes are being written, of the extraordinary accomplishments of the Williams sisters, Venus and Serena, both of them simultaneously sitting atop the world of tennis—a reflection not only of their own talent and determination, but of the long-term drive and courage of their parents. I'm thinking of those black men and women who are rising to the top in politics, the corporate world, higher education, and so on, and in their way pushing forward the dynamic of advancement that the Civil Rights Movement of the 1950s and 1960s expressed so forcefully.

For me, however, the most powerful and poignant expression of Black America's legacy of striving was expressed by the most maligned sector of black people: the black poor and unemployed. For, in the late 1990s, when the effects of the decade's booming economy finally reached all the way to the bottom of the economic ladder and provoked the creation of millions of low-wage jobs in the service sector, it was they who rushed to fill them. That was shown by a study of more than 300 metropolitan areas done by the National Bureau of Economic Research and released in the late spring of 1999: It found that black males, aged 16 to 24, with only a high school education at best, were working in greater numbers and earning bigger paychecks than ever before. The study also found, by the way, that levels of reported crime had fallen most sharply in those areas of the country where declines in joblessness had been the greatest. It was the black poor, in other words, who drove the black unemployment rate down to a record postwar low of 7.2 percent in April of 2000—and in the process refuted three decades' worth of tendentious rhetoric about the black poor being ensnared in a so-called culture of poverty—which kept them from understanding the value of work—blah, blah, blah.

Of course, the point of all that rhetoric was to write these black people off. Even some black people—shame on them!—bought it. But many of the black poor did not, and when they got a chance to show who they real-

Afterword

ly were, they did so speedily. The black poor showed us that they don't need any condescending lectures about what work means, what it enables one to do, and how it enables one to feel about one's self. They just need opportunity—as James Brown put it another way three decades ago: I don' want nobody to give me nothin', just open up the door, I'll get it myself. ...

So, for my money, with all that the rising black working and middle classes have done since the 1960s to follow what the writer Albert Murray described in his novelized memoir, The Spyglass Tree, as the indelible "ancestral imperative to do something and become something and be somebody," it's been the black poor who have most dramatically reminded us that one doesn't have to be highly formally educated and wear white collars and speak perfect English to have the right values. It's their behavior which has best exemplified the sustaining humanity of black people: a powerful optimism in the face of daunting odds; a willingness to work hard; a refusal to let the persistence of significant obstacles (racism) discourage them from trying to better themselves. It is the black poor whose behavior best exemplifies black people's determination to praise the mutilated world.

Martin Luther King, Jr. said in the "Mountain Top" speech on the last full night of his life that we as a people would get to the "Promised Land." That's the phrase, the prediction that has always captured the popular imagination.

But I've always been caught, and motivated, more by what he said in the speech just before that: He said: "We've got some difficult days ahead."

I've always asked myself: When he said "days," was he speaking of real time, or was he speaking metaphorically?

It was the latter, I think, which is perfectly in keeping with another facet of our legacy: the Struggle, to push back the borders of injustice and racism, to hew a place of comfort and opportunity out of a harsh environment, to make America live up to the American Dream.

So, our task—the task of those who seek the destruction of inequality in all of its forms and the expansion of justice—is to go on, while praising the mutilated world. You could put our task another way: You could say that our mission is wrapped up in the words of the late civil rights hero, James Farmer, who wrote in his autobiography of the danger he and the other activists faced in the South. He wrote: "Living was tenuous in Movement days. But the reaching toward happiness ennobled life for this nation." Such a wonderful way of putting it. So romantic. So poignant. So resonant with history. So resonant with hope. The only way to redeem the sins of the past, and the sins of the present, to redeem the lives of our neighbors and of the many thousands gone, is to ennoble this nation and this world by enabling more of our fellow human beings to reach toward happiness.

To do that, we have to commit ourselves, in whatever ways we can, to The Dream, and therefore to The Work. For only by committing ourselves to The Work can we have any hope of realizing The Dream. My brother, Lloyd, put it directly in a poem he sent to me several years ago. Since then, it's always been my reminder of what my responsibility is, of what is the responsibility and the mission of those who seek a just world.[2] This is its message:

Hard Work

In the cold light of winter
You recognize your fear
You are Miniver Cheever
Living everywhere else
Save here.
Ever the eternal dreamer
Lost in worlds unseen
Transfixed by the devastating beauty
Of wonders pure and philistine.

The time from there to here
A light-year's day on the sun
Must be crossed another way
If ever to be done.
Only work can make the dream

Afterword

The dream from here now
Future-past already
Whenever the spirit bows.
Only work can make the dream.
Reality is hard work.

feature

Ten Important Contributions Black America Made to America in the Twentieth Century

1. The Integration of the U.S. Army in 1948

African Americans have had to fight the nation's political and military establishment in order to fight for their country since the nation's founding. In the wake of the sacrifices blacks made both in the European and Asian theaters of the war and on the home front during World War II, the agitation among blacks to integrate the military increased sharply in the late 1940s. On July 26, 1948, President Harry S. Truman, bypassing a hostile Congress, issued Executive Order 9981 mandating the "equality of treatment and opportunity for all persons in the armed services without regard to race, color, religion, or national origin."[1]

2. The founding of *Ebony* Magazine

John H. Johnson founded Johnson Publishing Company and its flagship magazine, *Ebony*, in November 1942 on a shoestring budget: He had taken a loan of $500 for which the collateral was his mother's furniture. His first office was as a room in the law office of one of Black Chicago's most prominent lawyers. But Johnson's, and his wife's Eunice's, business acumen, combined with the new post-war assertiveness of Black America propelled *Ebony* (and its primary sister publications, *Jet Magazine* and *Negro Digest*) during the civil rights years of the 1950s and 1960s to the front rank of influential American magazines.

feature

3. The publication of *Invisible Man*

Nothing had prepared the world for Ralph Ellison's novel, *Invisible Man*, which he published after five years of work in 1952. The book, whose protagonist and narrator is never named, struck like a thunderclap. It spent four months on the bestseller lists, won the National Book Award, and made Ellison's reputation as a giant of literature. In a 1965 survey, 200 of the nation's most prominent critics, authors, and editors named it "the most distinguished single work: of the postwar era." At its publication, Langston Hughes had called it "a stunning blockbuster of a book that will floor and flabbergast some people, bedevil and intrigue others, and keep everybody reading right through its explosive end."

4. The passage of the civil rights acts of the 1960s

From the Supreme Court's repudiation of legal segregation in the 1954 *Brown v. Board of Education* of Topeka decision through the late 1960s, America's racial dilemma was played out not only in courtrooms and the halls of Congress, but in the streets of its cities, and its highways, and its back roads of dusty fields. The *Brown* decision, and the Montgomery bus boycott the following year unleashed the long pent-up determination of Negro America to have its full-fledged rights of American citizenship—Now! The mass-action nonviolent campaign of the Civil Rights Movement produced two great congressional acts, the Civil Rights Act of 1964, and the Voting Rights Act of 1965. Those acts, which banned racial discrimination from all sectors of American public life and guaranteed African Americans their right to vote in the South, made America a democracy in fact, not just in rhetoric.

5. The Montgomery to Selma March, 1965

When a sea of civil rights marchers, led by Martin Luther King, Jr. and many prominent Americans from all walks of life, slowly walked down the streets of Montgomery, Alabama on March 25, 1965 at the end of The Montgomery to Selma March, it ended an era of organized, state-sanctioned violent white resistance to the American struggle to expand democracy. The march had grown out of the Movement's efforts in Selma, Alabama to register Negro citizens to vote. The state-sanctioned resistance produced one of the most dramatic incidents of the civil rights years: the police attack of early March on nonviolent marchers at the Edmund Pettus Bridge in Selma. The attack, captured in film and photographs, shocked the nation and the world, provoked thousands of Americans to heed King's call to come to Alabama and march for justice, and led to the passage of the 1965 Voting Rights Act.

6. The appointment of Thurgood Marshall to the United States Supreme Court

A shrewd judge of people, a wily legal strategist and courtroom general, an indefatigable activist for and guardian of civil rights, Thurgood Marshall (1908 - 1993) was one of the giant figures of twentieth-century American life. This would have been so even if President Lyndon Baines Johnson had not appointed him to the high court on June 13, 1967; or had not previously appointed him as his Solicitor General in 1965; or President John F. Kennedy had not appointed him in 1961 to the U.S. Court of Appeals for the Second Circuit. For, before those appointments—which in themselves underscored the mid-century progress African-Americans had made—Thurgood Marshal was a central strategist of and participant in the NAACP's long, diligent campaign to destroy legal segregation in education and all sectors of American life. He served on the Supreme Court for 24 years, retired because of ill health in 1991, and died on January 24, 1993 at the age of 84.

7. The advent of affirmative action in the late 1960s

In the early 1960s, even as the struggle in the South to secure basic civil rights for blacks was being waged, civil rights leaders, including Martin Luther King, Jr. and the National Urban League's executive director, Whitney M. Young, Jr., were declaring that, after the decades of a fierce racial discrimination in both the public and private sector, more than the destruction of racist laws was needed to produce equality of opportunity.

feature

He urged the federal government to take positive steps—affirmative action—that black Americans had an equal access to the society's goods and resources. President John F. Kennedy implemented an affirmative action policy requiring that contractors doing business with the federal government take steps to protect their employees against discrimination because of race, creed, color or national origin. President Lyndon Baines Johnson went further. In 1965 he issued Executive Order 11246, which mandated that the government seek not "just equality as a right and a theory but equality as a fact and equality as a result." The order was later expanded to include gender equality as well.

8. The rise of African Americans to the chief executive offices of Fortune 500 corporations in recent years

In the late 1990s, three decades after the civil rights victories had dismantled the legal bulwarks of racial discrimination in the United States and affirmative action had opened white colleges and universities and corporations to significant numbers of people of color, a small number of African Americans have risen to the very top of Fortune 500 companies. Kenneth I. Chenault is chief executive officer of American Express; Richard D. Parsons is chief executive of AOL Time Warner; E. Stanley O'Neal is soon to become chairman and chief executive of Merrill Lynch; and Franklin D. Raines is chairman of Fannie Mae. [The latter two are also trustees of the National Urban League.] These are the most prominent of the evidence of the greater opportunities available to Black Americans in the corporate sector. But, as Raines notes in his essay in this issue ("What Equality Would Look Like"), one has to maintain the proper perspective about these advances. As welcome and inspiring as they are, if there were a full measure of equality in America. "We would have 62 African Americans running Fortune 500 companies, instead of just four. And we would have 590 more African Americans serving on boards of Fortune 1000 companies." And, of course, a significant proportion of those greater numbers would be women.

9. The appointments of Colin Powell as Secretary of State, and Condoleeza Rice as National Security Adviser in the administration of President George W. Bush

On December 16, 2000, President George W. Bush named General Colin I. Powell (U.S. Army-ret.) as his Secretary of State, the first African-American to be nominated to head the nation's foreign-policy establishment. The next day, President Bush named his longtime foreign policy expert, Condoleeza Rice, as his administration's national security adviser. The appointments were hailed in bipartisan fashion, and rightly so, given the superb qualifications each brought to his and her respective post. But they also represented something more than just more "firsts" for Black America. In the context of the deep spread of federal appointments of African Americans by the Clinton Administration (which included the late Ron Brown as Secretary of Commerce), the appointments of Powell and Rice and other blacks indicate that both parties now realize no administration can be considered legitimate unless those occupying their top policy-making posts in some significant measure themselves represent the diversity of the American people.

10. Jesse Jackson's campaigns for the Presidency in the 1980s

In 1972 Congresswoman Shirley Chisholm, of New York, had bravely defied the conventional wisdom of both the larger society and a considerable segment of the black political establishment by campaigning for president. Her perseverance in a lonely cause remains deserving of greater examination. But it was the Reverend Jesse L. Jackson, Sr.'s two campaigns for the presidency in 1984 and 1988 which, by galvanizing Black America's national black political ambitions, helped it fight the conservative tide of the Reagan and Bush (I) administrations and got it ready to play a crucial role in the victories of President Bill Clinton in 1992 and 1996. Despite the controversies which shadowed those campaigns, in the 1988 Democratic primaries, Jackson won seven million votes—a third of the total Democratic votes cast—and came to the national convention with more than 25 percent of the delegates. This was the exercise of a

feature

black electoral power that the American people—black or white or other—had never before seen, and it was a signal individual, and group, achievement.

Notes

1. Source: Gail Buckley, *American Patriots: The Story of Blacks in the Military from the Revolution to Desert Storm*, Random House, 2001, pp. 336-41.

appendix I

History of the National Urban League

The National Urban League, which has played so pivotal a role in the 20th-century Freedom Movement, grew out of that spontaneous grassroots passage to freedom and opportunity that came to be called the Black Migrations. When the U.S. Supreme Court declared its approval of segregation in the 1896 *Plessy v. Ferguson* decision, the brutal system of economic, social and political oppression quickly adopted by the white South rapidly transformed what had been a trickle of African Americans northward into a flood.

Those newcomers to the North soon discovered they had not escaped racial discrimination. Excluded from all but menial jobs in the larger society, victimized by poor housing and education, and inexperienced in the ways of urban life, many lived in terrible social and economic conditions.

Still, in the degree of difference between South and North lay opportunity, and that African Americans clearly understood.

But to capitalize on that opportunity, to successfully adapt to urban life and to reduce the pervasive discrimination they faced, they would need help. That was the reason the Committee on Urban Conditions Among Negroes was established in 1910 in New York City. Central to the organization's founding were two remarkable people: Mrs. Ruth Standish Baldwin and Dr. George Edmund Haynes, who would become the committee's first executive secretary. Mrs. Baldwin, the widow of a railroad magnate and a member of one of America's oldest families, had a remarkable social conscience and was a stalwart champion of the poor and disadvantaged. Dr. Haynes, a graduate of Fisk University, Yale

Appendix **I**

University and Columbia University (he was the first African American to receive a doctorate from that institution), felt a compelling need to use his training as a social worker to serve his people.

A year later, the committee merged with the Committee for the Improvement of Industrial Conditions Among Negroes in New York (founded in New York in 1906), and the National League for the Protection of Colored Women (founded in 1905) to form the National League on Urban Conditions Among Negroes. In 1920, the name was shortened to the National Urban League.

The interracial character of the League's board was set from its first days. Prof. Edwin R. A. Seligman of Columbia University, a leader in progressive social service activities in New York City, served as chairman from 1911 to 1913. Mrs. Baldwin took the post until 1915.

The fledgling organization counseled black migrants from the South, helped train black social workers and worked in various other ways to bring educational and employment opportunities to African Americans. Its research into the problems blacks faced in employment opportunities, recreation, housing, health and sanitation, and education spurred the League's quick growth. By the end of World War I the organization had 81 staff members working in 30 cities.

In 1918, Dr. Haynes was succeeded by Eugene Kinckle Jones, who would direct the agency until his retirement in 1941. Under his direction, the League significantly expanded its multifaceted campaign to crack the barriers to black employment, spurred first by the boom years of the 1920s, and then by the desperate years of the Great Depression. Efforts at reasoned persuasion were buttressed by boycotts against firms that refused to employ blacks, pressure on schools to expand vocational opportunities for young people, constant prodding of Washington officials to include blacks in New Deal recovery programs and a drive to get blacks into previously segregated labor unions.

As World War II loomed, Lester Granger, a seasoned League veteran and crusading newspaper columnist, was appointed Jones' successor.

Outspoken in his commitment to advancing opportunity for African

Americans, Granger pushed tirelessly to integrate racist trade unions, and led the League's effort to support A. Philip Randolph's March on Washington Movement to fight discrimination in defense work and in the armed services. Under Granger, the League, through its own Industrial Relations Laboratory, had notable success in cracking the color bar in numerous defense plants. The nation's demand for civilian labor during the war also helped the organization press ahead with greater urgency its programs to train black youths for meaningful blue-collar employment. After the war those efforts expanded to persuading Fortune 500 companies to hold career conferences on the campuses of Negro colleges and place blacks in upper-echelon jobs.

Of equal importance to the League's own future sources of support, Granger avidly supported the organization of a volunteer auxiliary, the National Urban League Guild, which, under the leadership of Mollie Moon, became an important national force in its own right.

The explosion of the Civil Rights Movement provoked a change for the League, personified by its new leader, Whitney M. Young, Jr., who became executive director in 1961. A social worker like his predecessors, he substantially expanded the League's fund-raising ability and, most critically, made the League a full partner in the Civil Rights movement. Indeed, although the League's tax-exempt status barred it from protest activities, it hosted at its New York headquarters the planning meetings of A. Philip Randolph, Martin Luther King, Jr., and other civil rights leaders for the 1963 March on Washington. Young also was a forceful advocate for greater government and private-sector efforts to eradicate poverty. His call for a domestic Marshall Plan, a 10-point program designed to close the huge social and economic gap between black and white Americans, significantly influenced the discussion of the Johnson administration's War on Poverty legislation.

Young's tragic death in a 1971 drowning incident off the coast of Lagos, Nigeria, brought another change in leadership. Vernon E. Jordan, Jr., formerly executive director of the United Negro College Fund, took over as the League's fifth executive director in 1972 (the title of the office was changed to president in 1977).

Appendix I

For the next decade, until his resignation in December 1981, Jordan skillfully guided the League to new heights of achievement. He oversaw a major expansion of its social service efforts, as the League became a significant conduit for the federal government to establish programs and deliver services to aid urban communities, and he brokered fresh initiatives in such League programs as housing, health, education and minority business development. Jordan also instituted a citizenship education program that helped increase the black vote and brought new programs to such areas as energy, the environment and nontraditional jobs for women of color. He also developed *The State of Black America* report.

In 1982, John E. Jacob, a former chief executive officer of the Washington, D.C., and San Diego affiliates who had served as executive vice president, took the reins of leadership, solidifying the League's internal structure and expanding its outreach even further.

Jacob established the Permanent Development Fund to increase the organization's financial stamina. In honor of Whitney Young, he established several programs to aid the development of those who work for and with the League: the Whitney M. Young, Jr. Training Center, to provide training and leadership development opportunities for both staff and volunteers; the Whitney M. Young, Jr. Race Relations Program, which recognizes affiliates doing exemplary work in race relations; and the Whitney M. Young, Jr. Commemoration Ceremony, which honors and pays tribute to long-term staff and volunteers who have made extraordinary contributions to the Urban League Movement.

Jacob established the League's NULITES youth-development program and spurred the League to put new emphasis on programs to reduce teenage pregnancy, help single female heads of households, combat crime in black communities and increase voter registration.

Hugh B. Price, appointed to the League's top office in July 1994, has taken its reins at a critical moment for the League, for Black America and for the nation as a whole. A fierce, market-driven dynamic described as globalization is sweeping the world, fundamentally altering economic relations among and within countries. In the United States that dynamic is reshaping the link between the nation's citizenry and its economy, and at least for the moment, is fostering enormous uncertainty among individuals and tensions among ethnic and cultural groups.

That economic change, and the efforts of some to roll back the gains African Americans have fashioned since the 1960s, have made the League's efforts all the more necessary. Price, a lawyer by training, with extensive experience in community development and other public policy issues, has intensified the organization's work in education and youth development; in individual and community-wide economic empowerment; and in the forceful advocacy of affirmative action and the promotion of inclusion as a critical foundation for securing America's future as a multiethnic democracy.

appendix II

Statistical Overview

As much as in essays and news articles the state of Black America can be seen in the statistics and tables of public agencies and private organizations. *The State of Black America* has always presented a sample of statistical information apart from a particular volume's essays which demonstrate that fact.

Top 10 Producers of African American Bachelor's Degree Recipients in the Physical Sciences: 2000

COLLEGE/UNIVERSITY	STATE
Xavier University of Louisiana	Louisiana
Lincoln University	Pennsylvania
Morehouse College	Georgia
Howard University	Washington, DC
Florida A&M University	Florida
Southern University of New Orleans	Louisiana
Tennessee State University	Tennessee
Grambling State University	Louisiana
Norfolk State University	Virginia
Dillard University	Louisiana

Note: All Institutions are HBCUs; highlighted institutions are UNCF member colleges and universities. **Source:** Frederick D. Patterson Research Institute (2001) analysis of Integrated Postsecondary Education Data System

Appendix **II**

Districts Represented by Black Members of Congress, 2001

STATE	DISTRICT	PRINCIPAL CITY	BLACK PERCENT OF VOTING-AGE POPULATION[1]
Alabama	7	Montgomery	67
California	9	Oakland	24
California	32	Los Angeles	33
California	35	Los Angeles	27
California	37	Compton	36
District of Columbia	At-Large	Washington, D.C.	56
Florida	3	Jacksonville	45
Florida	17	Miami	50
Florida	23	Ft. Lauderdale	55
Georgia	2	Columbus,	37
Georgia	4	Decatur	51
Georgia	5	Atlanta	51
Illinois	1	Chicago	72
Illinois	2	Chicago	69
Illinois	7	Chicago	59
Indiana	10	Indianapolis	31
Louisiana	2	New Orleans	62
Maryland	4	Silver Spring	74
Maryland	7	Baltimore	61
Michigan	14	Detroit	77
Michigan	15	Detroit	67
Mississippi	2	Greenville	61
Missouri	1	St. Louis	55
New Jersey	10	Newark	57
New York	6	Jamaica/Queens	50
New York	10	Brooklyn	33
New York	11	Brooklyn	60
New York	15	Manhattan	65
North Carolina	1	Fayetteville	47
North Carolina	12	Charlotte	42
Ohio	11	Cleveland	60
Oklahoma	4	Oklahoma City	7
Pennsylvania	2	Philadelphia	59
South Carolina	6	Florence	58
Tennessee	9	Memphis	61
Texas	18	Houston	36
Texas	30	Dallas	39
Virgin Islands	At-Large	St. Thomas	NA
Virginia	3	Richmond	53

*Based on 2000 U.S. Census Bureau figures available before 2000 Census redistricting.

MEMBER OF CONGRESS	MEMBER'S PARTY	FIRST YEAR IN OFFICE
Earl F. Hilliard	D	93
Barbara Lee	D	98
Diana E. Watson	D	'01
Maxine Waters	D	91
Juanita Millender-McDonald	D	96
Eleanor Holmes Norton	D	91
Corrine Brown	D	93
Carrie Meek	D	93
Alcee Hastings	D	93
Sanford D. Bishop, Jr.	D	93
Cynthia McKinney	D	93
John Lewis	D	87
Bobby Rush	D	93
Jesse L. Jackson. Jr.	D	95
Danny Davis	D	97
Julie Carson	D	97
William J. Jefferson	D	21
Albert Wynn	D	93
Elijah Cummings	D	96
John Conyers, Jr.	D	65
Carolyn C. Kilpatrick	D	97
Bennie G. Thompson	D	93
William Lacy Clay. Jr.	D	'01
Donald Payne	D	88
Gregory W. Meeks	D	98
Edolphus Towns	D	83
Major Owens	D	83
Charles B. Rangel	D	71
Eva Clayton	D	92
Melvin L. Walt	D	93
Stephanie Tubbs Jones	D	99
J.C. Watts, Jr.	R	95
Chaka Fatteh	D	95
James E. Clyburn	D	93
Harold E. Ford, Jr,	D	97
Sheila Jackson Lea	D	95
Eddie Bernice Johnson	D	93
Donna M. Christian-Christensen	D	97
Robert C. Scott	D	93

Source: Joint Center for Political and Economic Studies.

Appendix: Black Elected Officials in the U.S. by State 11970 and 2000

STATE	1970 TOTAL	2000 TOTAL	STATE	1970 TOTAL	2000 TOTAL
Alabama	88	731	Nebraska	2	6
Alaska	1	3	Nevada	3	14
Arizona	7	14	New Hampshire	0	3
Arkansas	55	502	New Jersey	73	247
California	105	236	New Mexico	3	4
Colorado	7	19	New York	74	320
Connecticut	31	71	North Carolina	62	498
Delaware	9	24	North Dakota	0	0
District of Columbia	8	204	Ohio	89	309
Florida	36	226	Oklahoma	36	104
Georgia	40	582	Oregon	0	7
Hawaii	1	0	Pennsylvania	49	186
Idaho	0	0	Rhode Island	2	10
Illinois	74	621	South Carolina	38	540
Indiana	30	83	South Dakota	0	0
Iowa	5	13	Tennessee	38	177
Kansas	5	19	Texas	29	475
Kentucky	41	62	Utah	0	3
Louisiana	64	701	Vermont	0	1
Maine	0	0	Virgin Islands	NA*	39
Maryland	43	176	Virginia	36	250
Massachusetts	8	31	Washington	4	24
Michigan	110	340	West Virginia	1	21
Minnesota	8	18	Wisconsin	7	31
Mississippi	81	897	Wyoming	1	0
Missouri	65	196			
Montana	0	0	**TOTAL**	**1,469**	**9,040**

*No Available data was gathered for Virgin Islands in 1970   Source: JCPES

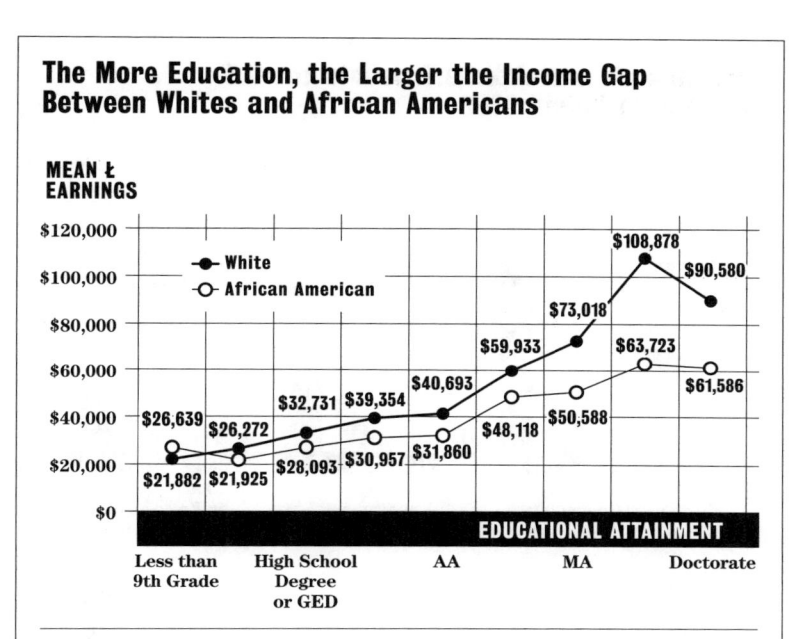

The More Education, the Larger the Income Gap Between Whites and African Americans

MEAN ₤ EARNINGS

Educational Attainment	White	African American
Less than 9th Grade	$21,882	$26,639
9th-12th Grade	$26,272	$21,925
High School Degree or GED	$32,731	$28,093
Some College	$39,354	$30,957
AA	$40,693	$31,860
BA	$59,933	$48,118
MA	$73,018	$50,588
Professional	$108,878	$63,723
Doctorate	$90,580	$61,586

Source: Frederick D. Patterson Research Institute 2001 Analysis of Current Population Survey 2000 Data, U.S. Census Bureau. **Note:** At the lowest level of education (less than 9th grade), African Americans earn more than whites. However, beginning with a 9th-12th grade education and continuing through a professional degree, whites earn increasingly more money than African Americans. At the doctorate level, the earnings gap narrows, but only slightly.

Appendix II

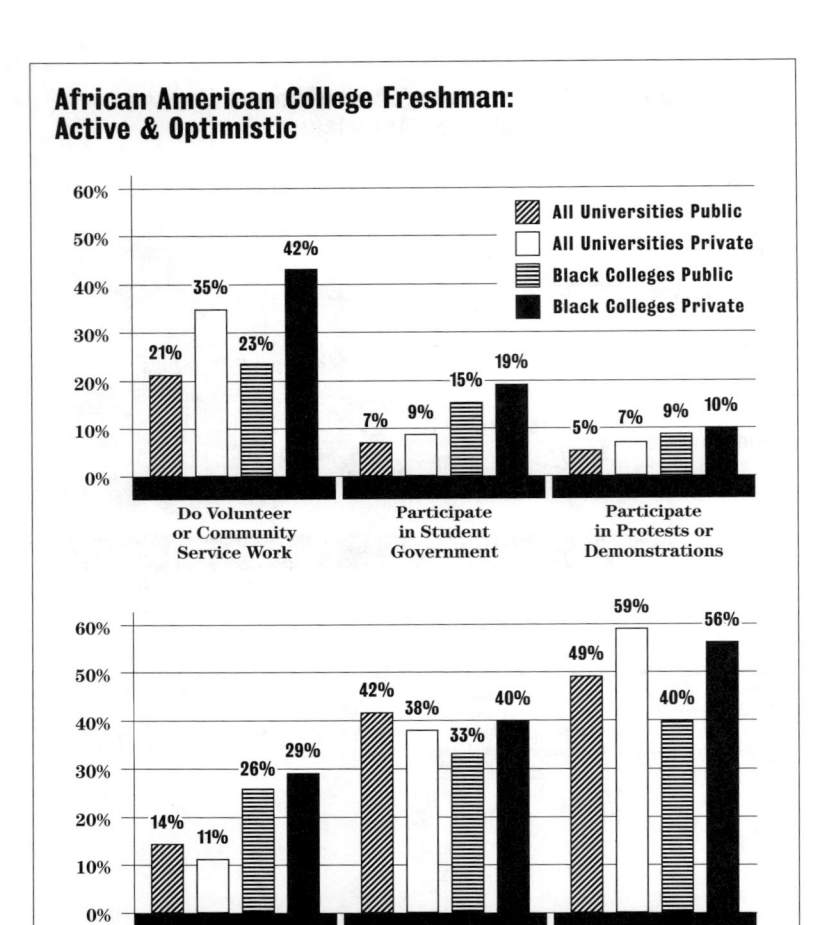

African American College Freshman: Active & Optimistic

Legend:
- All Universities Public
- All Universities Private
- Black Colleges Public
- Black Colleges Private

Category	All Univ. Public	All Univ. Private	Black Colleges Public	Black Colleges Private
Do Volunteer or Community Service Work	21%	35%	23%	42%
Participate in Student Government	7%	9%	15%	19%
Participate in Protests or Demonstrations	5%	7%	9%	10%
Join a Fraternity or Sorority	14%	11%	26%	29%
Get a Job to Pay For College Expenses	42%	38%	33%	40%
Be Satisfied With Your College	49%	59%	40%	56%

Source: The Frederick D. Patterson Research Institute Newsletter, Dec. 2001. Sax, L.J., Astin, A.M. Kom. W.S., & Mahoney, K. M. (2001). *The American Freshmen National: Norms for Fall 2000*. Cooperative Institutional Research Program, Higher Education Research Institute, UCLA and the American Council on Education. **Notes:** Students at private black colleges are more likely than their counterparts at public black colleges and at all other universities to do volunteer or community service, participate in student government, participate in student protests or demonstrations, and join a fraternity or sorority. They are equally likely as students at private institutions to get a job to pay for college expenses and to be satisfied with their college.

African American Educational Attainment Increased by Leaps and Bounds Since 1940

Percent of people 25 years old and over who have completed 4 or more years of high school: 1940-2000

YEAR	TOTAL			WHITE			AFRICAN AMERICAN		
	Total	Male	Female	Total	Male	Female	Total	Male	Female
1940	25%	23%	26%	26%	24%	28%	8%	7%	8%,
1950	34%	33%	36%,	NA	NA	NA	14%	13%	15%
1959	44%	42%	45%	46%	45%	48%	21%	20%	22%
1970	55%	55%	55%	57%	57%	58%	34%	32%	35%
1980	69%	69%	68%	71%	71%	70%	51%	51%	51%
1990	78%	78%	78%	79%	79%	79%	66%	66%	67%
2000	84%	84%	84%	88%	89%	88%	79%	79%	78%

Source: The Frederick D. Patterson Research Institute Newsletter, Dec. 2001. US Census Bureau. **Notes:** •In the early part of this century, it used to be that only a few young people attended school. Those who did were mostly whites, and they often did not even reach the 8th grade. •Between 1940 and 2000, however, the number of whites aged 25 and older who have continued their education through high school has more than doubled (+372%), and the number of African Americans has increased by an incredible 2460%!

Appendix II

Characteristics of Poor Children in America: 2000

	NUMBER POOR (in thousands)	% POOR
Total	11,633	16.2%
White	7,328	13.0
Non-Hispanic White	4,222	9.4
Black	3,526	30.9
Asian and Pacific Islander	459	14.5
Hispanic (May Be Any Race)	3,330	28.0
Mexican American	2,554	29.9
Puerto Rican	280	29.7
Central City	5,049	24.4
Suburb	4,185	10.8
Rural (Non-metropolitan)	2,399	19.2
Northeast	1,913	14.1
Midwest	2,253	13.8
South	4,413	17.8
West	3,055	17.7
Related to Head of Household	11,086	15.7
In Married Couple Family	4,271	8.2
In Female Headed Family	6,121	39.8
In Male Headed Family	694	20.4

Source: Children's Defense Fund, 2002

School Enrollment

Public elementary and secondary school enrollment in grades K-12 (in thousands), by grade level, with projections: Fall 1965-2011

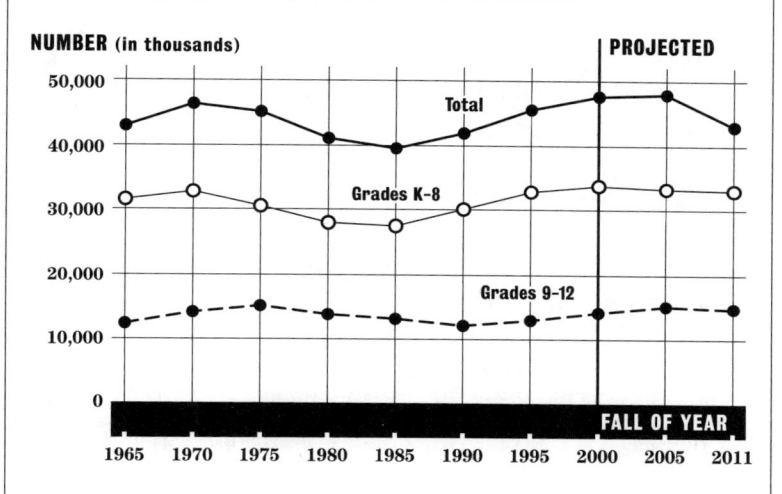

Note: Includes most kindergarten and some nursery school enrollment. Source: U.S. Department of Education, NCES. Common Core of Data (CCD), various years, and (2001) *Projections of Education Statistics to 2011* (NCES 2001-083).

Appendix **II**

Enrollment in Early Childhood Education Programs

Percentage of children ages 3-5 who were enrolled in center-based early childhood care and education programs, by child and family characteristics: Selected years 1991-2001

RACE/ETHNICITY	1991	1993	1995	1996	1999	2001
White	54.0	53.5	56.9	57.1	60.0	59.0
Black	58.3	57.3	59.5	64.7	73.2	63.7
Hispanic	38.8	42.8	37.4	39.4	44.2	39.8
POVERTY STATUS						
Below poverty	44.2	43.3	45.1	43.8	51.4	46.7
At or above poverty	55.7	56.0	58.8	59.1	62.3	59.1
POVERTY STATUS AND RACE/ETHNICITY						
Below poverty						
White	41.0	39.6	43.4	39.4	43.2	46.1
Black	55.4	53.2	54.9	60.9	72.2	60.1
Hispanic	34.4	37.2	30.1	32.6	41.2	36.2
At or above poverty						
White	56.4	56.0	59.6	60.3	62.6	60.8
Black	61.8	62.6	66.1	69.0	74.1	66.2
Hispanic	42.2	48.1	43.8	45.1	46.8	42.4

Note: Estimates are based on children who had not entered kindergarten. Center-based programs include day care centers, Head Start, preschool, nursery school, prekindergarten, and other early childhood programs. Children without mothers in the home are not included in estimates concerning mother's education or mother's employment status. **Source:** U.S. Department of Education, NCES. National Household Education Surveys Program (NHES), "Parent Interview" survey, various years.

Past and Projected Elementary and Secondary School Enrollments

Public elementary and secondary school enrollment in grades K-12 (in thousands), by grade level, with projections: Fall 1965-2011

FALL OF YEAR	TOTAL	GRADES K-8	GRADES 9-12
1990	41,217	29,878	11,338
2000	47,051	33,545*	13,506
2005	47,536	33,091	14,445
2010	47,131	33,034	14,096

* Projected

Status Dropout Rates, by Race/Ethnicity

Status dropout rates and number and percentage distribution of dropouts ages 16-24, by selected characteristics: October 2000

CHARACTERISTIC	STATUS DROPOUT RATE (percent)	NUMBER OF STATUS DROPOUTS (thousands)	POPULATION (thousands)	PERCENT OF ALL DROPOUTS
Total	10.9	3,776	34,568	100.0
SEX				
Male	12.0	2,082	17,402	55.1
Female	9.9	1,694	17,166	44.9
RACE/ETHNICITY[1]				
White	6.9	1,564	22,574	41.4
Black	13.1	663	5,058	17.6
Hispanic	27.8	1,456	5,237	38.6
Asian/Pacific Islander	3.8	54	1,417	1.4

[1] Due to relatively small sample sizes, American Indians/Alaska Natives are included in the total but are not shown separately. **Note:** Percentages may not add to 100.0 due to rounding. Details may not add to totals due to rounding. **Source:** U.S. Department of Commerce, Bureau of the Census, October Current Population Survey, 2000.

Appendix II

Racial/Ethnic Distribution of Public School Students
Percentage distribution of public school students enrolled in grades K-12 who were minorities, by region: October 1972-2000

OCTOBER	WHITE	MINORITY ENROLLMENT — SOUTH			
		TOTAL	BLACK	HISPANIC	OTHER
1972	69.7	30.3	24.8	5.0	0.5
1973	69.6	30.4	24.8	5.0	0.6
1974	67.8	32.2	25.6	6.1	0.5
1975	67.4	32.6	25.2	6.6	0.7
1976	67.1	32.9	25.7	6.3	0.9
1977	67.5	32.5	26.3	5.5	0.6
1978	66.4	33.6	26.3	6.2	1.1
1979	68.6	31.4	24.6	6.0	0.8
1980	64.6	35.4	25.8	8.2	1.4
1981	64.1	35.9	25.9	8.5	1.4
1982	64.1	35.9	26.9	7.9	1.1
1983	63.9	36.1	26.0	8.6	1.5
1984	66.0	34.0	24.7	7.5	1.8
1985	63.4	36.6	25.9	8.8	2.0
1986	62.2	37.8	26.6	9.0	2.2
1987	61.9	38.1	26.3	9.6	2.2
1988	62.2	37.8	25.0	10.5	2.3
1989	61.7	38.3	26.1	9.9	2.4
1990	59.9	40.1	27.4	10.6	2.1
1991	59.5	40.5	27.7	10.3	2.5
1992	59.5	40.5	27.2	10.5	2.7
1993	60.1	39.9	26.4	10.7	2.8
1994	59.2	40.8	26.2	12.4	2.2
1995	59.0	41.0	27.0	12.1	1.8
1996	57.7	42.3	26.9	12.6	2.8
1997	57.0	43.0	27.0	13.4	2.6
1998	56.0	44.0	28.1	13.1	2.9
1999	55.3	44.7	26.9	14.8	3.0
2000	55.1	44.9	25.6	16.0	3.2

Note: Percentages may not add to 100.0 due to rounding. **Source:** U.S. Department of Commerce, Bureau of the Census. October Current Population Surveys. 1972-2000.

WHITE	MINORITY ENROLLMENT — WEST			
	TOTAL	BLACK	HISPANIC	OTHER
72.8	27.2	6.4	15.3	5.5
74.1	25.9	6.2	14.4	5.2
72.7	27.3	6.8	14.9	5.6
72.0	28.0	7.0	14.8	6.3
72.9	27.1	7.1	14.8	5.2
72.2	27.8	6.7	14.8	6.3
71.4	28.6	6.8	15.2	6.6
70.0	30.0	7.8	15.7	6.6
66.9	33.1	6.6	20.5	6.0
66.5	33.5	6.8	18.5	8.1
65.2	34.8	5.4	19.9	9.5
63.9	36.1	5.5	20.4	10.3
63.8	36.2	6.8	19.6	9.8
64.1	35.9	6.4	20.6	8.9
62.5	37.5	6.1	22.0	9.4
60.3	39.7	7.1	22.9	9.7
60.3	39.7	6.5	22.7	10.5
59.4	40.6	6.1	24.9	9.6
59.0	41.0	5.5	25.1	10.4
59.0	41.0	5.8	25.5	9.7
58.5	41.5	5.8	26.3	9.3
58.7	41.3	6.1	25.9	9.3
58.4	41.6	5.7	27.5	8.5
57.0	43.0	5.5	29.6	7.9
52.8	47.2	5.2	29.4	12.6
52.1	47.9	6.5	29.4	12.1
51.9	48.1	6.8	30.1	11.2
52.7	47.3	5.7	30.6	11.0
51.1	48.9	5.9	31.6	11.4

Appendix II

Educational Attainment with Some College

Percentage of 25- to 29-year-olds with some college,
by race/ethnicity and sex: March 1971-2000

MARCH	ALL*			WHITE		
	TOTAL	MALE	FEMALE	TOTAL	MALE	FEMALE
1971	33.9	38.5	29.4	36.7	41.7	31.8
1990	44.5	43.7	45.3	48.3	47.3	49.3
2001	58.4	54.4	62.5	64.8	60.5	69.1

MARCH	BLACK			HISPANIC		
	TOTAL	MALE	FEMALE	TOTAL	MALE	FEMALE
1971	18.2	16.5	19.5	14.8	19.6	10.4
1990	36.1	35.0	36.9	23.3	22.9	23.9
2001	50.5	46.7	53.6	32.2	28.3	36.3

* Included in the totals but not shown separately are other racial/ethnic categories. **Note:** "Some college" also includes those with a bachelor's degree or higher, The Current Population Survey (CPS) questions used to obtain educational attainment were changed in 1992. In 1994, the survey instrument for the CPS was changed and weights were adjusted. **Source:** U.S. Department of Commerce, Bureau of the Census. March Current Population Surveys, 1971-2001.

Educational Attainment with Bachelor's Degree or Higher

Percentage of 25- to 29-year-olds with a bachelor's degree or higher,
by race/ethnicity and sex: March 1971-2000

MARCH	ALL*			WHITE		
	TOTAL	MALE	FEMALE	TOTAL	MALE	FEMALE
1971	17.1	20.4	13.8	18.9	22.4	15.4
1990	23.2	23.7	22.8	26.4	26.6	26.2
2001	28.7	26.2	31.1	33.0	29.7	36.3

MARCH	BLACK			HISPANIC		
	TOTAL	MALE	FEMALE	TOTAL	MALE	FEMALE
1971	6.7	6.9	6.6	5.1	7.9	2.7
1990	13.4	15.2	11.9	8.2	7.3	9.1
2001	17.9	17.9	17.8	11.1	9.1	13.2

* Included in the totals but not shown separately are other racial/ethnic categories.
Note: The Current Population Survey (CPS) questions used to obtain educational attainment were changed in 1992. In 1994, the survey instrument for the CPS was changed and weights were adjusted. **Source:** U.S. Department of Commerce, Bureau of the Census. March Current Population Surveys, 1971-2001.

Colleges and Universities With the Nation's Highest Black Student Graduation Rates, 2000

(Ranked by the Highest Black Graduation Rate)

INSTITUTION	BLACK STUDENT GRADUATION RATE, 2000
Harvard University	92%
Amherst College	92
Vassar College	91
Princeton University	90
Haverford College	89
Brown University	88
Yale University	87
Duke University	86
University of Virginia	86
Williams College	86
Colgate University	85
Dartmouth College	85
Northwestern University	84
Stanford University	84
Washington University	84
Wellesley College	84

Source: NCAA. *The Journal of Blacks in Higher Education*, Spring 2002, No. 35, p.10.

Appendix II

The Percentage of All College and University Faculty Who Are Black Dropped From 6.5 Percent in 1999 to 6.1 Percent in 2001

Percentage of All Employed College and University Teachers in the United States Who Are Black

PERCENT

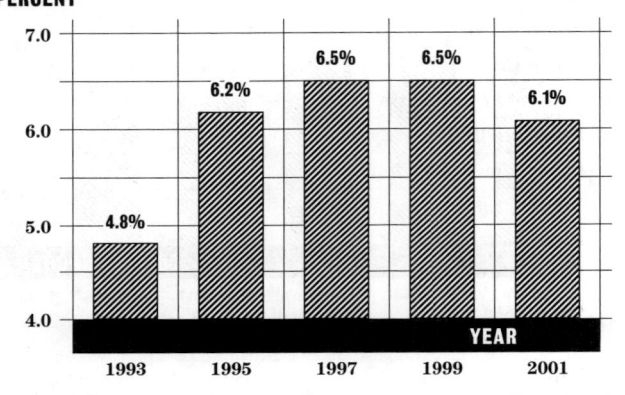

Year	Percent
1993	4.8%
1995	6.2%
1997	6.5%
1999	6.5%
2001	6.1%

Source: U.S. Department of Labor. *The Journal of Blacks in Higher Education*, Spring 2002, No. 35, p.12.

Blacks Make Up a Large Percentage of Student Athletes in Every Major College Sport Except Baseball

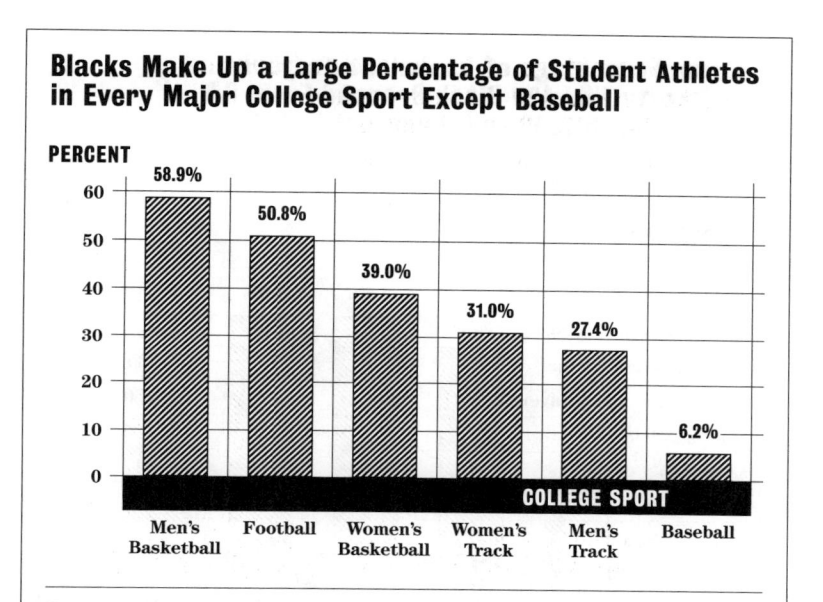

PERCENT

- Men's Basketball: 58.9%
- Football: 50.8%
- Women's Basketball: 39.0%
- Women's Track: 31.0%
- Men's Track: 27.4%
- Baseball: 6.2%

COLLEGE SPORT

Note: Data is for students on athletic scholarships at all 321 NCAA Division I colleges and universities. **Source:** National Collegiate Athletic Association – *The Journal of Blacks in Higher Education,* Spring 2002, No. 35, p.38.

Appendix II

Graduation Rates of Basketball Players at the Nation's 20 Highest-Ranked Men's Basketball Powerhouses*

(Ranked by Highest Black Graduation Rate)

INSTITUTION	WHITE RATE	BLACK RATE	DIFFERENCE
Stanford University	100 %	100%	0
Duke University	67	80	+13
University of Kansas	67	75	+8
University of Virginia	100	70	-30
Oklahoma State University	17	67	+50
Gonzaga University	25	60	+35
University of Illinois	33	50	+17
University of Miami	100	50	-50
Univ. of Southern California	NA	40	NA
Wake Forest University	33	36	+3
NATIONAL AVERAGE (Men's Basketball)	**52**	**35**	
University of Kentucky	100	29	-71
University of Georgia	67	25	-42
UCLA	100	22	-78
University of Alabama	67	17	-50
University of Florida	100	14	-86
University of Maryland	50	11	-39
University of Arizona	33	8	-25
University of Cincinnati	20	0	-20
University of Oklahoma	0	0	0
Syracuse University	100	0	-100

NA – There were too few white basketball players on athletic scholarship to make a meaningful statistical analysis. * As ranked by ESPN/USA *Today* (1-30-02)
Source: NCAA – *The Journal of Blacks in Higher Education*, Spring 2002, No. 35, p.39.

Graduation Rates of Basketball Players at the Nation's 20 Highest-Ranked Women's Basketball Powerhouses*

(Ranked by Highest Black Graduation Rate)

INSTITUTION	WHITE RATE	BLACK RATE	DIFFERENCE
Duke University	75%	100%	+25
Vanderbilt University	88	100	+12
University of Texas	56	100	+44
Baylor University	64	100	+36
University of Wisconsin	100	100	0
Virginia Tech	83	78	-5
University of Georgia	50	75	+25
University of Colorado	60	75	+15
University of Connecticut	64	75	+11
Iowa State University	67	67	0
Colorado State University	63	60	-3
Louisiana Tech University	80	60	-20
Texas Tech University	100	60	-40
University of Tennessee	80	57	-23
NATIONAL AVERAGE (Women's Basketball)	70	55	-15
Stanford University	100	50	-50
University of Florida	50	50	0
University of South Carolina	100	50	-50
University of Oklahoma	50	45	-5
Purdue University	57	38	-19
Kansas State University	64	0	-64

* As ranked by ESPN/USA *Today*, January 30, 2002. **Source:** NCAA – *The Journal of Blacks in Higher Education*, Spring 2002, No. 35, p.39.

Appendix **II**

Graduation Rates of Black Students and Student Athletes at Historically Black Colleges and Universities

(Ranked by the Difference in Graduation Rates for Black Athletes Compared to All Black Students)

INSTITUTION	ALL BLACK STUDENTS	BLACK ATHLETES	DIFFERENCE
Grambling State University	31%	58%	+27
Norfolk State University	22	42	+20
Howard University	48	66	+18
Texas Southern University	10	28	+18
Delaware State University	29	40	+11
Southern University	22	32	+10
Alcorn State University	40	49	+9
Alabama State University	21	29	+8
Morgan State University	39	45	+6
Hampton University	53	58	+5
Tennessee State University	40	45	+5
North Carolina A&T State Univ.	44	47	+3
Alabama A&M University	36	38	+2
Jackson State University	30	31	+1
Florida A&M University	44	33	-11

Source: NCAA – *The Journal of Blacks in Higher Education,* Spring 2002, No. 35,

Employment in the Year 2002:
Blacks Continue to Hold the Low Ground

Despite Major Gains in Education, African Americans Continue to Have a Very Large Percentage of Low-Paying Service Jobs While Whites Continue to Dominate High-Paying Professional Positions

THE WHITEST JOBS		THE BLACKEST JOBS	
OCCUPATION	**% BLACK**	**OCCUPATION**	**% BLACK**
Airline pilots	0.6%	Postal clerks	35.5%
Geologists	1.9	Orderlies	32.7
Physical therapists	2.5	Security guards	32.1
Biologists	3.0	Garbage collectors	30.8
Aerospace engineers	3.0	Welfare services aides	30.2
Architects	3.1	Pressing machine operators	29.0
Advertising executives	3.7	Bus drivers	28.6
Designers	3.9	Parking lot attendants	27.9
Veterinarians	4.0	Prison guards	26.8
Dentists	4.1	Meter readers	24.3
Mechanical engineers	4.2	Barbers	23.6
Insurance underwriters	5.4	Bill collectors	22.9

Source: *The Journal of Blacks in Higher Education*, Spring 2002, No. 35, p.82.

Appendix II

Black Student Athletes Graduate at a Rate Higher Than Black Students as a Whole*

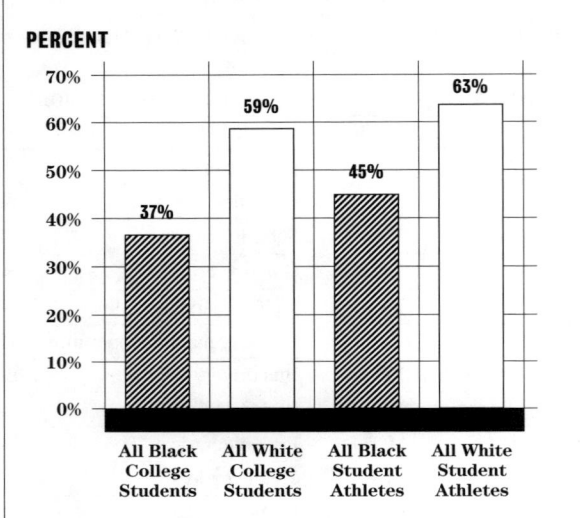

PERCENT

- All Black College Students: 37%
- All White College Students: 59%
- All Black Student Athletes: 45%
- All White Student Athletes: 63%

* Students on athletic scholarships at all 321 NCAA Division I colleges and universities. Rates are for students entering college in the 1991 to 1994 period and graduating within six years of matriculation. **Source:** National Collegiate Athletic Association – *The Journal of Blacks in Higher Education*, Spring 2002, No. 35, p.36.

appendix III

Special Research Report: Negative Effects of TANF on College Enrollment

This special research report was prepared by Kenya L.C. Cox, Research Analyst, and William E. Spriggs, Ph.D., Director, National Urban League Institute for Opportunity and Equality, Washington, D.C.

This special research report was prepared with the generous support of the Joyce Foundation

FOREWORD

In 1996, when the Personal Responsibility and Work Opportunity Reconciliation Act (PRWORA) passed, high school graduates who were recipients of the old Aid to Families with Dependent Children (AFDC) were 13 percent more likely to attend college than other poor women. In less than two years, under the new Temporary Assistance to Needy Families (TANF) program, welfare recipients were 7 percent less likely than other poor women to go to college. That is a 20-point swing to the disadvantage of welfare recipients. Nearly half of welfare recipients are high school graduates, so this is not an inconsequential policy effect. Further, according to the U.S. Census Bureau, in 2000, a woman without a high school degree earned $9,996, a woman with a high school diploma earned an average of $15,119 and an Associate's degree earned her $23,269. In contrast, a woman who earned a Bachelor's degree received $30,487, more than twice the earnings of a high school graduate. It would appear that reversing the negative effect of TANF on college enrollment would be a high priority, and that studying the policies that generated the negative outcome would also be a high priority.

This study, by Kenya Cox, a research analyst with the National Urban

Appendix III

League Institute for Opportunity and Equality, and William Spriggs, the Institute's Director, finds that state policies that limited TANF recipients' access to college by not counting it as a valid "work" activity significantly reduced the college enrollment of African-American TANF recipients. Increased hours spent working also lowered college enrollment, apparently accounting for much of the reduction in college attendance for welfare recipients. The results are robust, even when we control for differences in family size and differences in in-state community college tuition costs, there is a statistically significant switch so that women receiving TANF become less likely to attend college. Our findings show it is important for states to have the flexibility to allow college attendance, without limits placed on welfare recipients, and to count college credits as a legitimate work effort, to encourage college enrollment among TANF recipients.

One role for public policy analysts is to provide information for making smart decisions, not just politically driven decisions. That is the role the National Urban League Institute for Opportunity and Equality assumes in this report. Passions run high in debating welfare. In this debate, it is best to let the data speak. The early success of TANF in achieving job placements appears easy to understand. If a large share of college-ready women were pushed out of attending college and forced to compete with high school graduates for low wage jobs, then of course the TANF roles could fall, and former recipients receive jobs. But, the long run costs of that strategy is a massive under-investment in the skills of TANF recipients that will permanently lower their lifetime earnings, and at a time when the nation suffers from teacher and nursing shortages, perhaps deprive us all of the skilled work force we need. Perhaps more important is the long run effect on the recipients children, because we know the differences in life chances for children whose parents are better educated—better students, better health, and the list goes on. Policy makers would do well to understand the full implications of policies, where data clearly show negative effects.

Hugh B. Price
PRESIDENT, NATIONAL URBAN LEAGUE

EXECUTIVE SUMMARY

Despite reports that the Personal Responsibility Work Opportunity Reconciliation Act (PRWORA) of 1996 has been successful, this report shows that it has negative effects on TANF recipients' access to college. College enrollment at institutions TANF recipients predominantly attend, tell the story. For example, enrollment of welfare recipients at the City University of New York decreased from 27,000 in 1995 to 5,000 in 2000, indicating a drop of about 81.5 percent.

This report focuses on the impact (PRWORA) has had on the college enrollment of welfare recipients. Moreover, the study seeks to explain lower college enrollment rates among recipients in the post TANF period by examining the impact of specific state policies toward postsecondary education. State welfare policies under TANF placed limits on TANF recipients' access to college by not counting it as a valid "work" activity. This study found that these limits significantly reduced the college enrollment of welfare recipients, and especially that of African-American TANF recipients.

Data used for this study came from the 1997 and 1999 waves of the Urban Institute's National Survey of America's Families; this data reaffirms the trend seen at CUNY. Nationally, welfare recipients are attending college less after the passage of PRWORA; there has been approximately a 20-point drop in the college enrollment of all welfare recipients, relative to other poor women who were not recipients, and a 16-point drop for African-American recipients, over the first two years of TANF.

Clearly what was at work was not simply the passage of time, but a change in a set of policy variables that affected welfare recipients. We modeled those state policy variables that directly impacted college attendance by running logistic regression models and using college attendance as the dependent dichotomous variable. The focus was on those states that did not allow postsecondary education as a work activity and those states that limited the duration they would count college as a work activity. Many of the state TANF programs discourage college enrollment; in 1998, 25 states did not allow welfare recipients to count any time taking college courses toward their work requirement.

Appendix **III**

The result of our empirical research indicates that on average, state policies account for 13 percent of the drop in the probability that welfare recipients would enroll in college relative to other poor women after implementation of TANF. Overall, there is a substantial and statistically significant lowering of the odds that TANF recipients attend college after the implementation of TANF compared to pre TANF. Moreover, the decline in the probability of college attendance for TANF recipients occurred while there was, otherwise, an increase in college attendance among poor women. The most disturbing part of our finding was that African-American welfare recipients who reside in states with strict "work first" TANF programs are most affected.

This data cover a short period, only two years after welfare reform. Yet, they are able to show a dramatic decline in the probability of welfare recipients pursuing college. Given the current shortage of teachers and nurses, and computer technicians in America, this is an unintended consequence we all lose from. The talent pool within the welfare population is more diverse than is commonly recognized. So, it would be counterproductive to adopt a one-size-fits-all policy that limits the ability of states to design flexible programs that recognize it is important to maximize the lifetime earnings of welfare recipients.

INTRODUCTION

The purpose of this study is to determine what effect passage of the Personal Responsibility and Work Opportunity Reconciliation Act (PRWORA) has on the college enrollment of welfare recipients who have earned a high school diploma. Because nearly half of welfare recipients are high school graduates, this is an important effect to research. Two key effects are examined. First, a new social policy environment has evolved due to the fundamental change in social welfare policy, the removal of the entitlement status of welfare has limited the options of poor women who receive welfare to choose their own paths to self-sufficiency by increasing sanctions for choosing human capital development over immediately choosing work, and therefore under-investing in human capital. And, second, because of the discretion allowed by caseworkers without any checks for practices that discriminate, minority welfare recipients will be less likely than other poor women to pursue postsecondary education in states with aggressive "work-first" policies.

The imminent TANF reauthorization makes this question particularly important. Now is the opportunity to correct ineffective policy, or unintended consequences, so poor women can truly achieve financial independence. Using data from the Urban Institute's National Survey of American Families, our findings indicate how important it is for states to have the flexibility to allow college attendance, without limits placed on welfare recipients, and to count college credits as legitimate work effort, to encourage college enrollment among TANF recipients.

College enrollment of welfare recipients under AFDC and TANF indicate lower enrollment rates for welfare recipients in the post welfare reform period. For instance, since 1995, enrollment of welfare recipients at the City University of New York decreased from 27,000 in 1995 to 5,000 in 2000 (see Figure 1), a drop of about 81.5 percent (Applied Research Center, 2001). Data from the Urban Institute's National Survey of America's Families 1997 and 1999, which is used for this study, reaffirms the trend seen at CUNY. Nationally, welfare recipients are attending college less after the passage of PRWORA.

The result of our estimation shows a substantial and statistically significant lowering of the odds of TANF recipients to attend college in 1998 compared to 1996. Our model shows that, relative to other poor women who were also high school graduates, and who had similar sized families, that TANF and AFDC recipients were significantly more likely to attend college in 1996. Moreover, the decline in the probability of college attendance for TANF recipients occurred while there was, otherwise, an increase in college attendance among poor women. The most disturbing part of our finding was that college enrollment of African-American recipients is most affected by the change in state policy, where recipients are not allowed to count time spent taking college courses as a work activity.

The fact that education builds individuals' self worth is unquestioned. Yet, when poor women who are attached to the welfare system seek a college education but are limited or prohibited by the implementation of

Appendix III

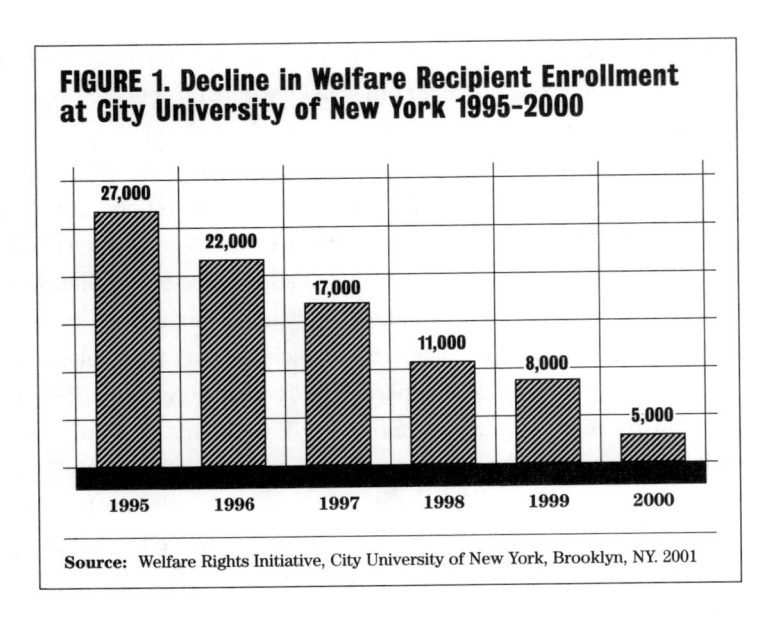

FIGURE 1. Decline in Welfare Recipient Enrollment at City University of New York 1995-2000

Year	Enrollment
1995	27,000
1996	22,000
1997	17,000
1998	11,000
1999	8,000
2000	5,000

Source: Welfare Rights Initiative, City University of New York, Brooklyn, NY. 2001

welfare reform policies, the obvious is ignored; more so than any other group, poor mothers need to build their human capital. Their low-income status stems from low wage earning capacity, more than the lack of work effort. They, especially, need to increase their chances of finding high wage jobs that are far more likely to be full time, and include health benefits and sick leave.

The correlation between education attainment and poverty reduction is well documented. The poverty rate of minority households substantially decreased by half after women heads of household attained only one year of postsecondary education (Sherman, 1990). Additional research examining the magnitude by which education can reduce the poverty status of women indicates that women with more postsecondary education were not likely to return to welfare rolls and most likely to escape poverty (Meyer and Cancian, 1997).

According to the U.S. Census Bureau, in 2000, a woman without a high school degree earned $9,996, a high school degree earned an average of $15,119 and an Associate's degree earned her $23,269. In contrast, a woman who earned a Bachelor's degree received $30,487, more than three times the earnings of a high school dropout (see Figure 2) (U.S. Census Bureau, 2001). This data indicates that attaining more education has incremental effects on the financial well being of working women.

The "work-first" philosophy currently underpinning federal welfare policy and a number of state TANF programs assumes a one-size-fits-all policy approach. This philosophy fails to consider the importance of educational attainment in promoting the economic well being of poor families. Research shows that better educated individuals are more likely to access better paying jobs, less likely to return to poverty, and more likely to have high-achieving children. Under AFDC, some recipients used their benefits to help subsidize their efforts to pursue postsecondary education opportunities and balance the responsibilities of parenthood.

Various researchers provide insight into welfare and education or training (APA, 1998; Bell, 2000). It is widely understood that education is key in reaching economic independence; this is especially true for minorities and women. Moreover, evidence shows that welfare recipients under AFDC were more likely to seek and receive training and education than

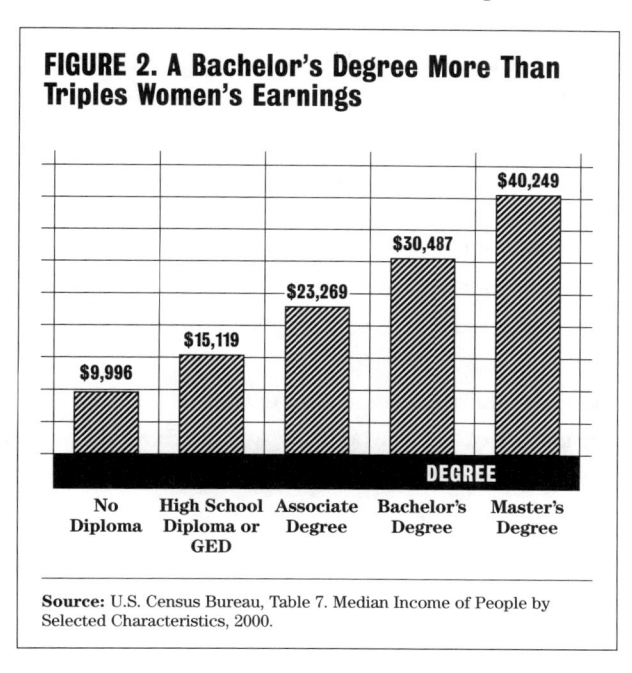

FIGURE 2. A Bachelor's Degree More Than Triples Women's Earnings

Degree	Earnings
No Diploma	$9,996
High School Diploma or GED	$15,119
Associate Degree	$23,269
Bachelor's Degree	$30,487
Master's Degree	$40,249

Source: U.S. Census Bureau, Table 7. Median Income of People by Selected Characteristics, 2000.

the general adult population (Bell, 2000). However, what is lacking in the research is an empirical investigation of the (PRWORA) policy impacts on the postsecondary educational attainment of welfare recipients. This kind of study is necessary to assess the effectiveness of PRWORA in promoting the development of human capital in TANF recipients in ways that truly boost their economic independence.

BACKGROUND AND PREVIOUS RESEARCH

Presently, federal welfare law requires that 50 percent of single-parent families and 90 percent of two-parent families receiving TANF be engaged in a work activity. Single-parent families are required to work 30 hours per week, however, if they have a child younger than six years old then the requirement drops to 20 hours a week. Two parent recipient families have slightly different requirements, they are required to work a minimum of 35 hours per week but if an infant of 12 months or less is in the household they are exempted from the work requirements.

New TANF reauthorization proposals in Washington, DC, including many being pushed forward in the House of Representatives and the Senate suggest setting work participation rates at 70 percent for all families receiving TANF and increasing the work requirement to 40 hours per week (Lyter, Oh and Lovell, 2002). Under these plans, the 40 hours can be divided into 24 hours of direct work and 16 hours of other constructive activities related to work or skill building, states define what is acceptable. In addition, although parents with infants would continue to be exempt from the work requirements, parents with children younger than six would see an increase in their required work participation to 40 hours per week.

There is anecdotal evidence of the detrimental impact that welfare reform, particularly of the type being pushed which would increase work at the expense of developing earning potential, has had on welfare recipients' ability to take college courses. College enrollment of welfare recipients under AFDC and TANF indicate lower enrollment rates for welfare recipients in the post welfare reform period. For instance, since 1995, enrollment of welfare recipients at the City University of New York decreased from 27,000 in 1995 to 5,000 in 2000, a drop of about 81.5 percent (Applied Research Center, 2002). This individual college enrollment trend raises the need to further investigate college enrollment of TANF recipients.

Generally, recipients complain that required work time constraints and other miscellaneous mandatory activities force them to interrupt their college education. Many recipients have voiced their concern about the amount of control welfare offices have over their time. Many activities seem to be counterproductive and do not appear to boost financial independence. One welfare recipient remarks, "when we could be caring for our children, looking for work that pays a living wage, or going to school, we are forced instead to deal with requirements for filling out papers; certification meetings after certification meeting; make work workfare placements; poorly planned academic classes and "dress for success" or weight loss classes; and jobs that pay us low wages for six months then fire us so that they can get another government tax credit (Applied Research Center, 2002)."

* The Importance of College Education to Poor Women's Economic Independence

The "work first" approach ignores important studies that chronicle amazing economic, personal, and familial success of women who have overcome barriers to complete their college education and obtain jobs that pay a decent living wage. These jobs provide access to health care, childcare and wealth building opportunities. Higher education has been one of the most promising pathways out of poverty. Although education does not eliminate racial and gender discrimination in the job market, the gap between the pay of women and men decreases with more education (U.S. Census Bureau, 2002). It is difficult for a woman head of household without any college degree to find a stable job that pays enough to support a family on one income. An average family receiving TANF benefits has three members, including two whom are children. The median earnings (meaning only half of all women make more) of a woman with a high school degree are about $15,000, barely above the official poverty thresh-

Appendix III

old for a family of three at 14,229 (U.S. Census Bureau, 2002).

Studies of people leaving welfare document the significant improvements some college has made on minority women's jobs, salaries, finances, family life, and self-esteem. (Gittell, Gross and Holdaway, 1993; Gittell, Schehl and Facri 1990; Johnson, 1991; Kates 1991). Survey results in six states reaffirm what we already know about the effects of education on poverty. Results of a 1990 survey administered in New York State indicated that 88 percent of welfare respondents who returned to college and graduated had been employed since graduation; over half were earning $20,000 and 7 percent were earning over $30,000 (Gittell, Schehl and Facri, 1990). Similarly, in Illinois, Tennessee, Pennsylvania, Washington and Wyoming, on average of 81 percent of females who graduated from college were continuously employed after graduation (Gittell, Gross and Holdaway, 1993). Those who completed a 4-year degree were the most likely to have left welfare for stable employment and adequate earnings to support a family.

Furthermore, research focusing on the impact of postsecondary education on the well being of minorities shows that with one year of postsecondary education minority women were able to decrease their poverty by half. African-American women with at least one year of postsecondary education as compared to high school graduates decreased their poverty from 51 percent to 21 percent, and Latina women decreased from 41 percent to 18.5 percent (Sherman, 1990). White women who achieved one year of postsecondary education realized smallest decreases; the drop in poverty was only 9 percent.

Postsecondary education provides the most effective means by which welfare recipients can become self sufficient through financial independence. Important players in the 2002 reauthorization of PRWORA should be encouraged to make welfare more effective at increasing families' economic independence. Evidence that current policy is not achieving the impact necessary for true economic independence abound. One-report shows, even five years after leaving the welfare rolls, nearly 80 percent of women are still raising their children in poverty (Kates, 1991).

* Unintended Consequences of Welfare Reform

More welfare recipients are eligible for postsecondary education than the public is led to believe (Bane and Ellwood, 1994). In fact, nearly half of welfare recipients have graduated from high school or obtained a General Equivalency Diploma (GED) (Center on Budget and Policy Priorities, 1993). Despite the desire and capacity to participate in postsecondary education, many welfare recipients under the new welfare reform law are discouraged from participating because of two factors: 1) states require recipients to work more and 2) states have elected to implement TANF programs that do not allow recipients to count time spent taking college courses toward their work requirement.

In order to receive benefits, students on welfare must get a job, even if the job causes them to drop out of school (APA, 1998). While everyone is pushing the theme of a better-educated workforce, too many caseworkers are telling welfare recipients to find jobs and drop out of college. It is estimated that community colleges will lose up to 60 percent of their welfare students as states are mandated to put larger proportions of their caseloads to work (Ritter, 1997). These trends are likely to continue if the Congress enacts welfare reauthorization that calls for a 40-hour workweek by 70 percent of the rolls.

Evidence suggests that work requirements under TANF result in mothers on TANF working more than mothers typically work in the general population. The Institute for Women's Policy Research analyzed mothers' work experience as reported for the year 2000. They find that only 36 percent of all mothers work year-round at 40 or more hours per week. The average number of hours mothers worked per week is less than 40; they work an estimated 30.9 hours a week (Lyter, Oh and Lovell, 2002).

Furthermore, under TANF, the type of education and training that can count toward work is restricted. The federal government limits education and training to one year. The devolution features of TANF allow states to be more restrictive than the federal law if they see fit. In 1996 about nine states did not count time spent pursuing postsecondary education toward the work requirements and in 1998, twenty-five states did not count it (Urban Institute, 2002).

Appendix III

* State Policies on Postsecondary Education

It is our belief that state policies are important in understanding whether poor women in general pursue postsecondary education and welfare recipients in particular. Many of the state TANF programs discourage college enrollment by refusing to count hours spent studying for college courses toward the work requirement. Some states understand the importance of postsecondary education in developing the human capital of their recipients and have passed policies reflecting this attitude. On the other hand, in 1998 states like California, New York and Pennsylvania, among 22 others, have not passed policies allowing welfare recipients to count education towards work requirements. Two of these three states constitute a large majority of the caseload; clearly limiting access to education in these states will decrease the number of recipients taking college courses.

DATA

Data used for this study came from the 1997 and 1999 waves of the Urban Institute's National Survey of America's Families (NSAF), a nationally representative survey of households that collects a wide range of program participation, economic demographic and program participation data. This data allows us to analyze the effects of both AFDC and TANF policy on the postsecondary educational attainment of welfare recipients. The survey asks questions about whether respondents were welfare recipients last year, so the first wave provides information about recipients in 1996. This data will provide a baseline on welfare recipients' college attainment before the full implementation of PRWORA.

In order to select a similarly situated subset of women to compare, both welfare recipients and women in poverty were identified. Welfare recipients under AFDC and TANF are both included in the analysis. The typical recipient family has one adult and two children. The poverty threshold for a family of three, including two children, in 1996 was $12,641 and in 1998 the poverty threshold was $13,133, women whose household income fell below this threshold were included in the sample. In addition, the age of this group of poor women was narrowed to 18 to 35 year olds. The purpose of narrowing the dataset was to examine the impact of state-level welfare policy pertaining to postsecondary education for those who have the greatest potential to attend college. Typically, in 1998 the majority of female college students were between the ages of 18 and 34; they constitute 75 percent of all female college students.[1]

The NSAF provided all of the individual level household characteristics used as covariates in the analysis, such as: number of family members and number of children younger than 6. It also provided race variables that are used to disaggregate the data to examine separate models for the total sample, African Americans and Latinas. State welfare policies toward postsecondary education are the variables of particular interest. Information to construct state policy welfare variables was obtained from the Urban Institutes' Welfare Rules Database, 1996 and 1998 state rules on postsecondary education were used. Table 1 identifies state policies toward postsecondary education in 1996 and 1998. Five states are highlighted, their total caseload is more than 50 percent of the national welfare caseload. Currently, three of the largest welfare caseload states did not allow recipients to count college toward their work activity requirements.

The focus is on two aspects of welfare reform: 1) federal policy and 2) more detailed state policy. Included in the analysis is a post PRWORA variable and two state level policy variables that pick up whether the state allows postsecondary education to count towards work requirements and states that limit the number of months that they will allow postsecondary education count towards work requirements.

MODEL SPECIFICATION

The model run was a logistic regression, the dependent variable, college enrollment, was operationalized by identifying whether the respondent had attended a college course in the previous year. Because the Urban Institute's NSAF data set oversamples poor people, these regressions were weighted, using a routine devised by the Urban Institute for use in logistic regressions. The model fitted was the following:

$$C[pr(Y=1)] = \beta_0 + \beta_{recipient} + \beta_{post} + \beta_{(recipient*post)} + \beta_{log(cost\ cc)} + \beta_{family\ size} + \varepsilon_i$$

Appendix III

TABLE 1: State Policy on Counting Postsecondary Education Towards the Work Activity Requirement

STATE	1996 COUNTS COLLEGE*	LIMITS COLLEGE**
Alabama	yes	2 year time limit
Alaska	yes	30 month time limit
Arizona	yes	2 year time limit
Arkansas	yes	no limit
California	no	
Colorado	yes	24 month time limit
Connecticut	yes	no limit
Delaware	no	
District of Columbia	yes	2 year time limit
Florida	yes	2 year time limit
Georgia	–	–
Hawaii	yes	no limit
Idaho	yes	4 year time limit
Illinois	yes	no limit
Indiana	yes	24 month time limit
Iowa	yes	30 month time limit for a 2-year degree; 40 months for 3 to 4 year degree
Kansas	yes	no limit
Kentucky	yes	4 year time limit
Louisiana	yes	no limit
Maine	yes	
Maryland	yes	no limit
Massachusetts	–	–
Michigan	no	
Minnesota	yes	no limit
Mississippi	yes	5 year time limit

* States incorporate into their AFDC or TANF program a provision which specifies that time spent pursuing postsecondary education will count towards that state's work activity requirement.
** Of those states that count time spent pursuing postsecondary education towards the work requirement, some elect to impose limitations on the duration of time that postsecondary education will be counted. For instance, numerous states limit the duration to a total of two years.

Source: The Urban Institute's Welfare Rules Database, 1996 and 1998. Note the five states that are highlighted have the largest welfare recipient caseload in both 1996 and 1998.

1998	
COUNTS COLLEGE	**LIMITS COLLEGE**
yes	2 year time limit
yes	no limit
yes	2 year time limit
no	
no	
no	
no	
no	
yes	2 year time limit
no	
yes	Must maintain a C grade point average
no	
no	
yes	1 year time limit
no	
yes	30 months for a 2-year degree; 40 months for 3 to 4 year degree
no	
yes	12 months time limit
no	
yes	12 weeks time limit
yes	24 months time limit
–	–
yes	no limit
no	
no	

continued

Appendix III

TABLE 1 CONTINUED: State Policy on Counting Postsecondary Education Towards the Work Activity Requirement

STATE	1996 COUNTS COLLEGE*	LIMITS COLLEGE**
Missouri	yes	24 months time limit
Montana	yes	no limit
Nebraska	yes	no limit
Nevada	no	
New Hampshire	yes	2 year time limit
New Jersey	yes	no limit
New Mexico	yes	no limit
New York	no	
North Carolina	yes	12 months time limit
North Dakota	yes	no limit
Ohio	yes	24 months time limit
Oklahoma	yes	no limit
Oregon	no	
Pennsylvania	yes	no limit
Rhode Island	yes	no limit
South Carolina	no	
South Dakota	no	
Tennessee	yes	no limit
Texas	yes	24 months time limit
Utah	yes	no limit
Vermont	yes	24 months time limit
Virginia	yes	no limit
Washington	yes	no limit
West Virginia	yes	2 year time limit
Wisconsin	no	4 year time limit for Associate's, 6 year time limit for BA
Wyoming	yes	

* States incorporate into their AFDC or TANF program a provision which specifies that time spent pursuing postsecondary education will count towards that state's work activity requirement.
** Of those states that count time spent pursuing postsecondary education towards the work requirement, some elect to impose limitations on the duration of time that postsecondary education will be counted. For instance, numerous states limit the duration to a total of two years.

Source: The Urban Institute's Welfare Rules Database, 1996 and 1998. Note the five states that are highlighted have the largest welfare recipient caseload in both 1996 and 1998.

1998 COUNTS COLLEGE	LIMITS COLLEGE
yes	24 months time limit
yes	no limit
yes	24 months time limit
no	
no	
yes	no limit
yes	no limit
no	
yes	12 months limit
yes	no limit
yes	24 months time limit
no	
no	
no	
yes	no limit
no	
yes	no limit
no	
yes	24 months time limit
yes	24 months time limit
yes	24 months time limit
no	
no	
no	
yes	no limit
no	

Appendix III

Where C is the variable capturing the response to the college attendance question, Recipient is a dummy variable (=1 if the respondent received AFDC or TANF benefits, =0 other poor women not receiving benefits in that year), POST is a dummy variable (=1 if the observation was after 1997, 0 otherwise), recipient*POST TANF is an interaction term, capturing the affect of being a recipient in the POST TANF period (=1 if a recipient in 1998, 0 otherwise), LOG(COST OF CC) is the natural logarithm of the average cost of in-state tuition for the community colleges in the respondent's state and FAMILY SIZE is the size of the respondents family.

The interaction term (recipient*POST TANF) allows us to perform a "difference-in-difference" look at the policy change brought on by TANF. All women in this sample were poor and high school graduates. In the short period studied, the major change was the institution of state level TANF policies, which had great variation to them. The 1998 variable, in this initial model captures the time change, and with it the policy change, and anything else that might change in such a short period. The interpretation of the interaction term is how did the broad policy change affect the target population of the policy change.

The model was run for a second time, but this time adding a set of state policy variables and covariates. This was done to isolate the specific changes between 1996 and 1998 that could affect college attendance, and to see if the interaction term (recipient*POST TANF) could be "explained" by their addition. Without the specific policy variables, it is impossible to make any reference about the impact of state policy. But, because we have included policy variables specific to 1998, they are correlated with the interaction term. Thus, their addition should lower the value of the interaction term, and also lower its significance as we now "include" the variables that make 1998 unique. Important control variables were also added. This was done to further control for variables that are known to limit women's activities.

$$C\ [pr(Y=1)] = \beta_0 + \beta_{recipient} + \beta_{post} + \beta_{recipient*post} + \beta_{log(cost\ cc)} + \beta_{family\ size} + \Sigma B + \Sigma \delta + \varepsilon_i$$

Where the ΣB symbolizes the state policy variables added, which included two state policy variables, both state policy variables were interacted with whether the respondent was a current welfare recipient: a dummy variable if the respondent's state did not count college toward fulfilling an AFDC or TANF work requirement (=1 if the state had such a policy, 0 otherwise); and a dummy variable if the respondent's state limited the amount of college attendance that could count toward fulfilling an AFDC or TANF work requirement (=1 if the state had such a policy, 0 otherwise).

Where $\Sigma\delta$ symbolizes the additional controls added, which included whether the respondent was a former recipient (intended to ferret out whether the apparent decline in current recipients attendance but increase in poor women's attendance was achieved by former recipients leaving welfare and now showing as poor women enrolled in college), usual hours worked a week by the respondent, and an interaction term to capture whether this had a different effect under TANF, the number of children 5 and younger (because when their children reach 3 in most states they are required to work, but the child is still too young to attend school), and two state policy variables, each interacted with whether the respondent was a current welfare recipient.

Model 2 was run again, but this time adding a set of state dummy variables. We created dummy variables for the five states with the largest welfare caseload in 1999. Recipients in California, New York, Texas, Pennsylvania, and Illinois make-up over half of the national welfare caseload.[2] We included the state dummy variables in the model to control for states with the largest caseloads because recipients in these states may be driving the results. Because of other peculiarities of these states, separately identifying them should make the model estimates more consistent.

$$C[pr(Y=1)] = \beta_0 + \beta_{recipient} + \beta_{post} + \beta_{recipient*post} + \beta_{log(cost\ cc)} + \beta_{family\ size} + \Sigma B + \Sigma\delta + \Sigma\vartheta + \varepsilon_i$$

Where $\Sigma\vartheta$ symbolizes the state dummy variables added.

For the coefficients in the models that are dummy variables, the var-

Appendix III

ious βs, can be used to calculate changes in probabilities by using the following formula:

$$\frac{P \cdot e^B}{(1-P) + P \cdot e^B} - P$$

Where P, is taken as the average (or mean) probability that an AFDC recipient in 1996 attended college compared to other poor women.

RESULTS

Figure 3 shows that initially, AFDC recipients were 13 percentage points more likely to attend college than other poor women in 1996, but this advantage changed in 1998 to a 7 percentage point disadvantage. That is a swing of 20 percentage points. For African Americans, figure 4 shows a similar swing. In 1996 under AFDC, African Americans were approximately 5 percentage points more likely to attend college than poor women but in 1998 this advantage changed and poor women became nearly 11 percentage points more likely than TANF recipients to attend college. This was a 16-percentage point swing. For Latinas the swing was less evident, in both years, 1996 and 1998 welfare recipients were more likely to be enrolled in college than other poor women. However, this group did exhibit a large decrease; in 1996 AFDC recipients were 16.4 percentage points more likely to attend college than other poor women but in 1998 they were only 4.9 percentage points more likely. The logistic regression analysis sets out to understand which specific variables could explain such a large swing.

* Econometric Model Results

Clearly what was at work was not simply the passage of time, but a change in a set of policy variables that affected welfare recipients. We modeled those state policy variables that directly impacted college attendance. Using the Urban Institute's "Welfare Rules Data Base" we modeled state policy toward allowing welfare recipients to attend college in two categories, as: those states that did not allow postsecondary education as a work activity and those states which allowed limited work activity credit for postsecondary education.

Table 2 presents results for three econometric models. For each model, results are presented for the full sample, African Americans and Latina women. Model 1 is the base model, which includes a dummy variable for welfare recipient (pre and post TANF), an interaction variable that picks up whether the respondent was a recipient after the implementation of TANF, average cost of a two-year public community college in the respondent's state and the number of people in the respondent's household. Results from the base Model 1 show what we expected. The sign for recipients taking college courses is positive, after the implementation of TANF college enrollment for poor women was up and significant, however, for welfare recipients in the post TANF period, after 1997, college enrollment decreased significantly. There are mixed results from the cost of community college that are difficult to interpret, but the coef-

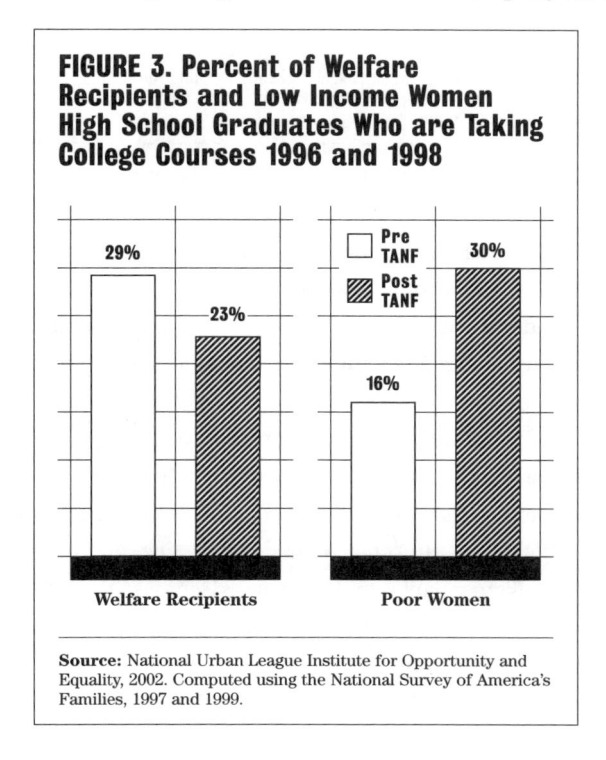

FIGURE 3. Percent of Welfare Recipients and Low Income Women High School Graduates Who are Taking College Courses 1996 and 1998

Welfare Recipients: 29% Pre TANF, 23% Post TANF
Poor Women: 16% Pre TANF, 30% Post TANF

Source: National Urban League Institute for Opportunity and Equality, 2002. Computed using the National Survey of America's Families, 1997 and 1999.

Appendix III

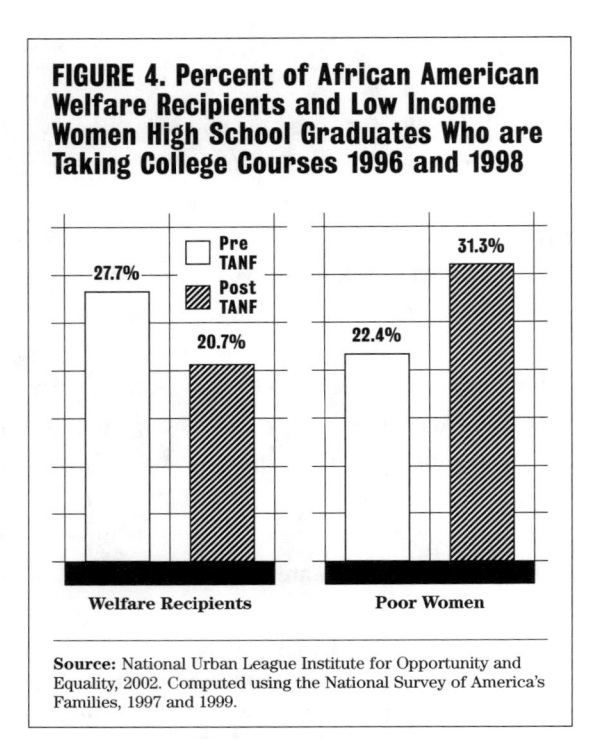

FIGURE 4. Percent of African American Welfare Recipients and Low Income Women High School Graduates Who are Taking College Courses 1996 and 1998

- Pre TANF
- Post TANF

Welfare Recipients: 27.7% / 20.7%
Poor Women: 22.4% / 31.3%

Source: National Urban League Institute for Opportunity and Equality, 2002. Computed using the National Survey of America's Families, 1997 and 1999.

ficient became more consistent once additional controls were included in the model. Family size also proves to be important in decreasing college enrollment. Generally, the results are similar for African Americans and the total sample. However, overall recipients were more likely than non-recipients to attend college than non-recipients, in the pre TANF period, while African-American and Latina recipients had a smaller advantage.

The impact of state policy variables on the interaction term (recipient*POST TANF), along with important controls, can be observed in Model 2. Changes in the interaction term from Model 1 to Model 2 parse out what happens to the college enrollment of recipients after implementation of TANF relative to other poor women. Overall, the inclusion of specific state policy variables and covariates decrease the magnitude and significance of the interaction term, showing how much of the post TANF experience they can explain.

According to Table 2, after controlling for state policies and important

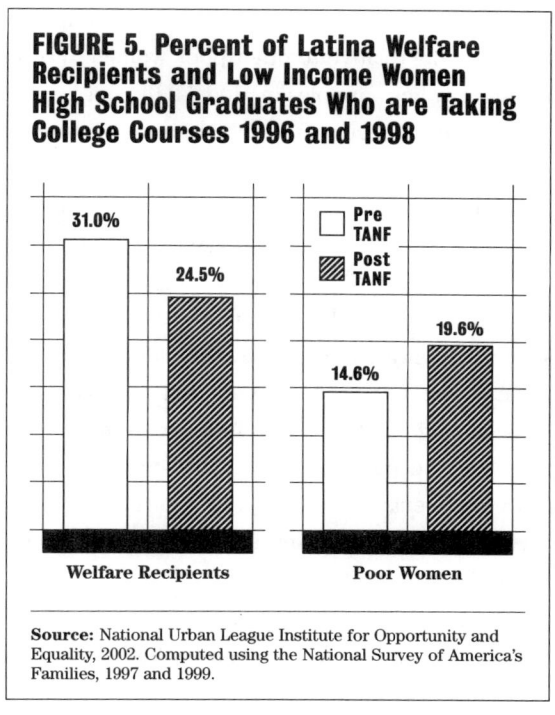

FIGURE 5. Percent of Latina Welfare Recipients and Low Income Women High School Graduates Who are Taking College Courses 1996 and 1998

Welfare Recipients: 31.0% (Pre TANF), 24.5% (Post TANF)
Poor Women: 14.6% (Pre TANF), 19.6% (Post TANF)

Source: National Urban League Institute for Opportunity and Equality, 2002. Computed using the National Survey of America's Families, 1997 and 1999.

covariates in Model 2, the coefficient estimate of the interaction term significantly decreased from

-1.175 to -.2466 and statistically it became undifferentiated from being 0 (that is, it lost its statistical significance). On average, state policies account for 13 percent of the drop in the probability that welfare recipients would enroll in college relative to other poor women after implementation of TANF.

Additional evidence that state policies significantly account for the difference in college enrollment is presented in Table 2. When we specifically examine African Americans, state policy significantly lowers the coefficient estimate for the interaction term in Model 2. Before the state policy variables were added, the coefficient estimate on the interaction term was -1.763 and significant at the 10-percent level. Once the policy variables are added in Model 2, the coefficient estimate on the interaction term changed to -0.8723 and it is no longer significant. This suggests that

Appendix III

for African Americans the policy accounts for differences in college enrollment by recipients relative to other poor women. For Latinas the addition of the state policy variables in Model 2 did not lessen the effect of the interaction term. This suggests that perhaps differences in the college enrollment of welfare recipient and poor Latina women are not wide enough to parse out the impact of state policies. It is also possible that 1998 is too early after TANF to see the impacts of state policies for Latina women.

Lastly, after controlling for the five states with the largest recipient caseload, the interaction variable for each group decreases further. More importantly, one of the state policy interaction variables that picks up whether recipients reside in strict "work-first" states indicates for African Americans the policy accounts for the difference in college enrollment between welfare recipients and other poor women. Model 3 indicates that college enrollment among African-American recipients in strict "work-first" states is significantly decreasing.

In conclusion, our results show that strict "work first" policies were able to explain a large portion of the drop in the odds ratio of college attendance for African-American welfare recipients. Roughly at least 10 percent of the drop in the probability for the average recipient to attend college can be linked to specific "work first" state policies that discouraged college enrollment. And, the addition of the policy variables lowers the statistical significance of the remaining gap, meaning we have captured much of the essence of what differed between 1996 and 1998 for welfare recipients.

Furthermore, our results show that there was not a simple shift of college attending welfare recipients into the pool of poor women attending college. Indeed, former recipients were significantly less likely to be attending college than current recipients. Compared to poor women, who were not current recipients, former recipients were 14.1 percentage points less likely to attend college. And, the state policy variables discouraging welfare recipients' college attendance also tended to lower college attendance of all poor women, though not significantly. Undoubtedly, the effect was in part because of the decline in the attendance of welfare recipients where earning college credit was not considered a work activity. But, the unintended consequence may have also been to discourage other poor women through a lack of peer models or uncertainty about the safety-net they may have felt they could no longer access.

POLICY RECOMMENDATIONS

This data cover a short period, only two years after welfare reform. Yet, they are able to show a dramatic decline in the probability of welfare recipients pursuing college. Given the current shortage of teachers and nurses, and computer technicians in America, this is an unintended consequence we all lose from. The talent pool within the welfare population is more diverse than is commonly recognized. So, it would be counterproductive to adopt a one-size-fits-all policy that limits the ability of states to design flexible programs that recognize it is important to maximize the lifetime earnings of welfare recipients. It is vitally important that college attendance, working toward a degree, be recognized as a legitimate work

TABLE 2. Logit Regression Results
(dependent variable = college course enrollment)

SELECT VARIABLES	MODEL 1 ESTIMATES		
	ALL (N=9,746)	AFRICAN AMERICANS (N=1,438)	LATINAS (N=1,289)
Recipient	.6535**	.7827	.6079
	(.2987)	(.5800)	(.5317)
POST TANF	1.456***	.9374***	1.358***
	(.1052)	(.3042)	(.2338)
Interact: Recipients * POST TANF	-1.175***	-1.763**	-.2775
	(.4063)	(.8017)	(1.109)
Ln (Cost of CC)	-.0525	.0250	.1155
	(.0765)	(.2998)	(.1916)
Family Size	-.3068***	-.2602***	-.3030***
	(.0423)	(.0876)	(.1096)
Intercept	-.2449***	-.6908***	-.0980***
-2 Log Likelihood Ratio	12549.322	1790.402	1488.986

* Statistically significant at 10 percent level. ** Statistically significant at 5 percent level.
*** Statistically significant at 1 percent level. (Standard Errors are in parenthesis)

Appendix **III**

Logit Regression Results (continued)
(dependent variable = college course enrollment)

SELECT VARIABLES	MODEL 2 ESTIMATES		
	ALL (N=6,412)	AFRICAN AMERICANS (N=1,097)	LATINAS (N=760)
Recipient	.5750 (.5358)	.6203 (1.016)	-.1125 (1.225)
POST TANF	1.466*** (.2865)	.6178 (1.017)	.8523 (.9413)
Interact: Recipients POST TANF	-.2466 (5843)	-.8723 (.8615)	.3710 (1.522)
Ln(Cost of CC)	-.1424 (.1066)	-.1389 (.3422)	-.0342 (.2617)
Family Size	-.0954*** (.0474)	-.1872*** (.1079)	-.0025*** (.1123)
States Limit College	-.0788 (.1766)	-.2964 (.5629)	.6394 (.5038)
Interact: Recipients in States that Limit College	.1421 (.5913)	.4141 (1.248)	-.3088 (2.131)
States No College	-.0261 (.1679)	.4596 (.6295)	-.0892 (.4022)
Interact: Recipients in States that Do Not Allow College	-.2224 (.5695)	-1.254 (1.042)	2.162 (2.083)
Usual Weekly Hours	-.0098*** (.0066)	-.0097*** (.0178)	-.0338*** (.0202)
Interact: Weekly Hours Worked Post TANF	-.0119 (.0084)	-.0038 (.0327)	-.0042 (.0294)
Children Age 5 and younger	-.9993*** (.0916)	-.3214*** (.2290)	-.9263*** (.2933)
Former Recipient	-.8711*** (.1678)	-.9442*** (.4357)	-.8983*** (.5296)
Intercept	1.028***	1.367***	.0246***
- 2 Log Likelihood Ratio	9059.997	1438.370	1007.207

* Statistically significant at 10 percent level. ** Statistically significant at 5 percent level.
*** Statistically significant at 1 percent level. (Standard Errors are in parenthesis)

Logit Regression Results (continued)

(dependent variable = college course enrollment)

SELECT VARIABLES	MODEL 3 ESTIMATES		
	ALL (N=6,412)	AFRICAN AMERICANS (N=1,097)	LATINAS (N=760)
Recipient	.6279 (.5361)	.5246 (1.033)	.6218 (1.532)
POST TANF	1.473*** (.2765)	.5885 (1.015)	.8223 (.9749)
Interact: Recipients POST TANF	-.2419 (.5750)	-.6720 (.8842)	.1460 (1.751)
Ln(Cost of CC)	.2759 (.2216)	.8615 (.5790)	.3234 (.7454)
Family Size	-.0929*** (.0457)	-.2235*** (.1002)	.0202*** (.1195)
States Limit College	.0313 (.1978)	-.3115 (.4820)	.7119 (.6979)
Interact: Recipients in States that Limit College	.1480 (.5950)	.6092 (1.147)	-.9368 (2.424)
States No College	-.2418 (.2157)	.7252 (.4423)	.1249 (.6839)
Interact: Recipients in States that Do Not Allow College	-.2840 (.5561)	-1.565* (.9118)	2.221 (1.751)
Usual Weekly Hours	-.0085*** (.0067)	-.0094*** (.0191)	-.0335*** (.0207)
Interact: Weekly Hours Worked Post TANF	-.0130 (.0084)	-.0107 (.0279)	-.0048 (.0302)
Children Age 5 and younger	-1.000*** (.0891)	-.2515*** (.2097)	-.9658*** (.3205)
Former Recipient	-.8589*** (.1653)	-.7862*** (.3693)	-.8900*** (.5643)
Intercept	-2.109***	-5.917***	-2.621***
-2 Log Likelihood Ratio	9059.997	1438.370	1007.207

* Statistically significant at 10 percent level. ** Statistically significant at 5 percent level. *** Statistically significant at 1 percent level. (Standard Errors are in parenthesis)

Appendix **III**

activity. The vast earnings differences between college and non-college educated women show that a college education is a proven way to financial independence. And, the educational attainment of the mother is one of the best predictors of a child's educational attainment. So, this would be a policy change to effect generations to come.

Works Cited

American Psychological Association (APA), *Making 'Welfare Work' Really Work.* Washington, DC, (1998).

Applied Research Center, *Welfare Reform As We Know It.* Oakland, CA: Grass Roots Organizing for Welfare Leadership, (2001).

Bane, M.J. and D. Ellwood, *Welfare Realities: From Rhetoric to Reform.* Cambridge, MA: Harvard University Press, (1994).

Bell, Stephen, *The Prevalence of Education and Training Activities Among Welfare and Food Stamp Recipients*, Series B, No. B-24, Washington, DC: Urban Institute, (October 2000).

Center on Budget and Policy Priorities. *States poised to adopt new program quality indicators: Learning for earning.* (Issue Brief 2). Washington, DC, (1993, April).

Kates, E.. *More than survival: Higher education for low income women.* Washington, DC: Center for Women's Policies Studies, (1991).

Lyter, D. M., Gi-Taik Oh and Vicky Lovell, *New Welfare Proposals Would Require Mothers Receiving Assistance to Work More than the Average American Mom; Child Care Inadequate*, Institute for Women's Policy Research, I WPR Publication #D445 (April 11, 2002).

Meyer, D.R. and M. Cancian. *Economic well-being of women and children after AFDC.* The La Follette Policy Report, 8(1), 10-14, (1997).

Ritter. *College off limits in welfare plan. USA Today*, p. 4(February 17, 1997).

Sherman. *College access and the JOBS program.* Washington, DC: Center for Law and Social Policy, (1990).

U.S. Census Bureau, Table 7. *Median Income of People by Selected Characteristics:* 2000, 1999, and 1998, (September 20, 2001).

Urban Institute, *Welfare Rules Database*, 1996 and 1998. Washington, DC: www.urban.org (2002).

Notes

[1] Computed from the Statistical Abstract of the United States: 2001, Table 263. College Enrollment by Sex and Attendance Status: 1983 to 1998.

[2] Data on the total TANF recipients by state is provided by The Administration for Children and Families at www.acf.dhhs.gov/news/stats/caseload.htm.

appendix IV

Index of Authors and Articles, 1987-2002

In 1987, the National Urban League began publishing *The State of Black America* in a smaller, typeset format. By so doing, it became easier to catalog and archive the various essays by author and article name.

The 2002 edition of *The State of Black America* is the eighth to contain an index of the authors and articles that have appeared since 1987. The articles have been divided by topic and are listed in the alphabetical order of their authors' names.

Reprints of the articles catalogued herein are available through the National Urban League, 120 Wall Street, New York, New York 10005; 212-558-5316.

Index of Authors and Articles
The State of Black America: 1987–2002

Afterword

Daniels, Lee A., "Praising the Mutilated World," **2002**, pp. 181-188

AIDS

Rockeymoore, Maya, "AIDS in Black America and the World," **2002**, pp. 123-146

Appendix **IV**

Business

Glasgow, Douglas G., "The Black Underclass in Perspective," **1987**, pp. 129–144.

Henderson, Lenneal J., "Empowerment through Enterprise: African-American Business Development," **1993**, pp. 91–108.

Price, Hugh B., "Beacons in a New Millennium: Reflections on 21st-Century Leaders and Leadership," **2000**, pp. 13–39.

Tidwell, Billy J., "Black Wealth: Facts and Fiction," **1988**, pp. 193–210.

Walker, Juliet E.K., "The Future of Black Business in America: Can It Get Out of the Box?," **2000**, pp. 199-226.

Diversity

Bell, Derrick, "The Elusive Quest for Racial Justice: The Chronicle of the Constitutional Contradiction," **1991**, pp. 9–23.

Cobbs, Price M., "Critical Perspectives on the Psychology of Race," **1988**, pp. 61–70.

Cobbs, Price M., "Valuing Diversity: The Myth and the Challenge," **1989**, pp. 151–159.

Darity, William Jr., "History, Discrimination and Racial Inequality," **1999**, pp. 153–166.

Watson, Bernard C., "The Demographic Revolution: Diversity in 21st-Century America," **1992**, pp. 31–59.

Economics

Alexis, Marcus and Geraldine R. Henderson, "The Economic Base of African-American Communities: A Study of Consumption Patterns," **1994**, pp. 51–82.

Bradford, William, "Black Family Wealth in the United States," **2000**, pp. 103-145.

———., "Money Matters: Lending Discrimination in African-American Communities," **1993**, pp. 109–134.

Burbridge, Lynn C., "Toward Economic Self-Sufficiency: Independence Without Poverty," **1993**, pp. 71–90.

Edwards, Harry, "Playoffs and Payoffs: The African-American Athlete as an Institutional Resource," **1994**, pp. 85–111.

Henderson, Lenneal J., "Blacks, Budgets, and Taxes: Assessing the Impact of Budget Deficit Reduction and Tax Reform on Blacks," **1987**, pp. 75–95.

———,"Budget and Tax Strategy: Implications for Blacks," **1990**, pp. 53–71.

———,"Public Investment for Public Good: Needs, Benefits, and Financing Options," **1992**, pp. 213–229.

Jeffries, John M., and Richard L. Schaffer, "Changes in the Labor Economy and Labor Market State of Black Americans," **1996**, pp. 12-77.

Malveaux, Julianne M., "The Parity Imperative: Civil Rights, Economic Justice, and the New American Dilemma," **1992**, pp. 281–303.

National Urban League Research Staff, "African Americans in Profile: Selected Demographic, Social and Economic Data," **1992**, pp. 309–325.

———, "The Economic Status of African Americans During the Reagan-Bush Era: Withered Opportunities, Limited Outcomes, and Uncertain Outlook," **1993**, pp. 135–200.

———, "The Economic Status of African Americans: Limited Ownership and Persistent Inequality," **1992**, pp. 61–117.

———, "The Economic Status of African Americans: 'Permanent' Poverty and Inequality," **1991**, pp. 25–75.

———, "Economic Status of Black Americans During the 1980s: A Decade of Limited Progress," **1990**, pp. 25–52.

Appendix **IV**

———, "Economic Status of Black Americans," **1989**, pp. 9–39.

———, "Economic Status of Black 1987," **1988**, pp. 129–152.

———, "Economic Status of Blacks 1986," **1987**, pp. 49–73.

Tidwell, Billy J., "Economic Costs of American Racism," **1991**, pp. 219–232.

Watkins, Celeste, "The Socio-Economic Divide Among Black Americans Under 35," **2001**, pp. 67-85.

Webb, Michael B., "Programs for Progress and Empowerment: The Urban League's National Education Initiative," **1993**, pp. 203-216.

Education

Allen, Walter R., "The Struggle Continues: Race, Equity and Affirmative Action in U.S. Higher Education," **2001**, pp. 87-100.

Bailey, Deirdre, "School Choice: The Option of Success," **2001**, pp. 101-114.

Bradford, William D., "Dollars for Deeds: Prospects and Prescriptions for African-American Financial Institutions," **1994**, pp. 31–50.

Comer, James P., Norris Haynes, and Muriel Hamilton-Leel, "School Power: A Model for Improving Black Student Achievement," **1990**, pp. 225–238.

Dilworth, Mary E. "Historically Black Colleges and Universities: Taking Care of Home," **1994**, pp. 127–151.

Edelman, Marian Wright, "Black Children In America," **1989**, pp. 63–76.

Freeman, Dr. Kimberly Edelin, "African-American Men and Women in Higher Education: 'Filling the Glass' in the New Millennium," **2000**, pp. 61–90.

Guinier, Prof. Lani, "Confirmative Action in a Multiracial Democracy," **2000**, pp. 333–364.

McBay, Shirley M. "The Condition of African American Education: Changes and Challenges," **1992**, pp. 141–156.

McKenzie, Floretta Dukes with Patricia Evans, "Education Strategies for the 90s," **1991**, pp. 95–109.

Robinson, Sharon P., "Taking Charge: An Approach to Making the Educational Problems of Blacks Comprehensible and Manageable," **1987**, pp. 31–47.

Rose, Dr. Stephanie Bell, "African-American High Achievers: Developing Talented Leaders," **2000**, pp. 41–60.

Sudarkasa, Niara, "Black Enrollment in Higher Education: The Unfulfilled Promise of Equality," **1988**, pp. 7–22.

Watson, Bernard C., with Fasaha M. Traylor, "Tomorrow's Teachers: Who Will They Be, What Will They Know?" **1988**, pp. 23–37.

Willie, Charles V., "The Future of School Desegregation," **1987**, pp. 37–47.

Wilson, Reginald, "Black Higher Education: Crisis and Promise," **198**9, pp. 121–135.

Wirschem, David, "Community Mobilization for Education in Rochester, New York: A Case Study," **1991**, pp. 243-248.

Emerging Ideas

Huggins, Sheryl, "The Rules of the Game," **2001**, pp. 65-66.

Employment

Anderson, Bernard E., "African Americans in the Labor Force,: **2002**, pp. 51-67

Darity, William M., Jr., and Samuel L.Myers, Jr., "Racial Earnings Inequality into the 21st Century," **1992**, pp. 119–139.

Hammond, Theresa A., "African Americans in White-Collar Professions," **2002**, pp. 109–121

Thomas, R. Roosevelt, Jr., "Managing Employee Diversity: An Assessment," **1991**, pp. 145–154.

Appendix **IV**

Tidwell, Billy, J., "Parity Progress and Prospects: Racial Inequalities in Economic Well-being," **2000**, pp. 287–316.

Tidwell, Billy J., "African Americans and the 21st-Century Labor Market: Improving the Fit," **1993**, pp. 35–57.

———, "The Unemployment Experience of African Americans: Some Important Correlates and Consequences," **1990**, pp. 213–223.

———, "A Profile of the Black Unemployed," **1987**, pp. 223–237.

Equality

Raines, Franklin D. "What Equality Would Look Life: Reflections on the Past, Present and Future, **2002**, pp. 13-27.

Families

Billingsley, Andrew, "Black Families in a Changing Society," **1987**, pp. 97–111.

———, "Understanding African-American Family Diversity," **1990**, pp. 85–108.

Hill, Robert B., "Critical Issues for Black Families by the Year 2000," **1989**, pp. 41–61.

Rawlston, Vanessa A., "The Impact of Social Security on Child Poverty," **2000**, pp. 317–331.

Stockard (Jr.), Russell L. and M. Belinda Tucker, "Young African-American Men and Women: Separate Paths?," **2001**, pp. 143-159.

Thompson, Dr. Linda S. and Georgene Butler, "The Role of the Black Family in Promoting Healthy Child Development," **2000**, pp. 227–241.

Willie, Charles V. "The Black Family: Striving Toward Freedom," **1988**, pp. 71–80.

Health

Christmas, June Jackson, "The Health of African Americans: Progress Toward Healthy People 2000," 1996, pp. 95–126.

Leffall, LaSalle D., Jr., "Health Status of Black Americans," 1990, pp. 121–142.

McAlpine, Robert, "Toward Development of a National Drug Control Strategy," 1991, pp. 233–241.

Nobles, Wade W., and Lawford L. Goddard, "Drugs in the African-American Community: A Clear and Present Danger," and 1989, pp. 161–181.

Primm, Beny J., "AIDS: A Special Report," 1987, pp. 159–166.

———, "Drug Use: Special Implications for Black America," 1987, pp. 145–158.

Housing

Calmore, John O., "To Make Wrong Right: The Necessary and Proper Aspirations of Fair Housing," 1989, pp. 77–109.

Clay, Phillip, "Housing Opportunity: A Dream Deferred," 1990, pp. 73–84.

James, Angela, "Black Homeownership: Housing and Black Americans Under 35," 2001, pp. 115-129.

Leigh, Wilhelmina A., "U.S. Housing Policy in 1996: The Outlook for Black Americans," 1996, pp. 188–218.

Military Affairs

Butler, John Sibley, "African Americans and the American Military," 2002, pp. 93-107

Music

Brown, David W., "Their Characteristic Music: Thoughts on Rap Music and Hip-Hop Culture," 2001, pp. 189-201

Appendix **IV**

Bynoe, Yvonne, "The Roots of Rap Music and Hip-Hop Culture: One Perspective," **2001**, pp. 175-187.

Overview

Price, Hugh B., "Still Worth Fighting For: America After 9/11," **2002**, pp. 9-11

Politics

Coleman, Henry A., "Interagency and Intergovernmental Coordination: New Demands for Domestic Policy Initiatives," **1992**, pp. 249–263.

Hamilton, Charles V., "On Parity and Political Empowerment," **1989**, pp. 111–120.

———, "Promoting Priorities: African-American Political Influence in the 1990s," **1993**, pp. 59–69.

Henderson, Lenneal J., "Budgets, Taxes, and Politics: Options for the African-American Community," **1991**, pp. 77–93.

Holden, Matthew, Jr., "The Rewards of Daring and the Ambiguity of Power: Perspectives on the Wilder Election of 1989," **1990**, pp. 109–120.

Kilson, Martin L., "African Americans and American Politics 2002: The Maturation Phase," **2002**, pp. 147-180.

McHenry, Donald F., "A Changing World Order: Implications for Black America," **199**1, pp. 155–163.

Persons, Georgia A., "Blacks in State and Local Government: Progress and Constraints," **1987**, pp. 167–192.

Pinderhughes, Dianne M., "Power and Progress: African-American Politics in the New Era of Diversity," **1992**, pp. 265–280.

———, "Civil Rights and the Future of the American Presidency," **1988**, pp. 39–60.

Price, Hugh B., "Black America's Challenge: The Re-construction of Black Civil Society," **2001**, pp. 13-18.

Tidwell, Billy J., "Serving the National Interest: A Marshall Plan for America," **1992**, pp. 11–30.

Williams, Eddie N., "The Evolution of Black Political Power", **2000**, pp. 91–102.

Religion

Lincoln, C. Eric, "Knowing the Black Church: What It Is and Why," **1989**, pp. 137–149.

Richardson, W. Franklyn, "Mission to Mandate: Self-Development through the Black Church," **1994**, pp. 113–126.

Smith, Dr. Drew, "The Evolving Political Priorities of African-American Churches: An Empirical View," **2000**, pp. 171–197.

Taylor, Mark V.C., "Young Adults and Religion," **2001**, pp. 161-174.

Surveys

Stafford, Walter S., "The National Urban League Survey: Black America's Under-35 Generation," **2001**, pp. 19-63.

Stafford, Walter S., "The New York Urban League Survey: Black New York—On Edge, But Optimistic," **2001**, pp. 203-219.

Technology

Dreyfuss, Joel, "Black Americans and the Internet: The Technological Imperative," **2001**, pp. 131-141.

Wilson Ernest J., III, "Technological Convergence, Media Ownership and Content Diversity," **2000**, pp. 147–170.

Appendix **IV**

Urban Affairs

Allen, Antonine, and Leland Ware, "The Geography of Discrimination: Hypersegregation, Isolation and Fragmentation Within the African-American Community," **2002**, pp. 69-92.

Bates, Timothy, "The Paradox of Urban Poverty," **1996**, pp. 144–163.

Bell, Carl C., with Esther J. Jenkins,"Preventing Black Homicide," **1990**, pp. 143–155.

Bryant Solomon, Barbara, "Social Welfare Reform," **1987**, pp. 113–127.

Brown, Lee P., "Crime in the Black Community," **1988**, pp. 95–113.

Bullard, Robert D. "Urban Infrastructure: Social, Environmental, and Health Risks to African Americans," **1992**, pp.183–196.

Chambers, Julius L., "The Law and Black Americans: Retreat from Civil Rights," **1987**, pp. 15–30.

———, "Black Americans and the Courts: Has the Clock Been Turned Back Permanently?" **1990**, pp. 9–24.

Edelin, Ramona H., "Toward an African-American Agenda: An Inward Look," **1990**, pp. 173–183.

Fair, T. Willard, "Coordinated Community Empowerment: Experiences of the Urban League of Greater Miami," **1993**, pp. 217–233.

Gray, Sandra T., "Public-Private Partnerships: Prospects for America…Promise for African Americans," **1992**, pp. 231–247.

Harris, David, " 'Driving While Black' and Other African-American Crimes: The Continuing Relevance of Race to American Criminal Justice," **2000**, pp. 259–285.

Henderson, Lenneal J., "African Americans in the Urban Milieu: Conditions, Trends, and Development Needs," **1994**, pp. 11–29.

Hill, Robert B., "Urban Redevelopment: Developing Effective Targeting Strategies," **1992**, pp. 197–211.

Jones, Dionne J., with Greg Harrison of the National Urban League Research Department, "Fast Facts: Comparative Views of African-American Status and Progress," **1994**, pp. 213–236.

Jones, Shirley J., "Silent Suffering: The Plight of Rural Black America," **1994**, pp.171–188.

Massey, Walter E. "Science, Technology, and Human Resources: Preparing for the 21st Century," **1992**, pp. 157–169.

Mendez, Jr. Garry A., "Crime Is Not a Part of Our Black Heritage: A Theoretical Essay," **1988**, pp. 211–216.

Miller, Warren F., Jr., "Developing Untapped Talent: A National Call for African-American Technologists," **1991**, pp. 111–127.

Murray, Sylvester, "Clear and Present Danger: The Decay of America's Physical Infrastructure," **1992**, pp. 171–182.

Pemberton, Gayle, "It's the Thing That Counts, Or Reflections on the Legacy of W.E.B. Du Bois," **1991**, pp. 129–143.

Pinderhughes, Dianne M., "The Case of African-Americans in the Persian Gulf: The Intersection of American Foreign and Military Policy with Domestic Employment Policy in the United States," **1991**, pp. 165–186.

Robinson, Gene S. "Television Advertising and Its Impact on Black America," **1990**, pp. 157–171.

Sawyers, Dr. Andrew and Dr. Lenneal Henderson, "Race, Space and Justice: Cities and Growth in the 21st Century," **2000**, pp. 243–258.

Schneider, Alvin J., "Blacks in the Military: The Victory and the Challenge," **1988**, pp. 115–128.

Appendix **IV**

Stewart, James B., "Developing Black and Latino Survival Strategies: The Future of Urban Areas," **1996**, pp. 164–187.

Stone, Christopher E., "Crime and Justice in Black America," **1996**, pp. 78–94.

Tidwell, Billy J., with Monica B. Kuumba, Dionne J. Jones, and Betty C. Watson, "Fast Facts: African Americans in the 1990s," **1993**, pp. 243–265.

Wallace-Benjamin, Joan, "Organizing African-American Self-Development: The Role of Community-Based Organizations," **1994**, pp. 189–205.

Walters, Ronald, "Serving the People: African-American Leadership and the Challenge of Empowerment," **1994**, pp. 153–170.

Ware, Leland, and Antoine Allen, "The Geography of Discrimination: Hypersegregation, Isolation and Fragmentation Within the African-American Community," **2002**, pp. 69–92.

Welfare

Bergeron, Suzanne, and William E. Spriggs, "The National Urban League and Social Welfare Policy: An Historical Perspective," **2002**, pp. 29-50.

Spriggs, William E., and Suzanne Bergeron, "The National Urban League and Social Welfare Policy: An Historical Perspective," **2002**, pp. 29-50.

Youth

Fulbright-Anderson, Karen,, "Developing Our Youth: What Works," **1996**, pp. 127–143.

Hare, Bruce R., "Black Youth at Risk," **1988**, pp. 81–93.

Howard, Jeff P., "The Third Movement: Developing Black Children for the 21st Century," **1993**, pp. 11–34.

McMurray, Georgia L. "Those of Broader Vision: An African-American Perspective on Teenage Pregnancy and Parenting," **1990**, pp. 195–211.

Moore, Evelyn K., "The Call: Universal Child Care," **1996**, pp. 219–244.

Williams, Terry M., and William Kornblum, "A Portrait of Youth: Coming of Age in Harlem Public Housing," **1991**, pp. 187–207.

appendix V

About the Authors

ANTOINE ALLEN is president of the Metropolitan Wilmington (Del.) Urban League. He earned a doctorate in Urban Affairs and Public Policy from the University of Delaware in 2001.

BERNARD E. ANDERSON is the Whitney M. Young Jr. Professor of Management at The Wharton School of the University of Pennsylvania. He was Assistant Secretary of Labor for Employment Administration Standards during the Clinton Administration.

SUZANNE BERGERON is Senior Legislative Policy Analyst at the National Urban League's Institute for Opportunity and Equality.

JOHN SIBLEY BUTLER is Professor of Management and Sociology at The University of Texas at Austin. His books include (with Charles C. Moskos), *All That We Can Be: Black Leadership and Racial Integration the Army Way*, published by Basic Books, 1996.

LEE A. DANIELS is Director of Publications for the National Urban League, editor of *The State of Black America*, and editor of *Opportunity Journal* magazine.

Appendix **V**

THERESA A. HAMMOND is associate professor of accounting and Ernst and Young Research Fellow in Diversity Studies at the Wallace E. Carroll School of Management at Boston College. Her book, *White-Collar Profession: African-American Certified Public Accountants Since 1921*, has just been published by the University of North Carolina Press.

MARTIN L. KILSON has taught at Harvard University since 1962 and is now Frank G. Thomson Research Professor. He recently finished a two-volume work, *The Making of Black Intellectuals: Studies on the African-American Intelligentsia*.

HUGH B. PRICE is President and Chief Executive Officer of the National Urban League. He is author of *Destination: The American Dream*, published by The National Urban League in 2001, and *Achievement Matters: Getting Your Child The Best Possible Education*, published by Kensington Publishing Corp. in 2002.

FRANKLIN D. RAINES is chairman of Fannie Mae and is a trustee of the National Urban League. He was director of the Office of Management and Budget during the Clinton Administration.

MAYA ROCKEYMOORE is Senior Resident Scholar at the National Urban League's Institute for Opportunity and Equality.

WILLIAM E. SPRIGGS is Director of the National Urban League's Institute for Opportunity and Equality.

LELAND WARE is the Louis I. Redding Professor of Law and Public Policy at the University of Delaware and chairman of the board of the Metropolitan Wilmington Urban League.